The Ideology of
Civic Engagement

The Ideology of Civic Engagement
AmeriCorps, Politics, and Pedagogy

SARA CARPENTER

Published by State University of New York Press, Albany

© 2021 State University of New York

All rights reserved

Printed in the United States of America

No part of this book may be used or reproduced in any manner whatsoever without written permission. No part of this book may be stored in a retrieval system or transmitted in any form or by any means including electronic, electrostatic, magnetic tape, mechanical, photocopying, recording, or otherwise without the prior permission in writing of the publisher.

For information, contact State University of New York Press, Albany, NY
www.sunypress.edu

Library of Congress Cataloging-in-Publication Data

Name: Carpenter, Sara, 1979– author.
Title: The ideology of civic engagement : Americorps, politics, and pedagogy / Sara Carpenter.
Description: Albany : State University of New York, [2021] | Includes bibliographical references and index.
Identifiers: LCCN 2020023303 (print) | LCCN 2020023304 (ebook) | ISBN 9781438481333 (hardcover : alk. paper) | ISBN 9781438481326 (pbk. : alk. paper) | ISBN 9781438481340 (ebook)
Subjects: LCSH: Service learning—United States. | AmeriCorps (U.S.) | Critical pedagogy—United States. | Democracy and education—United States.
Classification: LCC LC220.5 .C356 2021 (print) | LCC LC220.5 (ebook) | DDC 361.3/70973—dc23
LC record available at https://lccn.loc.gov/2020023303
LC ebook record available at https://lccn.loc.gov/2020023304

10 9 8 7 6 5 4 3 2 1

Contents

ACKNOWLEDGMENTS vii

CHAPTER ONE
A Shoulder to the Wheel: Dialectics and Democracy in
Critical Education Research 1

CHAPTER TWO
Community Service and "Learning" Democracy 35

CHAPTER THREE
The Social Organization of Community Service and
Civic Engagement in AmeriCorps 69

CHAPTER FOUR
The Actualities and Vacuities of Civic Engagement in AmeriCorps 107

CHAPTER FIVE
Civic Engagement and Community Service as Ideological Frame
and Practice 143

CHAPTER SIX
New Citizens for an Age of Uncertainty 171

CHAPTER SEVEN
Beyond a Better Democracy: Rehistoricizing and Rematerializing
Critical Education 201

NOTES	217
BIBLIOGRAPHY	237
INDEX	251

Acknowledgments

Acknowledgments are the final, and most difficult, part of a book project to write. This is inevitably because the community of people required to bring this text into being is so expansive it feels impossible to do justice to naming their contributions. Any piece of scholarship that takes time, and all decent scholarship takes a *long* time, means that I have crossed paths, had coffee with, chatted, listened, debated, and read from an endless networks of scholars, activists, educators, students, and community members. Each of these interactions has been meaningful and impactful to me and I thank these people for sharing their ideas, experiences, and insights with me. They have formed my thinking in obvious and subtle ways.

Nevertheless, there are many whom I can name and do so with deep gratitude.

To my research participants, who welcomed me into their experience in the AmeriCorps program and who provided me with much optimism during the research and who affirm in their actions every day that people sincerely want to be good to one another.

To the communities of scholars who have supported this work over the long path it took to final publication, especially the students and faculty in the Adult Education and Community Development program at Ontario Institute for Studies in Education of the University of Toronto and my colleagues in the Canadian Association for the Study of Adult Education, the Standing Conference on University Teaching and Research in the Education of Adults, the Adult Education Research Conference, and the Toronto Historical Materialism group. Special thanks to Daniel Schugurnesky, Roxana Ng, Alan Sears, and John Holst.

To the community of friends who assembled to support me so that I could complete this work, providing shelter, food, transportation, emotional support, and encouragement: Jeri Lu Mattson, Don Esperson, Nan and John Kari, David Holliday, Meg Erke, Martha Malinski, Scott Shoemaker, Sarah Humpage, Lindsay Schwab, Rob Zelada, Shana Mengelkoch, Bill Reichard, Oded Burger, Michael Eaton, Paul Van Cura, Phil Sandro, Joel and Faith Krogstad, Lynn Englund, John Wallace, Jane Plihal, Anthony Cushing, Antony Chum, Eddie Farrell, and Michael Colley.

To my friends and colleagues who created spaces for me to do this work, making sure that I had gainful employment and encouraging me to pursue my interests and passions: Megan Burnett, Carol Rolheiser, and June Larkin.

To the editors who have kept after me and taken care with my work: Stephan Dobson and Danielle Stewart are talented, brilliant, patient, and kind people. Michael Rinella has shepherded this text in its final march and I am grateful for that work and encouragement.

To the women I have walked with in research and struggle, Bethany Osborne, Soheila Pashang, Bahar Biazar, Sheila Wilmot, Sheila Gruner, Bonnie Slade, Hongxia Shan, Srabani Maitra, Soma Chatterjee, Kiran Mirchandani, Nadya Weber, Shama Dossa, Tara Silver, Shirin Haghgou, Genevieve Ritchie, Chandni Desai, Shahrzad Arshadi, Himani Bannerji, Helen Colley, Roxana Ng, and Paula Allman.

To Amir Hassanpour, who taught me not to be afraid of a fight. To Shahrzad Mojab, who did everything above and more.

And finally, Sue, Graham, Matt, Jody, Duncan, and Ethan, who get behind and let me do my thing and take care of me along the way.

Chapter One

A Shoulder to the Wheel

Dialectics and Democracy in Critical Education Research

In the fall of 2008, I began research into the question of civic engagement movements and practices in the United States. It was an auspicious time to ask questions about the promotion of forms of political participation, as the economy of the United States was beginning its most rapid decline in recent memory. The resulting public debates surrounding financial regulation, debt, and economic crisis pushed the relationship between democracy and economy into sharp relief. The nightly news became filled with images not only of protests and occupation movements, but also their violent repression by the state. Tear gas, batons, and municipal police with military-style armaments were common images. The fiscal crisis of 2008 was, and remains, a devastating crisis in capital accumulation and, as with all crises in capitalism, it is those least able to weather such violence that must endure it. This "global slump," combined with decades of cuts to public services, was in actuality a "human recession."[1]

In the United States, the crisis resulted in a massive growth in unemployment, home foreclosures, bank failings, public service reduction, and increased poverty. Given, as Stuart Hall argued, that race is "the modality through which class is lived,"[2] these sharp declines disproportionately impacted the material and social well-being of communities of color.[3] Already, by the time I began fieldwork and the country celebrated the inauguration of Barack Obama in January of 2009, the fallout of the crisis was felt in the communities I entered for my research. Home foreclosures abounded, joblessness was pervasive; people were awash in material and social insecurity and young adults felt this crisis acutely. In response to the crisis, the Obama administration pushed through several major pieces of legislation within their first six months. One of these, the American Recovery and Reinvestment Act of 2009, colloquially known as "the stimulus plan," provided a staggering amount of public funds to imploding financial corporations as well as an injection of resources into public infrastructure development. A second piece of legislation, the 2009 Edward Kennedy Serve America Act, made substantial resources available for the promotion of community service and volunteerism programs, specifically through the Corporation for National and Community Service (CNCS), an independent federal agency. These pieces of legislation, and the relationship between them, aptly characterize the response to the crisis by the American government: fiscal bailouts for private financial institutions and increased public service rhetoric for private citizens. As Obama argued in his promotion of the 2009 summer volunteerism campaign "United We Serve," it was time for American citizens to muster up their ethic of civic duty and get to work fixing the problems in American communities.[4] If everyone was to put their "shoulder to the wheel" and volunteer their labor in local communities, we could work our way out of the crisis and its fallouts. The "wheel" of recovery and progress would turn only with the collective might of the American citizenry behind it. It was time, Obama argued, for us to be good citizens.

This particular moment in history signaled an opportune time to raise critical questions about the realities of democracy and citizenship in the United States. For more than two decades, voices from higher education, civil society, and various facets of American government had been wondering what to do about the so-called democratic deficit in the United States. Following September 11th and the subsequent occupations of Afghanistan and Iraq, even more voices joined a chorus of concern about the status and vitality of American democracy, if not liberal democracy itself. Jean Bricmont asked how it was that, since the end of the Cold War, democracy and human rights had become the perfect justifications to wage war and violate, even desecrate, human rights themselves.[5] Similarly, Ellen Meiksins Wood asked how the United States government had been able to convince its citizenry that feminism and liberalism were good reasons to go to war.[6] The anti-globalization movement, most visibly in their yearly demonstrations against the G8 and the G20, raised to public view the very troubling relationship between democracy and corporate power. Their actions echoed, in some ways, the important debates that demand that democracy be understood through its relationship to two other social phenomena: capitalism and imperialism.

However, those concerned with the vitality of American democracy, and particularly the engagement of individual citizens, largely ignored these concerns, as if these theorists of democracy were speaking past one another. One reason for this speaking-past-each-other phenomenon can be described by what Slavoj Žižek called "fidelity to the democratic consensus." This fidelity

> means acceptance of the present liberal-parliamentary consensus, which precludes any serious questioning of the way this liberal democratic order is complicit in the phenomena it officially condemns, and, of course any serious attempt to imagine a different sociopolitical order. In short, it means: say and write whatever you like—on condition that you do not actually question or disturb the prevailing political consensus. Everything is allowed, solicited even, as a critical topic: the prospect of a global ecological catastrophe; violations of human rights; sexism, homophobia, anti-feminism; growing violence not only in faraway countries, but also in our own megalopolises; the gap between the First and the Third World, between rich and poor; the shattering impact of the digitalization of our daily lives . . . the problem is that all this occurs against the background of a fundamental *Denkverbot*: a prohibition on thinking.[7]

For myself, Žižek's argument became even more salient during a crisis that was deeply connected to the fiscal crisis and that once again provoked US police to take to the streets in full military gear, shooting protesters with tear gas and rubber bullets. That incident was the rebellion in Ferguson, Missouri, following the murder of Michael Brown by a police officer in August of 2014. It is worth noting that Obama's actions following that event were decidedly less responsive than they were in 2008.[8] The murder of Black Americans by police should prompt us to ask how it is that democracy can be, as Žižek notes above, "complicit in phenomena which it officially condemns."

Through the notion of "fidelity," Žižek identifies one of several central paradoxes in our democracies; we are free to think critically, to engage in critique, but not to develop a revolutionary imagination. We are able to imagine the expansion of the franchise, the weakening of borders for a more cosmopolitan or globalized citizen, or even the possible re-creation of a social welfare state. These discourses about the full realization of citizenship, in all its civic and social dimensions, typically come to us through debates around equality and equity. These conversations are not premised on the idea that we may need to consider, as Žižek argues, the complicity of our political order in both the emergence and re-creation of these violations. The problem of imagining and realizing an alternative social formation to our current condition is the central pedagogical challenge of critical education work, both in classrooms and communities. I have found, however, that this problem rarely expresses itself in the terms described above. Rather, what we contend with in educational spaces is what Teresa Ebert called the "modernist contradiction," which emerges in our experiential reality when the democratic promise of political equality collides with the visible, visceral reality of material inequality, organized and expressed through interrelations of race, nation, gender, sexuality, ability, origin, and language on a global scale, and which is necessarily a class relation.[9] This contradiction produces instability in the psychic, affective, cultural, intellectual, and political life of us all; how to understand it and what to do about it could be understood as one of the core political questions of our historical moment.

I have also noticed in my teaching that, once confronted with the complexities of our social formation, the immediate question of concern becomes what one's individual role might be in addressing the paralyzing complexity of human suffering as well as forms of violence and dispossession in our communities. It is here that I found myself, in many different ways over the past twenty years, contending with the discourse of civic engagement. As a discourse, civic engagement posits a way of addressing the challenges posed by the contradictions we face every day; it is a proffered path to navigate our allegiance to democracy with our reality of inequality, violence, degradation, and suffering. At its core is an assertion that there is a deeply transformative relationship between participating in democracy and the learning necessary to create an enlivened democracy that can address all manner of social problems. This imagined participation in democracy takes many forms, from electoral politics and lobbying to civic associations and block clubs, but in recent years the most popular and discussed form within educational theory is community service. In elementary, secondary, and higher education, the influence of this discourse appears as service-learning. In higher education, it also goes by phrases such as civic engagement or community-university partnership or public scholarship. In adult education, we focus on the cultivation of civil society. The common trait across these various articulations is a theory of change, an argument that if we (citizens, young people, university students) participate in community (or volunteer, serve, work), then we will be better citizens, exhibiting values of civility, tolerance, and participation; skills and capacities of deliberation, advocacy, and pragmatic problem solving; increased empathy, passion, and commitment; and knowledge of government structures and paths to social change. We may even deepen our understanding of the structural roots of inequality in our society. The argument continues that from this wealth of experience and knowledge will come the tools necessary to create a more humane life for all. For most educators, the site of this learning is "the community," amorphous as that maybe, or, more specifically, civil society. It is a powerful progressive vision, richly full of "if-then" causal claims.

After many years of intersecting with civic engagement as an activist, an educator, and a researcher, I became concerned, theoretically and pedagogically, with a key question: How can democracy be compatible with human deprivation and degradation? Through experiences garnered in community organizations around migrant justice, antipoverty activism, and antiracism work, I discovered there was another way to phrase this question: *Under what conditions* does democracy become compatible with human deprivation and degradation, as well as the destruction of the planet and our ecosystem? Through my work in community education, primarily with young adults, I learned that this question can be extended into the terrain of pedagogical consideration by asking *through what means* are young people incorporated into *what kinds* of democracy?

To address these questions, it is exceedingly important that we understand how youth and adults come to understand the relationship between the category of citizen and the problems and possibilities of democracy. This text is an attempt to explore these question through what I refer to as the civic engagement movement, which is both a discursive and pedagogical movement to cultivate particular forms of political participation amongst young adults in the United States and, increasingly, internationally. I began this research by trying to understand what young people learn about citizenship and democracy through their participation in the American federal civic engagement and national service program AmeriCorps and by spending a year conducting ethnographic research within an AmeriCorps community. I spent this time with two AmeriCorps programs in the Midwest, participating in their Corps activities as well as service projects, regional gatherings, local conferences, and training activities. I interviewed program directors, state commission employees, consultants, and trainers. I had numerous off-the-record conversations about the program with service supervisors, school officials, community members, and educators. Most importantly, I spent extensive time with AmeriCorps members, speaking with them individually and in groups that met regularly. When I asked for volunteers to participate in the research, I expected perhaps a dozen AmeriCorps members, twenty if I was lucky, would be interested, given the time commitment I requested. To my surprise, and ultimate edification, nearly fifty of them signed up. I found out very quickly that they had a great deal of interest in the questions I was asking. After spending so much time with them and coming to understand better their aspirations and intentions, it is my belief that the sort of analysis I offer here is necessary to ultimately realize the beliefs in democracy and social change many of them hold.

This research was also inspired by my own participation in various institutional initiatives for civic engagement and citizen participation in the United States as a student, educator, and activist. These initiatives are pervasive; they exist in numerous arenas of everyday social life, including the state, educational institutions, civil society, the labor market, and the private sector. They have formed in response to massive transformations in global political economy and state organization that have thrown the relationships between citizen, state, and market into increasingly deeper forms of crisis and contradiction. It became clear over time that within this historical moment, a particular form of citizenship has arisen, one that is based on notions of participation and community and forges new roles for citizens in the everyday social relations of capitalism. However, as an educator, particularly one who identifies with the traditions of critical adult education, I found that an investigation into the pedagogy of civic engagement within a community service program became much more than identifying the discursive operation of the concept. Rather, an attempt to understand what civic engagement means within such a program, and how the young people within the program understand it, became a reexamination of the relationship between ideology, epistemology, experience, and pedagogy. It became an opportunity to examine what modes and forms of abstraction are present, or what is rendered invisible or obscured, when we talk about being "good citizens" and doing "good work" in communities. More than anything, this text charts the course of a journey to understand the politics of civic engagement in the American federal government's most explicit attempt to cultivate civic and political participation among young adults. This journey, however, led deeply into the theorization of ideology, not just as the content of ideas but also as an epistemological and pedagogical practice in educational contexts.

In order to take up the project I have outlined, I require some specific and complex analytical tools. This text is steeped in particular traditions of analysis building from Marx and Engels's work in *The German Ideology*. I have also relied heavily on feminist and antiracist scholars who seek to extend dialectical historical materialist analysis into the study of capitalist social relations, educational philosophy, and empirical inquiry. Empirically, this research follows the path laid out by Dorothy Smith as Institutional Ethnography (IE), and in what follows in this chapter I discuss in more depth the premises of this approach. From these literatures I draw heavily on the theorization of ideology, consciousness, and praxis, which I believe are key conceptual tools in critical education. These tools allow us to examine how people learn through the everyday and every night experience of living and my discussion and application of them are infused throughout the text. Finally, this study is premised on the idea that we must contend with history—how the past appears in our present and our present conditions our future. We must also contend with the notion that this past, present, and future is made by people, in relation with our environment, and that in order to be radical, we must go to the root of these active, social relations.

Using Dialectics to Investigate Democracy and Learning

One of the central claims of those advocating civic engagement is that it is a form of citizenship education that can address a wide range of issues including conflict and war, migration, racism, ecocide, poverty, terrorism, corporate malfeasance, and the "democratic deficit." As much as I believe that these arguments require investigation and critique, I also think it is important to recognize that demands to reconceptualize citizenship and participation stem from sincere concerns about changes in the global landscape. Today we live with a tremendous contradiction; we have not managed to materialize the kind of equality and justice that our belief in democracy promises to provide, nor have we been able to stem the forces that create inequality and injustice. Today we live in a world in which global income inequality has not only been forced to extremes, but in which poverty and juridical frameworks regularly expel people from society, pushing many to the furthest margins.[10] We also find ourselves in a state of permanent war in which imperialist nations continue to battle over the expansion of markets and territory and which forces millions of people out of their homes and fleeing across international borders.[11] The condition of life, for all species and our planet, is very serious and understanding the various contradictions that compose this social reality is very difficult.

My experience as an educator leads me to believe that our approaches to, and understanding of, citizenship and democracy do not address this contradiction between increasing political participation and increasing forms of human suffering, nor do they give us the intellectual or political tools necessary to critically engage the world in which we live or to embark on social transformation. The pedagogical spaces I work within, including classrooms, communities, and workplaces, are filled with individuals interested in difficult questions of change, leadership, and justice. I regularly encounter learners who are paralyzed by the impasse between a professed value for community and a deepening disregard for the welfare of others, particularly those we construct as different from ourselves along lines of race, origin, sexuality, gender, nation, ability, religion, and class. This impasse permeates the society in which they live; it presents itself as an obstacle to their own sense of justice at the same time that they struggle to understand how this impasse is also part of their own thinking and acting. In the popular vernacular of this moment, many of them want to be "woke." I watch them struggle with questions of ethics, representation, policy, and reform at the same time that they do not interrogate the kind of social and material relations that lead to the very forms of violence they seek to address. They are unable to question in what kind of society these conditions would be deemed legitimate or even tolerable. There is nothing new about this challenge; I think it has occupied all of those whom we look to for guidance on how to change our society. Every feminist, antiracist, anticolonialist, anticapitalist thinker and actor has struggled with these same challenges.

Under conditions of bewilderment and paralysis, being a "good citizen" seems as decent a place to start as any. However, I believe that it is time to reread the problem of learning democracy from a Marxist-feminist perspective. Only in this way can citizenship education be explored not as practice, pedagogy, experiment, movement, or as an *idea*, but as a social relation bound up in the racialized and gendered relations of capitalism, expressed through relations of exploitation and oppression. What does it mean, however, to read democracy and education from a Marxist-feminist perspective? Many might associate Marxist feminism with wages for housework campaigns and critiques of the institution of marriage. We have heard for many years that Marxism and feminism constitute an "unhappy marriage."[12] Certainly many understand this as the limits of what such a theoretical orientation has to offer. There are many different iterations of such a framework, meaning that many activists and scholars with diverse political aims have laid claim to the terminology. In what follows, I want to outline what a Marxist-feminist approach means to me and why I've adapted it to ask questions about citizenship and democracy, which are not usually taken up from this standpoint. An effort to read democracy, citizenship, and learning through such a framework requires specific conceptual tools, the most important of which is historical materialist dialectics. The struggle to understand dialectics has occupied this research and has served as both a point of departure and arrival. Going forward I explain what dialectics means in the context of this research and how it relates to Institutional Ethnography, which is the approach to research I've utilized in this study. I also outline how investigating the project of civic engagement in the AmeriCorps program might look from a dialectical and Marxist-feminist perspective.

A Historical Materialist Dialectical Approach

When I use the term *dialectics*, I am evoking a complex philosophical tradition with many different avenues of development. The word dialectics does not mean the same thing to all people. One approach is that dialectics is a mode of reasoned argumentation. In this classical construction, two rational individuals have differing perspectives. They attempt, through argumentation and logic, to resolve their differences amicably and come to an agreed-on conclusion. There are many possible outcomes. One of these two individuals might argue the other into submission. They might agree they are both wrong about some things and come to a third conclusion. They might agree to disagree, although this would likely not be satisfactory for a disciple of logic and rationality. One of them might also become belligerent and use physical force or social power to subdue the opponent. At this point, our rational individuals have strayed out of rationality, however, and into another common terrain of human interaction. The very act of logical argumentation could be considered to be a terrain of epistemic violence. These possible outcomes of rational intercourse, when extended into the terrain of recognition, form the basis of Hegel's famous master-slave dialectic. Hegel's dialectics, and his approach to logic, have been hugely influential in continental philosophy and social theory more broadly. It is worth noting, however, that we can make a differentiation between insights gained through the application of dialectical analysis and reflection on Hegel's dialectical method itself. These are necessarily related in that a great deal of the philosophical elaboration of Hegelian dialectics has been made through reflection on the *types* of analyses produced utilizing the approach. Perhaps the most contested and debated issues have arisen around Hegel's dialectics of history or philosophy of history. These debates, which I am not going to cover here, have to do with attempts to use Hegelian dialectics to explain, and sometimes predict, historical change and to produce a more substantial framework through which to articulate the forces of historical transformation.

What this scholarship points toward is that dialectics is a philosophical tool; it is a not a theory in the traditional sense of an explanation of reality that emerges through an abstraction from empirical data or is conceived a priori through a claim to logical reasoning. It is a way of conceiving of reality ontologically in order to conceptualize it in particular ways, that is, epistemologically. For this reason, there is a difference between the dialectical approach of Hegel and of Marx (and subsequently other Marxists such as Lenin). As I mentioned earlier, much of my work in this research has been an attempt to understand Marx's dialectics through its empirical application as he and Engel's outlined in *The German Ideology*, and not only as a philosophical object of inquiry. Bertell Ollman has persuasively and consistently argued that the key to understanding Marx's approach to dialectics is to understand it ontologically, that is to understand it involves conceptualizing our social world through intricately inner-constituted relationships.[13] According to Paula Allman, Marxist or historical materialist dialectical conceptualization

> involves apprehending a real phenomenon as either part of or the result of a relation, a unity of two opposites that could not have historically developed nor exist as they presently do outside the way in which they are related.[14]

Dialectics itself is an organic way to conceive social reality, since it explicitly seeks to avoid the objectification and reification (turning relations and processes into things) of social phenomena. Bertell Ollman argued that

> [d]ialectics is not a rock-ribbed triad of thesis–antithesis–synthesis that serves as an all-purpose explanation; nor does it provide a formula that enables us to prove or predict anything; nor is it the motor force of history. The dialectic, as such, explains nothing, proves nothing, predicts nothing, and causes nothing to happen. Rather dialectics is a way of thinking that brings into focus the full range of changes and interactions that occur in the world.[15]

I would make one slight amendment to the wording here and suggest that dialectics does not bring *into* focus the complex relationships of the world, but rather brings *our* focus, as thinkers, to these relationships. Once we have conceived of social phenomena as relations and processes rather than "things," our way of thinking is directed toward the form of these relationships. This further requires that we engage with the historical specificity of these relationships and processes and investigate how they relate to the broader historical context in which we encounter them. In other words, thinking dialectically requires us to think relationally, contextually, historically, and materially. When applied to a question concerning democracy, this shifts the inquiry dramatically to ask questions about the historical emergence of democracy and the kinds of political, cultural, and material relationships that constitute our "democracy" in our given moment.

From the standpoint of historical materialist dialectics, one of the major challenges is to reject idealist conceptions of social reality. To think in an idealist fashion is not to use the word in the typical sense, as in that which is "best" in a given situation (e.g., the ideal solution). Rather, when Marx uses this term he is referring to philosophical traditions that locate the origin of social reality in the human mind and in modes of consciousness. In their search to locate philosophical inquiry in a conception of the world that would allow them to understand how particular conditions of life emerge, change, change again, and can be willfully, consciously transformed by human beings (following Marx's famous edict that point of philosophy is not to interpret the world but change it[16]), Marx and Engels identified several modes of thought as particularly problematic and obstructionist. These idealist conceptions not only begin in philosophical abstractions, laden with the assumptions and values of the person doing the conceptualizing; they are then put to use to interpret reality instead of using empirical inquiry to try and understand what is happening. Further, even when empirical inquiry is utilized, it can be used to create an abstraction that is then put to work to determine what is happening in social reality. Ironically, this kind of empirical, positivist research performs the same kind of abstraction and determination as an idealist construction. The key, they argued, is to think historically as well as materially, to try and understand any given aspect of our reality in its deeply historical constitution and expression and also to understand how that social reality is composed through human activity. In this way, thinking materially means something very specific to me. It is does not mean thinking economically or in terms of economic relations as systems of the production and distribution of material goods. Thinking materially, and dialectically, means neither treating social reality as a force outside of human beings nor as an object that materializes out of nothing (what Dorothy Smith, following Marx, would call a "mystical" sociology). Rather, Marx and Engels argued that we should understand our social reality as being produced by human beings through their activity, which is necessarily socially organized.[17] The social organization of human activity is not just the mere act of doing something, however. It includes the ways in which we think about and conceptualize our activity as forms of consciousness under particular historical produced conditions and relations. When we endeavor to think using historical materialist dialectics, we are thinking through historical specific modes of human social relations.

Let me provide some examples related to this research in order to further elaborate this mode of thinking. In what follows, I want to apply dialectical conceptualization to three key areas that constitute this research: learning, democracy, and inquiry. First, I will apply a dialectical conceptualization to how I think about learning and the formation of consciousness. Second, I will provide a few thoughts on how utilizing dialectics changes my thinking on democracy, but also on what constitutes the materiality of society and how that materiality is organized through socially differentiated relations (e.g., race and gender). Third, I will elaborate on the approach to research that has been used in this study, that of Institutional Ethnography. I will provide a detailed discussion here of how Institutional Ethnography guides inquiry toward the empirical method outlined in *The German Ideology*.

Dialectics and Learning

In order to articulate what dialectics means in the context of this research, it is necessary to extend the concept into the domain of knowledge and knowledge production. When we assert that young people learn democracy, for example, through experiential and participatory pedagogies, we implicitly utilize a conception of the reality that is experienced (ontology) and how it can be known or transformed into knowledge (epistemology); we call this relation "learning." Ontology and epistemology are themselves categories used to describe a lived relation, specifically the relation between being and knowing, which we also describe as praxis. Whether we like it or not, human beings tend to ponder their existence and the nature of their reality. We have a long historical record of asking ourselves questions about what we know and how we know it as well as what exactly constitutes our ability to know, perceive, understand, speak, and act. Without recapping that entire school of philosophical inquiry, I will say that my inclination is toward a relational articulation of knowing and being; specifically, I find affinity with a conceptualization in which they cannot be separated from each other.

There is great diversity in human approaches to conceptualizing their lived experience. Students in the social sciences will likely be familiar with some of the major paradigms through which we have historically framed our thinking about the relation between what is reality and how it can be known. In the positivist paradigm we conceive of reality as independent of human consciousness. This applies to both our physical world and the social lives of our species. Both are ""natural" in this regard. There is a good deal of interdependence between a positivist paradigm and what we might regard as a rigid materialist approach, one in which a determining or causal relation is attributed to that which is "objective" or "real." For example, some of the recent developments in neuroscience research have led many to argue that human consciousness is not so mysterious; it is rather the outcome of the basic functioning of the brain. In this approach, the biology of the brain determines consciousness. In a constructivist or interpretivist paradigm, however, we give precedence not to the objective character of reality but to the subjective. It is understood that what we believe is real is largely just that, a belief. These beliefs are not natural or outside of human beings; rather, they are made by human beings in groups. For this reason we can think of reality, particularly our social reality, as socially constructed. A constructivist might respond to a neuroscientist by arguing that brain mapping can tell us how the brain functions, for example, how it sorts and processes stimuli, but it cannot tell us why some stimuli are meaningful to a person nor can it tell us why some systems of meaning have more social power than others and thus are more readily taken up through perception and interpretation. Meaning is something made both socially and individually and it is fully inscribed with cultural constructions, past experience, and emotions. Meaning is not a biological reflex from this perspective. An extreme version of a constructivist perspective might argue that nothing is real outside of human consciousness. A tree is only a tree because human beings have assigned it such an existence and given it a name. A more moderate perspective might argue that there is a natural reality, but that social reality is an entirely different thing and the two cannot be understood using the same conceptual tools. A critical iteration of this perspective would assert that human consciousness is not only a social construction, but the social constructions we create to interpret and act in our world are never politically or ethically neutral. Nevertheless, from this standpoint the power to determine what constitutes social reality is given to human consciousness.

There are perspectives, however, that reject a dichotomy between the objective and the subjective characterization of social reality, no matter how stretched. Those working within these perspectives aim to conceive of being and knowing as relational entities. For example, I do not claim to be well educated in or understand deeply the epistemologies and ontologies of many Indigenous cultures, but I recognize that many of those who articulate these worldviews begin from radically different premises than the paradigms I have described above. The tradition I am more familiar with is the historical materialist tradition, which despite having many of its own tributaries (some of which trickle to dead ends or end up reproducing the dichotomy described in the previous paragraph) also has a way of conceptualizing being and knowing as relational when historical materialism is conceived of dialectically. In this tradition, it becomes clear that neither the subjective nor the objective have a determining power; rather, they are formed through their relation to one another; in other words, dialectically.

Thus, there is another way to approach the relationship between thinking and being or experience and learning. This approach draws philosophically from Marx and Engels's work to reject both idealist and more objectivist materialist forms of philosophy. This approach is predicated on a conceptualization of our material and social reality as the conscious, sensuous activity of human beings in relation with one another and with our natural world under definite historical conditions.[18] Paula Allman provided the most sophisticated application of this philosophy to the field of education, although her argument is limited to Marx and Engels's work and requires extension by feminist, antiracist, and anticolonial educators.[19] Nevertheless, the analytical tools she gleaned from Marx's articulation of praxis as well as her understanding of historical materialism as a philosophy of inner relations provides a radical departure from the kind of conceptualization of learning offered by John Dewey, the pragmatist philosopher of education who is deeply popular in conversations about democracy and learning. The basis of this conceptualization is Marx's theorization of consciousness, which, as argued by Allman, is best understood as praxis.

Praxis is a commonly utilized concept in educational theory. It is largely understood to articulate a relation between theory and action. For some the relation is linear or sequential, resulting in a formulation that proceeds as act-reflect-think-act or act-reflect-act-reflect. In this conceptualization, the relationship between theory and action is related to limits; the limit of theory is tested in practice and practice provides the ultimate test of the validity of theory. This is a pragmatic, and somewhat instrumentalist, interpretation of the concept. This iteration of praxis reduces the concept to a unified articulation of reflective action such that it is externally related to theory. In this conceptualization, theory and praxis, working together, constitute aspects of a whole, but each retains a distinct, external form. None of this grasps the complexity of epistemological and ontological positions that led Gramsci to refer to historical materialism as "the philosophy of praxis."[20]

Marx identified the source of this fragmentation when he argued the following, in the first thesis on Feuerbach:

> The chief defect of all hitherto existing materialism (that of Feuerbach included) is that the thing, reality, sensuousness, is conceived only in the form of the *object or of contemplation*, but not as *sensuous human activity, practice*, not subjectively. Hence, in contradistinction to materialism, the *active* side was developed abstractly by idealism—which, of course, does not know real, sensuous activity as such. Feuerbach wants sensuous objects, really distinct from the thought objects, but he does not conceive of human activity itself as *objective* activity.[21]

This passage is worth taking time to consider, because Marx articulated the central problem that leads us toward the error of an externally related conceptualization of experience and learning: the problem of ontology, or what constitutes reality. His critique focuses on the way in which reality is conceptualized; he is speaking of the relation between epistemology and ontology, that is to say, between knowing and being. He specifically objected to conceptualizations of social reality as something either "in the form of the *object*"—fixed, static, and objective—""*or of contemplation*"—created solely by the human mind. He critiqued Feuerbach for being unable to address social reality as the creation of human activity itself. Human activity, however, is not mindless practice, but *sensuous*, that is, having to do with the senses. In other words, social reality, materiality, is made real through the conscious activity of human beings. As well as being subjective and conscious, it is *also* objective, a concrete activity by people within historical, human social relations, in order to create the social reality in which we live. Thus, understood as internal (rather than external) relations, the subjective (conscious) person and the objective (material) reality is articulated through the concept of praxis.[22]

The implications of this argument for the theorization of learning are far reaching, and I have written about them extensively elsewhere and in collaboration with Shahrzad Mojab.[23] To articulate a relation between epistemology and ontology as praxis means to understand the relationship between consciousness and practice dialectically as an internal relation. Thus, our thoughts, feelings, ideas, and interpretations are, in Allman's words, "conceptualized dynamically, as the sensuous, active experience of human beings in the material world. Therefore, at any one moment in time, consciousness is comprised of thoughts that arise from each human being's sensuous activity."[24] In other words, our consciousness (thought) and experience (practice) are internally, not externally, related and cannot be separated from one another on the terrain of experience itself. This can only happen epistemologically, through an act of abstraction.[25] This counters explanations of experiential learning as having prereflective characteristics or of being reliant on a linear or sequential theorization of praxis.

Further, theory, as a form of abstraction, is a way of making sense of the world around us through generalizations.[26] Theories are always present in our consciousness as "the consciousness of any human being will also include thoughts that have arisen external to the individual's own sensuous activity, that is, from other people's sensuous activity both historically and contemporaneously."[27] These theories are present in our thinking through numerous processes of learning, both those that are empirical and formal, such as schooling, those that are cultural and informal, such as socialization, and, importantly, those that are somewhat mystical, such as ideology. Thus, our experience in and of social reality is an active, conscious process. The world in which we live is not a "text," unless such a text can be both read and written at the same time. When we conceive of praxis as a process of producing meaning through experience, then it becomes clear that learning is an existential and ongoing process, one that is active and produced through social relations. This can include the intentional pedagogical intervention of another person, which in turn shapes how we experience praxis and come to name some experiences as learning. Taken in such a way, the idea that only certain forms of experience are educative can be clearly understood as normative and, moreover, as reliant on the tearing apart of one's sensuous conscious activity into reified forms of "experience" and "learning."

The reification of experience in our thought is reliant on processes of abstraction, which have both an epistemological and ontological dimension.

Epistemologically, abstraction involves, through conceptualization, the taking apart of the relations and processes that constitute our material reality. To abstract is to literally remove a social phenomenon or experience from the relations in which it was produced. For example, as I write, I can see a road beyond my window. To reify the road is to conceptualize it as a mass of rocks mixed with tar, lined with paint, and edged in concrete sidewalks. It is a thing, an objective thing, a road, on which people are walking and, largely, ignoring one another and their surroundings. In conceptualizing the road in this way, I have abstracted all human relations and processes out of its creation and rendered it inert, given, and static, and not the concretization, literally, of a complex human process. If I wish to understand this road in its constitutive human relations, to render its existence as the creation of people, I will have to think about the people who made the road, the conditions of their labor, and the accumulation of the raw materials for its construction. I will also have to consider the rationale for the building of the road, how it was determined necessary, and for what purpose. If I want to go further and explain the existence of the road in this space outside my window I will have to acknowledge that it is here for a purpose, which is to move people and commodities. If I go further I will see the decision to build the road is the result of previous decisions in history, the most important of which was the decision by Canadians, and their European forefathers, to build a settler colony on the banks of the North Saskatchewan River and dispossess the Dene, Cree, Nakota Sioux, Blackfoot, and Saulteaux First Nations of their traditional lands.

However, when I leave today, and I walk down the road, I will not be "experiencing" these relations. I will feel concrete under my feet, I will hear the noise of the city, and I will wish I had a warmer coat. I might reflect on how sad it is that no one smiles at anyone or makes eye contact. I might lament how most of the people I can see from my position on the road are locked away from me inside of cars. I might be aggravated that walking home will involve traversing dangerous intersections where the road and the sidewalk have been built to facilitate the movement of cars and not pedestrians. I might pass people who are living on the road and do not have access to a safe, warm place to sleep. I might wish there were more essential services available to me in storefronts instead of across wide swaths of treacherous parking lots. I might just wish someone would plant some trees or flowers and make the experience of the road more pleasant. I might wish I'd taken the bus. In other words, I will experience the effect of the relations that constituted the road and all I find along the way, but not experience the relations themselves. They will be rendered distant, abstract, obscure, and ephemeral in my experience. This is the ontological component of abstraction. Nevertheless, the relations are present in the road. The road could have been created through other relations, but it was not. The road is the embodiment of those relations.

Marx's argument, across numerous works, was that the material relations of capitalism, as a mode of life, create a sensuous world of fragmentation, abstraction, and displacement on a global scale. These social relations, operating across borders and through time, as well as the forms of consciousness we use to organize our understanding of our world, create a lived reality of abstraction

> wherein the components of the relations not only appear to exist independently but in some cases also develop an independent existence and are experienced as such and also where some of these relations are only experienced in objectified forms that also obscure their relational origin.[28]

Thus, my experience of abstraction and the naturalization of that abstraction in my consciousness is part of the epistemology as an *ideological* process, in which ideology is understood as a *way of knowing* and not just *what* is known. In other words, it is an ideological mode of thinking to conceptualize experience as an experience "of" or "between" self and society rather than an experience within social relations. To decide that these relations, which form the historical and material ground of experience, are unimportant would be a normative and political decision on my part. If I decide that a road is just a road and the traditional territory on which it is situated is not important, and neither are the people who were displaced and murdered in order to seize the land on which the road was built, then I have made a decision about the relationship between knowledge and power. However, most of the time these decisions are not easily available to us. Knowledge, theory, and concepts come to us already made by other people through history, formed through this process and carrying with them forms of social power. Thus, our experience of the social world, our praxis, must contend with these forms of knowledge in order to a make meaning and conceptualize our everyday lives. To the extent that we are aware of these processes and challenge ourselves to look beyond what is immediately available to us, we may be able to confront the insidious power of ideology in our thought and practice.

On one level, the connection between learning, ideology, and democracy is quite apparent, particularly in an era of "fake news" and when our commitment to uncovering the link between knowledge and power has never been more necessary. However, working within an approach of historical materialist dialectics, I must proceed with a skeptics eye toward the question of learning democracy. This discussion of the complexities of learning from a Marxist-feminist standpoint points toward understanding learning as a form of praxis and as a constant negotiation of the meaning of material reality while at the same time sifting through pervasive ideological constructions. "Learning democracy" is in no way exempt from this process, particularly when democracy is the source of many important ideological processes.

Dialectics and Democracy

Using historical materialist dialectics does not just mean studying human labor or work, which is often the terrain with which Marxism is most associated. This is largely due to the explanatory power of Marx's analysis of capitalism, which was itself a project of applying his formulation of historical materialist dialectics to the study of political economy. If you look closely at *Capital*, much of what you see is Marx critiquing idealist explanations of how economies operate. For example, his argument to move from looking at money and wages to looking at capital and labor.[29] Marx also worked to understand the role of the state in his present society, but the method of his thinking can be applied to understand the evolving forms of state and capital that we see today. It requires, however, a major shift in how we conceptualize democracy. Our typical conceptualization of democracy is that there is a central truth to this political formulation that is contained within the word itself; democracy means rule by the people. We are taught that this central truth was present in Athenian democracy, in Roman democracy, in more ancient and egalitarian peasant societies, and that it is present in modern, liberal democracies. Historical material dialects would require us to ask if this is in fact true and to study how those societies actually organized themselves politically and materially. It would push us to examine the actual historical emergence of our present form of democracy and to ask how our political relations are actually concretized, that is, made objective in daily life. It would require us to study democracy not from the standpoint of what we believe it to be, but from investigations into how we actually organize our lives socially and particularly how we organize power. It would not allow us to get out of the very contradictions within democracy that I identified earlier, specifically the contradiction between the ideals of equality and justice and the reality of deeply divided societies that are anything but equal and just.

It would also require us to be very critical of the conceptual economy we use in our understanding of democracy. In order to ground this discussion a bit more, let me provide an example of how using dialectical conceptualization changes the orientation of scholarship. One category that is central to this research is the notion of civil society. Civil society is an old and loaded term in social theory. Today we typically use it to refer to a nongovernmental, extra-economic arena in which citizens conduct their affairs, usually in some sort of collectivized manner, away from the influence of the state and the market. The political logic of the "third way" of the late 1990s emphasizes this exact point; the most effective terrain of citizen engagement is civil society.[30] This notion of civil society, however, is very particular to the most recent development of liberal capitalist political formations. The term itself dates back to pre-Christian philosophy, but according to Ehrenberg three major historical periods have marked its development: feudalism, the Enlightenment, and modern capitalism.[31] Sayer further argued that the term cannot be used in a transhistorical way.[32] As a category we use to express our conceptualization of social life, it is necessarily specific in a historical mode of social relations.

In the contemporary use of the term, civil society is used to refer to an arena of public life that is associational, common, and often called the public sphere.[33] This use of the term references a space in which individuals are free to interact with one another away from the conditioning influences of the market and the state. This "free" individual of civil society, who today is necessarily a citizen although a citizen free from "the state," emerges from the Enlightenment understanding of the term. Callinicos argued that Hegel took his understanding of civil society from the British and Scottish political economists.[34] In this tradition, civil society is understood as the arena of man's productive, competitive, private interests. Women and reproductive labor were excluded from these conceptions. For Hegel, civil society referred to men (and again not women) in their personal and economic relations rather than political or public relations.[35] For Sayer (1985), the use of civil society by the early political economists and philosophers such as Rousseau and Hegel is highly ideological and coincident with their own explorations of the "moral basis of the emerging capitalist social order."[36] These theorists deployed the term *civil society* in contrast to the social, political, economic, and cultural orders of feudalism, which were rapidly degrading. The new civil society was composed of isolated individuals in their "natural" state: egoist, competitive, autonomous. In this philosophical tradition, these individuals existed socially only by virtue of their universal consent to a social contract based on self-interest with their relations mediated through legal frameworks.

Marx also used the term *civil society*, but he moved through Hegel's articulation of the term into a different dialectical conceptualization of the category. For Marx, individuals in their productive lives only *appear* as isolated individuals within the social relations of capitalism. Processes of dispossession, privatization, and the division of labor that characterized the development of capitalism not only confined individuals within their labors and enclosed commons used for material subsistence, but transformed previous forms of community through changing social bonds, the mobility of labor, and the destruction of traditional communal forms, both political and material.[37] This destructive process, which Marx referred to as "so-called primitive accumulation," eradicated one manner of social relations and replaced them with a capitalist division of labor and dependency on the market.[38] In this way, the conceptualization of an isolated "civil society" by political economists and philosophers is a historical category specific to capitalist social relations. From a historical materialist and dialectical standpoint, such a conceptualization is highly problematic. How is it possible to identify a terrain of human activity that is separate from the state and the market, that is, a space isolated and fragmented from all other social relations? It would have to be a vacuum in society, which, quite frankly, does not exist.

Thus, Marx and Engels use the term very differently. It is the sum of human labor, social organization, and forms of consciousness that Marx calls "civil society." For Marx, the term, as the Enlightenment theorists have employed it, cannot be used transhistorically; this individualization of people only becomes possible when the development of productive forces detaches productive relations from previous communal forms and thrusts competitive atomized individualism into the center of human relations. Thus, in Marx's conception of the term, civil society is the category we use to refer to our actual productive and reproductive lives under capitalism and all the various social practices and relations related to those labors. In other words, civil society is the arena of class struggle.

However, given that civil society is composed of all of these forms of "human intercourse," we can also understand civil society as the material base of society, which I understand to be necessarily gendered and racialized relations. Himani Bannerji argued that in *The German Ideology*, Marx and Engels provide us with an understanding of civil society, of the mode of production, as a complex, evolving social-historical space filled up with various forms of social consciousness, social organization, and social practices.[39] Marx and Engels provide a very slight and casual opening for an analysis of gender in civil society when they discuss productive forces and productive relations as both productive *and* reproductive. From this we can expand the argument that the social organization of labor in a given mode of production does not just include labor that makes new "things," per se, but labor that remakes life itself, that reproduces the conditions of life every day. Similarly, several important feminist works have challenged the notion that the "appropriation of nature" only includes transformation of the physical environment and not the appropriation of women's bodies in the service of reproduction.[40] In this way we can draw in sexuality and gender as two forms of the social organization of civil society and, even further, that gender and sexuality constitute forms of exploitation within capitalism.[41] Further, we can move forward with the historical evidence, particularly in the context of colonialism and slavery as crucial components of capitalist development, that race is an equally important organizer of labor. We have a tremendous wealth of scholarship providing examples of how race, class, and gender are inseparable social relations that also constitute not just the organization of labor, but also other social practices and, very importantly, forms of social consciousness. In this way, Bannerji argues that civil society and the mode of production is concretized through the social practices that organize it, specifically social practices predicated on notions of race and gender.[42] Race and gender arise as irresolvable social realities that give shape and form to the everyday practices of capitalist accumulation.

In this trajectory, civil society is understood not in an idealized fashion, but as a conceptual means of describing social life that both emerges from the dialectical conceptualization of productive forces and relations of production and also references these dialectical relations. This is the conceptualization of the term that I bring to this research. In this notion of civil society, individual lives and forms of social cooperation are seen as mutually determining relations; the individual is a social being, social life is individual life. What this means is that human agency cannot be located in its spatial relation to institutions such as the state or the market, but as part of the complex conflagration of relations of production and reproduction of a mode of life. In this way, an individual can never exist as autonomous or abstracted from these relations, as the contemporary formation of civil society predetermines. Rather, with a dialectical conceptualization of the term

I am able to fully immerse research into a notion such as "citizenship" as part of these relations. It also allows me to see that only through a mode of thinking that negates a dialectical conceptualization could I arrive at "civil society" as an autonomous terrain of citizen activity.

Bringing a dialectical conceptualization of democracy to this research on the AmeriCorps program and on civic engagement more broadly requires me to do a few things all the time. The first is to resist utilizing a pre-existing determination of what democracy is or means. This means I am constantly working to understand how democracy is conceptualized within the program and by the participants rather than imposing a framework of what it means on to them. Second, it means trying to always ground the research and my own modes of thinking in their historical specificity. Third, it requires not divorcing democracy as a political relation from other social relations. This means that I am endeavoring to understand not just what AmeriCorps members are learning about democracy as an abstract category, but really what they are learning about society and about claims regarding how we should live. This has meant trying to understand their thinking as evolving modes of consciousness that are formed dialectically to the practical activity they have taken up in doing community service in "civil society." This shift is ontological in nature and it is for that reason that Institutional Ethnography, as a dialectically conceived approach to inquiry, is the most appropriate for this research.

An Ontological Shift from Subjects to Relations: Dialectics and Institutional Ethnography

There is another aspect of this ontological and epistemological shift in conceptualizing learning that requires elaboration of the approach to inquiry that guided this research. If we go forward with the argument I have made here, it has to be recognized that social relations are *social*, not individual, and that empirically establishing how those social relations are socially organized is key to understanding how a social process, such as learning democracy through service, is constituted. For this reason, I used the approach of Institutional Ethnography, a form of sociology that seeks to actualize the philosophical method of inquiry outlined in *The German Ideology*.[43] Institutional Ethnography has evolved through the work of Dorothy Smith since the 1980s and is used widely as an approach to inquiry in the social sciences. It has been less utilized in education and even less so in the United

States. Nevertheless, it offers important analytical tools to understanding how the particular form of "learning democracy" put forth by the federal government through the project of AmeriCorps. This approach, which is informed by Dorothy Smith's work on a new materialist method of analysis and on dialectical historical materialist approaches to understanding political praxis, which she refers to as a sociology for people, directs my attention away from how knowledge and power operate to impose, suggest, or discipline particular subjectivities and toward what people are actively doing in particular institutional contexts and how their activity is socially organized. I am and have always been interested in the question of how people learn and on what terms they constitute knowledge through their experience. As Smith has argued, "To know is always to know on some terms."[44] I do not want to begin from the premise that subjects are discursively constituted. I do not want to make discourse into an active subject and reify it, thus obscuring the active role of people in the making of social reality. In fact, I am concerned that, following Smith's argument, to do so would reinforce "the traditional separation of the bases of consciousness from the local historical activities of people's everyday lives."[45] I do not want to examine the constitution of AmeriCorps members as subjects, that is, how they are made into "civically engaged youth" through the discourse operationalized within the program. I am interested in what AmeriCorps members "do" that constitutes civic engagement within their program, what they learn from it, and how their "doings" are socially organized. My interest is in the "doings" of civic engagement and not just the discourse.

To study the social relations through which people learn requires an approach to research that begins with people's everyday activities. This position asserts that social reality is constituted through the organized social activity of individuals. Thus, inquiry is directed not at a reified notion of society, but through empirical examination of how people work and relate and how consciousness is formed through this social activity. It is then understood that modes of consciousness, including ideas, theories, and categories, arise not through abstraction, but through human social relations and the relations between humans and the material world. In this conception the individual and the social cannot be ontologically separated, as they are in traditional forms of inquiry. Rather, the individual and the social are dialectically related, meaning that individual action and consciousness have an inner relation with the social totality within which individual lives are lived. This dialectic of individual-social-material relations is particularly evident in Marx's theory of consciousness, which postulates that "we actively and sensuously experience these relations; therefore our consciousness is actively produced within our experience of our social, material, and natural existence."[46]

This ontology, the materialist dialectic of social-individual-material relations and consciousness, is the ontology taken up through the project of institutional ethnography. The aim of this approach is both to understand the organization of social relations, but also to understand how consciousness is shaped in this process. The problem faced by Smith is the question of how one *actualizes* inquiry into this conception of the social. Given our entrenchment in the abstractions and mystifications of traditional forms of inquiry, how should we go about understanding the social relations in which we are bound up and their expression in modes of consciousness, some of which constitute forms of ideology? Smith's answer is to begin by making an ontological shift in conceptualization.[47] This shift requires the researcher to work from an explicit theorization of the social, which Smith has defined as individuals plus their doings plus coordination. Working from this definition, and Marx's ontology, inquiry must always begin with individuals and their actual experiences and practice. In making this shift, the researcher moves away from understanding the social world as a collection of concepts divorced from people's everyday experience and that determine what is happening in reality. These sorts of concepts are the target of much of Marx and Engels' critique in *The German Ideology* and characterize the "violent abstraction" they identify as ideological critique. Making this shift requires a researcher to invert the interpretive paradigm, to avoid reification of individuals and their meaning making process as directed toward society, that is, as separate objects of inquiry, and to conceptualize the dialectical formation of social-material relations and human consciousness.

It is important to remember that the caveat of Marxist ontology is the understanding that social relations and social reality are not necessarily of one's own making.[48] Individuals work within historical processes, inheriting material and social relations from the past. Thus, individuals must constantly contend with history, the forms of knowledge produced through that history, and with the complexity created, in that their relations take place within a larger mode of social relations. Smith argues that given this definition of the social, there is some social mechanism through which human relations are coordinated and organized over time and space.[49] This mechanism, however, is not an "out there" entity such as structure (a "blob-ontology"), but is itself a process and a relation.

Here Smith builds on Marx and identifies this "something" as ruling relations and discourses.[50] Ruling relations and discourses are core concepts to both the approach and method of Institutional Ethnography. The ruling relations are the subject of much confusion among students of Institutional Ethnography. Given the emphasis on institutions and texts within the approach, the ruling relations are sometimes mistaken for bureaucracy, certain individuals, or even the texts or discourses themselves. Ruling relations are not a thing, system, or people, nor are they an equivalent concept to domination or hegemony. The concept of ruling relations runs contrary to a structural ontology that sees power outside of social relations. Given Smith's emphasis on Marxist ontology, the ruling relations are a "complex of objectified social relations that organize and regulate our lives in contemporary society."[51] Smith has also been known to refer to the ruling relation as *the relations that rule* or *relations of ruling* in order to dispel an interpretation of ruling relations as a top-down hegemonic exercising of power. Ruling relations are "forms of consciousness and organization that are objectified in the sense that they are constituted externally to particular people or places."[52] This external construction points toward the translocal coordination of activity and social relations.

Smith's articulation of objectified social relations and forms of consciousness is complex. It draws together many facets of Marx's ontology and critique of idealism, particularly components of ideology and consciousness. In Marx's original conception, human consciousness is developed through the dialectical relationship between practice and thinking (praxis). Following Paula Allman's interpretation of Marx's theory of consciousness, consciousness can be distorted when we rely on ideological forms of reason and draw on abstracted, idealist categories to organize our thinking.[53] Consciousness can also be critical when we follow a historical-materialist dialectical form of reasoning that exposes the inner relations and contradictions within social relations and modes of production.

Smith expands on this notion of consciousness to conceptualize ruling relations as objectified forms of social consciousness.[54] Smith sees the ruling relations as a historical development over the last hundred years of imperialist capitalist development—a process through which consciousness clearly expresses its objectified character in that it *appears* as a force outside of individuals that organizes and coordinates their activities. This assertion thus makes the argument that the ruling relations are primarily ideological in the sense that they rely on objectified methods of reasoning to create objectified consciousness and explanations abstracted from individual experience. Ruling relations, however, do not just frame how we interpret or understand the social world; they also coordinate how we act within these relations. This process happens through the dialectical relationships between consciousness and action (praxis). As we think about the world, we act accordingly; as we experience, we condition our thinking. The exploration of the ruling relations in Institutional Ethnography is an exploration of the dialectic of consciousness, action, and social relations that are coordinated through texts as much as anything else.

Within Institutional Ethnography the concept of the ruling relations is very closely tied to the notion of discourse. The term *discourse* is a loaded word in the social sciences, and I will say from the beginning that Smith's conception of discourse is quite different from its other usages. Discourse, for Smith, stems from looking at the way social relations, individual actions, and consciousness are organized in a particular way.[55] More popular notions of discourse, typically following Foucault, conceptualize discourse as forms of power embedded in language, in particular acts of speaking, statement, and text.[56] This form of discourse, however, still locates knowledge outside individuals and their experience and it acts to impose particular subjectivities on individuals.[57] Smith discusses the form of discourse as power in language as important to the study of ruling relations. From her perspective, Foucauldian discourse analysis explicates a particular dimension of the ruling relations, and it can be seen as a complementary process to textual analysis in Institutional Ethnography as it "captures the displacement of locally situated subjects."[58] However, this form of discourse

> leaves unanalyzed the socially organized practices and relations that objectify, even those visible in discourse itself. Its constitutional rules confine subjects to a standpoint in discourse and hence in the ruling relations. They eliminate the matrix of local practices of actual people that brings objectification of discourse into existence.[59]

For institutional ethnographers discourse refers not just to language, but also to the totality of social relations mediated in texts (broadly defined to include electronic media and text-based exchanges of all sorts). A discourse is not an entity of knowledge existing outside individuals; rather, a discourse is a particular arrangement of social relations in which people are active participants.

This difference is best explained in Smith's discussion of institutional discourses.[60] These are discourses embodied in particular institutions or complexes of social relations. An example might be the discourse of teacher-student relationships. This discourse coordinates activity within the institutional setting of the school, but it also organizes relations between individuals and knowledge. It is embedded with relations of power and domination, but it is a discourse that teachers, students, parents, administrators, politicians, and the general community participate in every day. They enact this discourse and bring it to life. Discourse can be understood as the particular arrangement of social relations coordinated and organized through ruling relations and it is crucial for critical reflection. When institutional ethnographers begin their inquiry with a problematic, understood as the grounding of the research in the everyday world, the researcher develops this problematic in concert with critical reflection on their own location within a discourse, also known as standpoint.[61]

Given this methodological orientation, one of the primary tasks of my research is to further understand the institutional discourses of citizenships within the contemporary ruling relations of democracy within the United States at this historical moment in the imperialist development of capitalism. This kind of inquiry will hopefully lead me in a direction opposite to the typically discursive research into citizenship. Discursive research in the field of education has proven extremely useful in demonstrating how deeply political ideology embeds itself within curriculum and the consciousness of educators. However, it provides no ground for the emergence of those ideologies; that type of explanation is impossible without a historical materialist orientation to the production of knowledge. Thus, in this research I will pursue the "good citizen" not just as a discursive construction, but as an active, social relation that young people struggle to recognize, internalize, negotiate, and activate.

It is Smith's contention that discourses and the ruling relations are observable through the ways in which they are embedded in talk, texts, and institutions. Institutional Ethnography maintains a special and dynamic focus on texts as the central mediating body of ruling relations. Ruling relations are conceived of as embedded within texts, whereas the historical development of a text-mediated society brought the ruling relations into existence. Contemporary society has developed into a social reality dependent on texts for communication, organization, and regulation. Historical developments of technology, particularly print and now computer technologies, allow for the mass replication of texts across time and space, thus instilling in texts a regulatory function across multiple local sites of activity.[62] Texts are also embedded within institutions and operate through institutions to coordinate social relations. Texts embedded in institutions and the institutional discourses they create are the primary focus of institutional ethnography. Texts embedded in institutions almost take on a life of their own. According to Smith, "the materiality of the text and its replicability create a peculiar ground in which it can seem that language, thought, culture, formal organization, have their own being, outside lived time and the actualities of people's living."[63] This understanding of text makes clear the relationship between the way texts function in society and the objectified consciousness of the ruling relations.

Smith uses the term *text* in a broad manner. Text does not just refer to written language, but to other forms of representation, including images, that are replicated and produced across multiple sites. However, Smith also rejects poststructuralist theorizing on texts that places them solely within the interpretive realm. Texts are actual things, made through human labor, that exist in an actual space. They are taken up by readers in different times and activated in different ways. Texts exert a regulatory capacity, but they are much more than sets of rules or directives that readers blindly follow. Smith and Schryer argue that

> coordinating people's doings through the multiplication of identical texts takes for granted that a given text will be interpreted in different local contexts. Texts penetrate and organize the very texture of daily life as well as the always-developing foundations of the social relations and organization of science, industry, commerce, and the public sphere.[64]

In this way, texts function in a manner similar to the ways in which Marx and Engels described how abstract conceptualizations help to order consciousness.[65] But texts go beyond this function in that they also organize behavior and coordinate action. Ellen Pence's institutional ethnography on domestic violence demonstrates this dual process.[66] Through her inquiry, Pence shows how texts utilized by police in the course of domestic violence intervention not only shape the consciousness of police on gender-based violence, but also coordinate their actual practice of policing these offenses, ultimately leaving social relations of patriarchy unchallenged, thereby putting at risk the safety of victims and offering perpetrators impunity. Texts function as the carriers of institutional discourses, making explicit the ways in which individuals are "hooked in" to larger social relations through these institutional processes.

Texts, institutional texts in particular, work as organizers and coordinators of social relations. This is the very process described by the concept of ruling relations. Based on Smith's understanding of texts, it is easy to see that texts are an integral part in the formation of institutional discourses. Institutional discourses are embodied and enacted through texts. However, Smith cautions us not to interpret those relations as ones in which discourses and texts dictate activities. Rather, we should see discourses and texts as "providing the terms under which what people do becomes institutionally accountable"[67] and so institutionally actionable. They frame activities, agents, subjects, behaviors, relations only in institutional terms, using institutional categories. This ideological process again obscures and evacuates individual experience and the "hooking in" of social relations. In this way, institutional texts and discourses produce regulating discourses. Explication of the regulating discourse and the mapping of its associated social relations is the ultimate goal of institutional ethnography.

In this section I have discussed how utilizing historical materialist dialectics as an approach to inquiry influences my thinking around the two major areas of inquiry in this study, learning and democracy, and how I can empirically approach the question of "learning democracy." Approaching this research through the lens of dialectical conceptualization directs my attention to the social relations that constitute the material ground on which any form of meaning making or knowledge can be produced. These social relations are understood to be activity produced by people, coordinated across space and time, and taking place within definite, historical relations. In other words, the focus of this research shifts, from a dialectical standpoint, from learning to praxis.

The Arch of the Book

Drawing from the approach to inquiry that I've described in this chapter, the analysis provided in this text has several aims that are related more broadly to critical education scholarship and pedagogical effort. The first aim is to understand what civic engagement means in this historical moment. I set out to understand civic engagement as a pedagogical endeavor and an attempt to cultivate particular forms of political consciousness among young people. In attempting to answer these questions, I arrived at what is now the second aim of this book: to move beyond a critique of ideology as thought content and ideas and to ground the critical exploration of ideology in critical education scholarship in socially organized human practices, both epistemological and pedagogical. This effort led to the third aim of this book, which is to demonstrate how a theorization of democracy and democratic participation without a theorization of capitalism and its constitutive relations might deliminate the theorization of critical educational responses in very crucial and dangerous ways.

I want to provide fair warning that this book does not proceed in an entirely tradition manner. Often in academic texts we tell the story abstractly, that is theoretically, at the outset and then proceed to weave empirical demonstration throughout, followed by discussion of the findings. I have endeavored to do something different here and which is more in keeping with the approach to inquiry I have laid out in the previous sections of this chapter. There is an arch to this text. It begins with the case at hand: the movement for civic engagement as a pedagogical mode of incorporating young people into democracy. Following this, I provide two chapters of detailed data analysis of the AmeriCorps program. I then continue with a chapter of examining the data before returning to the question of theory. It is in the final chapters of this text that I aim to return to a larger social and historical context and to ask questions regarding the implications of this research. In this way it may feel as if the end of the story is the beginning, but I believe this is as it should be; the point of arrival in any inquiry should transform into a point of departure as well.

I begin in chapter 2 by situating this study within several intersecting threads of a debate concerning the decline of democratic engagement in the United States. This debate, which centers around concerns expressed as "the democratic deficit," has provided us, over the last thirty years, with renewed efforts to promote "good" and "active" citizenship. There have been many articulations of what good and active citizenship might mean, stemming from many facets of political philosophy, but one crucial concept in this literature is that of civic engagement. In chapter 2, I detail some of the parameters or ways in which the concept of civic engagement has been utilized to ground a movement aimed at the renewed political incorporation of young people. This has primarily happened through the high traffic and currency of the concept within higher education and its articulation through the pedagogy of service-learning. As a pedagogical claim, the link between service-learning and civic engagement is based in part on a philosophy of education and democracy that stems from the work of John Dewey, and I spend some time in the chapter 2 examining these claims. I then introduce the case that this research examines: the AmeriCorps program in the United States as an example of a state-sponsored service-learning and civic engagement program. As I've previously stated, my aim in exploring this program is to understand further what sorts of ideas around citizenship and democracy are promoted by the American federal government through this civilian national service model. I did not set out to explore how young people learn to be civically engaged in this program; rather, I was interested in what the program is attempting to teach.

As such, this study did not begin from the premise that civic engagement is something that can be measured, qualitatively or quantitatively, and that I could do so by examining its actualization in the community service model utilized in the AmeriCorps program. Despite the fact that the title of this book is the ideology of civic engagement, I did not go out looking for such an ideology per se. Rather, I wanted to understand practically and materially what is happening in the everyday reality of the AmeriCorps volunteers and how the claim that their service is a way to learn democracy actually played out in their experience. To do this I had to understand what actually constitutes their daily activity as volunteers. In keeping with an approach to inquiry grounded in historical materialist dialectics, I could not begin with the perception and appearance of community service; instead, I had to understand how young people come to serve in specific spaces and in specific ways under the auspices of the AmeriCorps program. Chapter 3 details this process by explicating the ways in which various federal regulations organize the daily practice of volunteers, program directors, and other stakeholders. Specifically, I examine the ways the rules and procedures of the program narrow the terrain of learning from the vastness of civil society to a very narrow type of not-for-profit and municipal organization. This is accomplished through texts that articulate processes such as funding mechanisms and evaluation criteria that determine the eligibility of organizations for funding, as well as the type of organizations that are deemed suitable as grounds for learning democracy. This process depoliticizes the work of AmeriCorps members in important ways, ensuring that community service is only carried out in contexts that are nonpartisan. However, this process also ensures that volunteer labor is aimed exclusively at changing the behavior of individual service recipients. This process is organized through federal regulations concerning not only so-called permissible activities, but also through the use of organizational tools in the grant-funding process that require social problems and interventions to be conceptualized in limited ways. The outcome of this processes presents community service as a logical and effective means to address a range of social problems and needs and to effectively obscure the role of the state or public policy in the creation or expression of forms of social inequality.

In chapter 4, I continue this analysis by asking what constitutes a theory of civic engagement in such a learning environment. After documenting the historical emergence of the emphasis on civic engagement within the AmeriCorps program, I examine both the explicitly curricular components of the program that are intended to produce civic engagement as well as the discourses of civic engagement that circulate within the programs. What is key in this analysis of civic engagement is its movement to the center of institutional priorities to the point that it becomes a performance measure of the program. I ask what the articulation of civic engagement through the logic of performance measures has to do with its pedagogical elaboration in the program, especially as it translates to actual pedagogical activities such as civic engagement activity plans and community service experiences. Throughout this process I document how AmeriCorps members struggle to make sense of learning activities aimed at cultivating civic engagement, but separated from, and often set in opposition to, their daily experiences of service work in contexts of acute poverty, racism, and social crisis. I argue that ultimately the construct of civic engagement is inseparable from other ideological forms within the program and relies on epistemologies based in abstraction and reification to articulate what constitutes democracy and citizen participation.

In chapter 5, I synthesize the ethnographic data on the program and expand the discussion of ideology to argue the importance of recognizing ideology as a *practice* within the program and not just as the circulation of particular ideas. This discussion focuses on two of the most central forms of social consciousness circulating within the AmeriCorps program as it relates to civic engagement: the relation of the citizen to the state and the locating of the roots of social inequality in individual or cultural behavioral pathologies. Utilizing the approach of institutional ethnography I interrogate how civic engagement acts as an ideological frame for community service and democracy in the AmeriCorps program, providing a set of ideas and practices through which a variety of activities can be articulated and enacted as a form of democracy that locates the impetus of social crisis in particular individuals and communities while directing attention away from the role of the state and capital in the reproduction of oppression and exploitation.

In chapters 6 and 7 I turn to the implications of this analysis. In chapter 6, I anchor the analysis of the ideology of civic engagement within two levels of explanation. First, I examine the relationality between my analysis and various articulations of the neoliberalization of citizenship. To do this I articulate my own understanding of the concept of neoliberalism and what may be some of the limitations of its use as an explanatory framework. I then argue that we can push deeper into understanding the core contradictions between capitalism and democracy when we investigate the historical emergence and forms of ideology within capitalist democracy. I argue that it is more productive to locate an understanding of the ideology of civic engagement within the central political and material contradictions within a capitalist mode of production. In chapter 7 I extend this discussion into some concluding remarks on the implication of this analysis for the theorization and practice of critical education. Specifically I argue for the need to rehistoricize and rematerialize our understanding of critical education praxis in order to not reproduce the kind of ideological work that happens within and through the concept of civic engagement. I also argue that rehistoricizing and rematerializing this work requires confronting the limitation of my own research on democracy, which has not gone far enough into understanding the importance of colonialism and imperialism as constitutive relations of capitalist democracy in the United States.

It is my hope that the research and theory discussed in this text can help educators to think through some of their own assumptions regarding how we engage young people and each other in trying to change the world. I began this research because of a realization I had about my own practice as an educator and my own proffered solutions to the challenges we face. At a certain point I found myself surrounded by the argument that any and all challenges faced by the communities with which I worked, ranging from sky-high electric bills and lack of health care to the intricate work of emerging from a violent colonial conflict, could be solved if we simply had more and better democracy. At the time, I had not considered how learning about democracy might lead to learning about other social problems, or rather learning about social problems in a particular way. What I have learned through this research into the ideology of civic engagement and its expression in the AmeriCorps program is that our democracy, or lack thereof, is an expression of paradoxically and often contradictory social relations we live within every day. In order to organize our way out of these terrible relations that create such suffering, we cannot rely on a conceptualization of them that normalizes the political and material relations that create them in the first place.

Chapter Two

Community Service and "Learning" Democracy

> In view of the great interest Americans of all ages and backgrounds have expressed since the attacks of September 11 in becoming more active citizens of our country, we believe we have a great opportunity—and responsibility—this coming year to strengthen AmeriCorps' value as a "school" for democracy.
>
> —2003 AmeriCorps Guidelines

There have been a great many "schools" for democracy in the history of the United States. Perhaps those most familiar to me, given my background in adult education, are the Settlement House movement of the later nineteenth and early twentieth centuries, the citizenship schools of the US civil rights movement, and the Highlander Folk School. Each of these experiments, with the exception of Highlander, which is still operating, attempted to craft pedagogical spaces that transcended social divisions among people in order to create a more fulsome democracy. The concept of "school for democracy" is often associated with the trade union movement as well and with the readying of everyday people to advocate, lobby, and, if need be, battle in their own best interests. In the adult education tradition, schools for democracy are usually places where people struggle for unrealized freedom, where they both make demands from those in power and participate in the making of democracy itself through those demands.

When considering K–12 education and higher education, the question of school and democracy becomes more difficult. Historically, schooling has included educating young people about the basic form and structure of government (civic education). There have been movements to inscribe in young people the moral character of good citizenship within democratic societies, such as cultivating an ethical orientation toward democracy, fostering care for the broader society, and inculcating a kind of individual discipline in students (moral and character education). There have been programs focusing specifically on helping young people understand the relationship, both historically and philosophically, between numerous forms of social difference and democracy (cosmopolitan, global, and inclusive citizenship education), and also long traditions of engagement and participation (e.g., citizenship education, participatory democracy). In addition there have been varied experiments in building actually existing democracy within schools and classrooms, experiments that take the approach that curricular reform is ultimately insufficient in preparing young people for active engagement in democracy. These models have not taken hold easily; instead, they have emerged through movements of educators, parents, academics, and policy makers who were concerned with the relationship between a healthy democracy, the education system, and a functioning citizenry. All of this is contrasted, or held in tension, with the reality that schools are also the place where young people are socialized into the dominant power relations of society and where they specifically learn and internalize race, class, and gender hierarchies.

The quotation that opens this chapter is from the 2003 AmeriCorps guidelines, written by then–CNCS CEO Leslie Lenkowsky. When the CEO of the CNCS proclaimed AmeriCorps as a "school" for democracy, she was indeed situating the program within a long history of scholarly production. The literature on how to go about making good citizens is extensive and diverse, capturing nearly every philosophical position on not only education itself, but democracy as well. This literature extends across an expansive terrain of the theorization of learning and education; it moves beyond the walls of schools and universities into communities and workplaces and even takes up public policy and modes of subject formation as inherently pedagogical. I believe that learning and education are different social processes. To me, following Peter Jarvis,[1] learning is an existential phenomenon. People are always learning, that is, always making meaning *of* their social reality *through* their social reality. Education, however, is purposeful pedagogical intervention in someone else's life and schooling doesn't necessarily have much to do with either education or learning. Education implies intention, action, and orientation. To claim that a set of experiences can be labeled with the term *school* is important to me, and thus begs the following questions: Who is organizing this school? What is the curriculum? And who is the pedagogue?

Demands for the cultivation of civic engagement largely stem from two parallel streams of thought. One is the now century-long call for civilian national service, which aims to cultivate not only participation in democracy but attachment to the nation. Proposals for civilian national service have ranged from the establishment of compulsory models of youth service, which can be found in both civilian and military forms in numerous countries, to job creation and vocational training models to the current model, which is entirely voluntary and linked to access to higher education. Throughout this century-long history of advocacy, a constant has been the argument that through service to the nation, young people will learn something about their role as citizens in a democracy and will feel more responsible for the state of the nation. This claim amounts, in terms of a theorization of learning, to a claim to informal learning or even a form of political socialization attached to the experience of service. A second, and more recent, movement has come primarily from higher education, with notable backing of the foundation sector. This movement has called for a reinvigoration of the public purpose of American colleges and universities and a revitalization of democratic learning as part of higher education. While this movement has included arguments concerning publicly oriented scholarship and administration, the calls for civic engagement in regards to students have emphasized the development of pedagogies that cultivate a range of articulations of good citizenship. These two streams came together most explicitly in the early 1990s when the American federal government began to utilize voluntary civilian national service as a means to "cultivate" a spirit of citizenship and service among all national service participants, but particularly in the young adults targeted by national service programs through tuition incentives. In this chapter, I want to explore these two streams of civic engagement and engage with the argument that community service is a way to learn democracy. I believe it is crucial to understand what is contained within such a claim and why different approaches to research are necessary in order to understand why the state would take up community service as a "school for democracy."[2] The purpose is to understand clearly how the relationship between the "experience" of community and the "learning" of democracy is delimited.

Civic Dis/Engagement as Academic Debate and Pedagogical Possibility

Most scholars interested in the debates concerning civic engagement will trace its emergence to the last decade of the twentieth century. The publication of Robert Putnam's initial 1995 article "Bowling Alone: America's Declining Social Capital" alerted many to the reality that the traditional forms of civic association in the United States were, if not in decline, most definitely in flux.³ I would argue that understanding the roots of our contemporary concern about a democratic deficit, particularly amongst those in government, should be traced at least back to the Trilateral Commission's publication of *The Crisis of Democracy* in 1975.⁴ I say "contemporary" because for much of American history there has been deep anxiety about the health of its democracy, and typically the threat to this health has been seen as immigrants, the poor, and formerly enslaved people. However, the Trilateral Commission's interests were very different from Putnam's; they were mostly concerned with a lack of trust in public institutions that was signaled by an "excess" of democracy—an excess that was expressed through public protest and a public sphere crowded with too many specialized interests from those who were, as the authors argued, "impatient with the distinctions of class and rank."⁵ Their concern focused on the erosion of commonality in the public sphere and the ability of the government to assert authority over the citizenry. Ten years later, the effect of policy reform under the Reagan administration caused another group of voices to decry the diminishing of democracy. This group, characterized by Robert Bellah's *Habits of the Heart* in 1985, brought attention to the erosion of the social welfare system and the dangers of festering material inequality.⁶ The 1980s laid the groundwork for the emergence of a powerful articulation of communitarian democracy, which contains internal debates reflecting radical to quite conservative arguments concerning the relationship among citizens, as well as between citizens and the state.

By the early 1990s, Kmylicka and Norman argued, in an important capture of the discussion at the time, that the "citizenship debate" was crossing over three major terrains of political thought: liberalism, communitarianism, and civic republicanism.⁷ It would be remiss not to note that academics are by no means in agreement with one another around the terms on which this deflation of democracy should be understood. In the literature on civic decline one can find the problem studied from seemingly endless perspectives. Every diagnosis that was proffered was, in the classical spirit of the academy, subjected to empirical and theoretical investigation. For example, there is no consensus about the extent of voter decline or decreases in civic participation. Nor is there agreement concerning indicators of trust, association, or social capital. It is telling that the terms on which we might research the health of democracy cannot be agreed up.

While the academic debate concerning the parameters and meaning of the so-called democratic deficit continued unabated, in the mid-1990s several key associations emerged to address the problem. Just prior to this period, in 1985, Campus Compact was formed as an association of American colleges and universities committed to revitalizing the civic mission of higher education. In 1993, the Corporation for National and Community Service was founded with the mission of cultivating citizenship through civilian national service. In 1996 the National Commission on Civic Renewal was established, and in 1998 it issued their report, *A Nation of Spectators: How Civic Disengagement Weakens America and What We Can Do About It*.[8] Each of these organizations had, in different ways, aligned themselves with the building argument that anemic democracy required an influx of citizen energy; individual citizens as well as major institutions, such as universities and the federal government, must become involved in the health of democracy through participation and active involvement in civil society.

In response to these academic and popular debates, citizenship education emerged as a substantive and contentious area of research and writing across the field of education, particularly in the post–Cold War context. In addition to academic discussions, a new energy emerged in policy circles for formalized citizenship education in schools. Today civic education has been remandated in schools, almost uniformly, across the United States and increasingly across Western Europe and other parts of the globe.[9] Educational scholars have responded to the call to understand youth civic development with a plethora of research, exploring every imaginable facet of the lives of young people.[10] Although civic education and citizenship education cannot be entirely conflated, the terms are used loosely depending on the philosophical orientation of an author. Citizenship education has also emerged under the blanket of conservative-oriented efforts for moral and character education and also within critical pedagogy and more social justice–oriented forms of education.[11]

As educational theorists from many subspecialties of the field traverse this terrain of the relationship between citizenship, education, and learning, they are actually theorizing the democratic subject and the political field. They are taking up the central questions of political philosophy as pedagogical problems: How could we live democratically as well as sustain and reproduce this democracy? In pursuing these questions, we engage with academics, politicians, contrarians, think-tank intellectuals, policy makers, and so on. I have argued elsewhere that several important characteristics can be observed in the literature on citizenship education.[12] The literature is highly dependent on ideal, abstract articulations of good citizenship that are based not in everyday experience, but in political theory. A vast amount of this literature is devoted to delineating the knowledge, skills, and attitudes of the good citizen and translating them into educative practice, which are in turn linked back to these ideal articulations of citizenship. This articulation of the *good* citizen is dialectically related to an articulation of the *bad* citizen, a construct that assumes many forms in the literature, the most popular of which are: the apathetic, disengaged, and perhaps antisocial youth; immigrants and Black Americans with an inferior or necessarily antidemocratic culture or intellect; and the dependent female, particularly one in receipt of public welfare programs. The overwhelming thrust of all of this academic production is the continued assertion that something is wrong with democracy in the United States, and more globally, that part of the solution to this crisis is the reformation of the citizen. A new citizen must emerge; one who is more engaged and active and who participates in new and innovative ways.

The most explicit call for civic engagement has come from within higher education. Funded by foundations such as Carnegie, Kettering, Spencer, and Ford, civil and political engagement are the fashionable trends in higher education. University officials have declared their intention to craft universities into institutions that serve the interests of democracy through the core activities of teaching and research.[13] Pedagogies and programs aimed at getting university students out into communities in order to generate civic capacities and values have flourished, while academics have recommitted themselves to the "public" and "democratic" purposes of knowledge production.[14] The civic engagement trend in higher education is part of a much larger body of work that focuses on the political and civic engagement of young people.[15]

It was not my intention with this research to measure the correspondence between a theoretical or philosophical conceptualization of civic engagement and its appearance in the reality of daily life for AmeriCorps volunteers. Rather, my aims were to understand what constitutes civic engagement within the confines of the program and, most importantly, what pedagogical and epistemological relations support that articulation. After sitting with the literature on civic engagement for several years, I came to the conclusion that it would be a particularly problematic exercise to define the concept of civic engagement based on existing literature and research. Put differently, I think any definition that might rally widespread agreement and support would be so vague and banal as to be meaningless, both in terms of its use in scholarship and its proposed political ethics. There are many, many debates on what exactly civic engagement means, what it looks like, how it can be understood empirically, and how it is similar or dissimilar to other concepts such as political engagement, community engagement, or participation. These debates reflect the wide diversity of interests and beliefs represented in competing conceptualizations of political life, the public sphere, and democracy. The result is conceptual chaos, a cacophony of voices, and a great deal of difficulty in navigating exactly what people mean when they use the concept. For some, this diversity of thought is an indication of the robustness of the concept and the debate itself is sufficient to signal that democracy is alive and well. There is nothing new about this situation; any novice student of political philosophy might be overwhelmed by how much intellectual labor has been devoted to the question of how we should live, materially, and how these relations should be organized, politically and culturally.

Despite this contested conceptual terrain, there have been some valiant efforts to bring coherence to the concept of civic engagement, and while some have even offered attempts at a definition, most have circled around familiar debates.[16] For example, should we distinguish political engagement, or engagement with electoral politics, from civic engagement and voluntary association in civil society? Is it possible to separate civic engagement from political engagement in the first place? What is civil society or the public sphere? What do we mean by engagement? This conversation could go on for many hundreds of pages, and I find the energy to fragment social life into heuristic bits to be an important epistemological act. There is further debate as to how civic engagement is conceptually alike or dissimilar to other attempts to capture the relationship between the citizen and the state as an *active* relationship. Active citizenship is perhaps the broadest catchall category used in articulations of civic engagement, especially within educational scholarship, as it is typically juxtaposed with the passive citizen. The passive citizen is the perfunctory citizen, doing the bare minimum of voting when required, paying taxes regularly and legally, and, in some more conservative critiques, passively consuming entitlements from the state. The active citizen, however, is engaged in some way, and the concept of engagement is often used to signal that this activeness on the part of the citizen involves some kind of labor. However, the scope of the activity of this citizen varies greatly depending on what kind of democracy one is describing. Radical democracy, participatory democracy, representative democracy, deliberative democracy, liberal democracy, to name just a few variations, require different kinds of activity from their citizens.

Defining the concept of civic engagement is made even more difficult when we see that it has been situated within a web of concepts (e.g., civil society, community, social cohesion, and association) and a diversity of frameworks for empirical investigations. It is obviously very difficult to talk about what civic engagement might mean apart from conversations about citizenship and democracy in the first place. This, I believe, is part of the reason for the popularity and helpfulness of Westheimer and Kahn's work on delineating, for educators, the various strains of democratic theorizing in the American context and their possible pedagogical implications.[17] For educational researchers, the implications of a concept such as civic engagement are complicated not just by competing political philosophies, but also by pedagogical debates and theorization of political learning expanding across citizenship education, civic education, political engagement, political socialization, and community engagement. This includes linkages to literatures related to critical consciousness, politicization or radicalization, social justice education, critical pedagogy, and even transformative learning. The philosophical contestation of the concept also becomes an empirical problem, raising the question of what approaches to research illuminate what aspects of the phenomenon. Because there is no agreed-on understanding of the concept, major research in this field has resolved this problem by, for example, choosing to measure sets of behaviors (such as volunteering or voting), skills (such as deliberation and debate), attitudes (such as tolerance), or knowledge (such as constitutionalism) and treating the appearance of these phenomena as an expression of "civic engagement." In this way, civic engagement is a conceptual abstraction and it is very unclear what it is meant to represent.

As might be clear from my comments, I believe trying to draw conceptual clarity on civic engagement out of the existing body of literature is a bit of a tail-chasing enterprise. It is not my intention to dismiss this research as if there is nothing to be learned or as if important observations have not been made. However, I am concerned that the majority of the research suffers from its attempt to impose philosophical problems on reality rather than beginning with the material conditions in which we live. There are many implications of such a conceptual move, but an obvious one is the multiplicity of issues I have raised above. Importantly, even the simplest attempts at definition start to break down when we ask questions about context. For example, what does democracy, or rule by the people, mean in the context of settler colonialism? What does citizenship as membership in a national body mean when that national body is an expression of the long morphology of white supremacy? What does civic engagement mean when political dissent is criminalized? It is worth acknowledging that these sorts of questions rarely emerge in the literature on civic engagement. Discussions of the concept also typically ignore, or take as an exception, the broader historical context of the formation of liberal democracies in North America. This is largely because the conversation around civic engagement is driven by *idealist* conceptions of political life. As I discussed in chapter 1, by idealist, I do not mean ideal as in the best possible circumstances; I mean ideal in the philosophical sense, as emerging from constructions of the mind rather than the actual materiality of day-to-day life. Said differently, civic engagement is largely a theoretical construct, a concept that contains certain assumptions, perspectives, values, and proposals about how we should live. As such, civic engagement is part of a conceptual economy within educational research around democracy. This conceptual economy

> provides a silent foundation for further knowledge projects. . . . It amounts to positing an unproblematic assertion of correspondence between social reality and its representation. . . . These epistemes of base concepts for creating knowledge are not bound by or produced solely within the "field" of the academic discipline, for example, of sociology. Rather, they are an intrinsic part of historical, socioeconomic, and political relations.[18]

The conceptual problem of civic engagement is thus not just in its incoherence, but its very emergence as a concept used to interpret political life and articulate that life in statements of value. Although it is a concept proliferated by academics and policy makers, it is one that emerged in a particular historical, social, material, and political context. It is also a concept that is used to guide practice, or pedagogy, in a particular way.

Thus far, I have argued that the ongoing debate about civic engagement is premised on assumptions regarding the form, content, functionality, and axiology of democracy more broadly. I have also argued that the concept of civic engagement contains a powerful if-then postulation; if we participate in our communities, then we will become better practitioners of democracy. I want to pursue slightly different if-then questions. While much research on the relationship between civil-society learning and democracy is evaluative in nature, my position is that the civic engagement argument is also a deeply abstracted formulation in need of serious interrogation. It begs a series of important questions. What kind of citizenship is "good citizenship?" What kind of democracy results from this formulation? What about the state? What about capital? If we adopt this orientation toward citizenship and learning, how will we organize and address social relations of inequality? What are the politics of this kind of citizenship? How do we incorporate young people in what *kinds* of democracy?

Stream One: National Service and Democratic Socialization

Over the last two decades, and even more so since September 11th and the 2008 recession, it is impossible to discuss community service programs in the United States without taking into consideration the Corporation for National and Community Service and the AmeriCorps program. I was first introduced to the AmeriCorps program when I worked in the not-for-profit sector, and the terms on which I was introduced to it, which involved being told by a program director that AmeriCorps members could not attend a community meeting on immigration policy, made me immediately curious about the program. The AmeriCorps program, whose history and organization are detailed below, is a federal program charged with "cultivating a culture of citizenship, service, and responsibility in America" through the project of civilian national service. AmeriCorps provides an ideal case study for interrogating the realities of community service as a state-sponsored practice for the promotion of democracy and civic engagement.[19]

While programs linking community service and civic engagement exist in school districts, universities, and community organizations across the country, the most expansive efforts by far as those of the Corporation for National and Community Service, also called "the Corporation" by many who work in its programs. The CNCS is an independent federal agency established in 1993 by an act of Congress and under the advocacy of the Clinton administration.[20] The CNCS has reorganized its programs and priorities several times since its founding; however, its primary mission is to "to improve lives and foster civic engagement."[21] Beginning in 2009, following its renewal through the Edward Kennedy Serve America Act, the CNCS has operated three programs: AmeriCorps, Senior Corps, and the Social Innovation Fund. Further, the AmeriCorps program has three subprograms: AmeriCorps Network (formerly AmeriCorps State/National), AmeriCorps Volunteers in Service to America (VISTA), and AmeriCorps National Civilian Community Corps (NCCC). Each of these branches of AmeriCorps have a slightly different focus and form, but are tied together through a commitment to community service as a meaningful form of civic engagement and as appropriate means through which to address problems in communities. The CNCS and its programs are situated at the intersection of two ways of talking about volunteer service; one is an argument for civilian national service that has been percolating in the United States since the early twentieth century and the other is a discourse around community service that has gained increased momentum since the mid-1980s. In what follows, I want to detail some aspects of the emergence of these two ways of talking about volunteer service and how they have come to coexist within the US federal government under the auspices of the CNCS.

Calls for civilian national service have existed since the early twentieth century. The concept has waxed and waned over time, but only became articulated through the language of civic engagement and civic renewal in the early 1990s. An examination of the history of civilian national service illuminates this form of service as a particular way for the state to cultivate its citizenry; in fact, it began in 1902 with such an argument. There are a variety of mechanisms by which governments seek to organize their national body; the majority of these are legislative and have to do with establishing who can and cannot be included in that body as citizens, both in terms of legal status and national identity.[22] The state also engages in pedagogical projects to cultivate citizenship. For example, there is a strong argument to be made that military service is one such pedagogical project. State-mandated civics curricula are perhaps the clearest example. Another historical example is the Division of Immigrant Education, established within the US Bureau for Education in 1914, to facilitate the Americanization program that coercively "democratized" new immigrants from eastern and southern Europe while reinforcing the exclusion from the national body of Black Americans, Asian immigrants, and Indigenous peoples from across North America and Mexico.[23] I argue that the national civilian service movement, which seeks to tie the labor of individuals on a voluntary basis to the needs of society in order to cultivate an attachment to the nation, should be understood in a similar light.

The history of civilian national service is often traced to an early argument made by philosopher William James, who advocated for a form of civilian national service that would be morally equivalent to military service. He argued that the conscription of young men into such service would build character and national identity and that

> numerous other goods to the commonwealth would follow . . . no one would remain blind as the luxurious classes now are blind, to man's relations to the globe he lives on, and to the permanently sour and hard foundations of his higher

life. . . . They would have paid their blood-tax, done their own part in the immemorial human warfare against nature; they would tread the earth more proudly, the women would value them more highly, they would be better fathers and teachers of the following generation.[24]

It is possible to interpret James's argument as a call to the traditions of public service and civic republicanism that "built" the United States. I say "built" because it is difficult to find among discussions of national service any reference to the labor of enslaved peoples, indentured servants, or colonized peoples. Rather, histories of national service often cite the Civilian Conservation Corps (1932–1942), one of the social programs of Roosevelt's New Deal during the Great Depression, as the first example of such civilian national service. Participants in the Civilian Conservation Corps built national parks, hydroelectrical systems, paved roads, and were part of the building of America's national infrastructure. The Corps, however, was not a civilian national service program; it was a social welfare program designed to put to work as many unemployed people as possible. Further, the infrastructure created by the Corps was not solely for the use of the public or the citizenry; some projects provided the basis for privatization and the accumulation of capital. For example, the Corps reseeded forests that had been commercially thinned only for those lands to be resold to corporate holders for commercial logging forty years later.[25] Thus, while the Civilian Conservation Corps may be heavily doused in civic rhetoric, its actualities are far more complicated and imbricated with interests of private accumulation.

I have often heard AmeriCorps described as a domestic Peace Corps, and it is the emergence of the Peace Corps in 1961 that is the most likely direct antecedent to today's forms of national civilian service. The Peace Corps was part of a complex post–World War II landscape in which the United States, Canada, and Western Europe were reconfiguring the landscape of imperialism globally. Their seeming control over the development of whole spheres of the globe required not only policy and dollars (such as the Marshall Plan and Truman's Point Four Program), but also human labor. Conveniently enough, international volunteerism was increasingly popular among privileged Americans and Europeans during the 1950s and '60s. The UN went so far as to assist in the formation of the International Secretariat for Volunteer Service (ISVS) in 1963. Donald Eberly, an influential policy advocate on the development of civil society and future White House staffer during George W. Bush's administration, founded a similar organization, the National Service Secretariat (NSS), in the United States in 1959. Early in his administration, John F. Kennedy proposed the Peace Corps as an opportunity to advance America's interests internationally, do good works, and promote a benevolent image of American development objectives in the face of opposition to the United States' postwar Marshall Plan for Europe and so as to expand development projects to "modernize" Latin America, Africa, Asia, and the Middle East.

The efficiencies of using volunteer labor to develop areas of deep poverty were also a possibility within the United States itself. In the early 1960s Walter Heller, chairperson of the White House agency the Council of Economic Advisors (CEA), chaired a series of discussions that led to the development of the War on Poverty Task Force. This task force, led by Sargent Shriver (who also led the first iteration of the Peace Corps), resulted in the 1964 Economic Opportunities Act (EOA). The EOA provided for massive infusions of federal dollars into poor communities and established a wide network of social service programs, including Head Start, Job Corps, the Legal Service Program (LSP), the Community Action Programs (CAPs), and the Office of Economic Opportunity (OEO). The models for these initiatives drew heavily from antipoverty initiatives led by the Ford Foundation and the President's Committee on Juvenile Delinquency and Youth Crime.[26] Following the success of two early experimental volunteer programs piloted with help from the National Service Secretariat, the Retired Seniors Volunteer Program and Foster Grandparents/Senior Companion programs, the 1964 legislation also authorized the organization of Volunteers in Service to America. VISTA became the first iteration of a domestic national civilian service program.

Around the same time that Kennedy established the CEA task force on poverty, he also commissioned the Task Force on a National Service Program, the first executive-level inquiry into the philosophy and feasibility of civilian national service. The energy behind the task force, and as a result many of its members, came from the Office of Juvenile Delinquency and Youth Crime in the Department of Justice under the leadership of Robert F. Kennedy.[27] The task force did not initially associate national service with the antipoverty agenda or with antipoverty work per se. The discussions included the value of national service in the care of those residing in public mental hospitals.[28] In fact, the Kennedy administration distinguished the national service proposal from a youth employment bill. He warned Congress that the youth employment bill was for youth in *need* of help while the service corps was for those who *could be* of help.[29] The legislation failed, and the proposal for civilian national service was added to Title VI: Administration and Coordination of the Economic Opportunity Act (1964). Here the legacy of national service became institutionally fused to government efforts to address the proliferation of poverty. Further, this moment is significant for its initial indication that the government made a qualitative differentiation between the recipient and the provider of service, between those who served and those who were served. The model of the Peace Corps provided the initial schematics for VISTA. Volunteers were recruited largely from university campuses, so much so that 95 percent of VISTA volunteers were white, middle-class, college-educated youth by the late 1960s.[30] However, the nature of their service necessitated that their training periods be condensed and decentralized to local communities. Thus, many nonprofit agencies and community organizations, such as the Hull House in Chicago and the YMCA, took over the training and supervision of the volunteers. They were also placed in other Economic Opportunity Act offices, such as Community Action Agencies (CAAs) and Job Corps.

In Gillette's oral history of the program, informants reported that it was a struggle in the early years to maintain the VISTA program as a civilian national service apart from the war on poverty.[31] VISTA was mandated to "help people help themselves," and its members were sent out to the poorest rural, urban, and reservation communities to work with the elderly, the unemployed, youth, migrant workers, and the disabled. There was local opposition to the program, with both participants and administrators admitting that "poor communities," euphemistic for communities of color, took issue with primarily white volunteers coming into the communities to "help."[32] We can see here the ways in which volunteer service in communities, under these conditions, maps onto and expresses existing social relations of power (such as class, race, and gender) in the context of the United States.

Civilian national service, and volunteer service more generally, experienced opposition throughout the 1970s and '80s. President Nixon was openly antagonistic to all War on Poverty and Great Society programs and reorganized VISTA under the auspices of the new ACTION Agency, which covertly redirected activities away from capacity building in poor communities and toward direct service activities with local not-for-profit organizations.[33] Reagan's administration further reoriented service programs to direct service projects, narrowly focusing on some of the most outward manifestations and conservative targets of ongoing poverty, including illiteracy, lack of job skills, unemployed youth, and women utilizing public welfare programs. Reagan, however, was not completely obstructive to efforts to increase volunteerism; he just had a completely different vision of the government's involvement. Reagan set about applying his "trickle-down" economics theory to volunteerism. It was thought that if the government cut federal funding to social programs, it would stimulate volunteerism and innovation in the not-for-profit sector; "the idea was that voluntarism would expand because people would make more donations, current donors would become more generous, more people would begin to volunteer, and current volunteers would devote more time to unpaid work."[34] Reagan and his advisers were completely wrong, but their vision did clearly articulate what would become a trend in the thinking of White House policy makers.

In the context of deepening economic inequality and the evisceration of social welfare provisions in the 1980s, several important academic texts began to emerge that linked the human toil of social deprivation to a new kind of citizen engagement. As part of the larger academic movement on communitarianism, authors such as Robert Bellah and Benjamin Barber gained support for their arguments that the rampant individualism of Reaganism had destabilized communities, resulting in social problems that could only be addressed through the reinvestment of citizen activity and a marked change in political culture. The revitalization of an active citizenry and the cultivation of a shared democratic vision for the nation were echoed by national service advocates and formally merged in Janowitz's landmark call for national civil service, which was furthered in subsequent publications by Charles Moskos.[35] Primarily military sociologists, Janowitz and Moskos argued that civic consciousness, understood by them as a sense of shared responsibility for shared institutions, was at the heart of democracy and patriotism.[36] They believed that this kind of consciousness could not be promoted without a system of national service. At the same time, President George H. W. Bush became the first Republican president to support the agenda of national service by forming the Commission for National and Community Service in 1990, with a mission to promote volunteerism and explore national service possibilities.[37] Bush also founded the Points of Light Foundation in 1990, which, under the reorganized entity Points of Light, continues to promote volunteerism. Moskos credited the strength of Janowitz's argument, coupled with the case made by national service advocates such as himself and Donald Eberly, in finally getting the attention of policy makers.[38]

Ultimately, the movement for national civil service culminated in the founding of the Corporation for National and Community Service and the establishment of the AmeriCorps program early in the Clinton administration.

The purpose of establishing the Corporation was "to concentrate national efforts on meeting certain unmet human, educational, environmental or public safety needs."[39] These needs were to be addressed by citizens at the level of the community. The establishment of the CNCS, however, cannot be understood simply as the realization of an idea whose time had come. Rather, the formalization and institutionalization of civilian national service occurred at a historical moment in which the entirety of the federal government was being both ideologically and materially reorganized. This reorganization, which was articulated by its advocates as a "reinvention" of government through entrepreneurial means, continued the work of the two previous decades to redefine the role of the state and public policy and the relationship of individual citizens to their government.[40] When Bill Clinton declared that the new CNCS would be a model of his plan to reinvent government, he articulated a crucial relationship in understanding national civilian service: the link between not just community service and reduced public spending, but the link between a new way of thinking about the role of government and the work of individual, private citizens.

The CNCS struggled in its first decade. While it grew steadily, it was stilling finding its stride in terms of the administration of its programs and the creation of a coherent identity for the organization. Several efforts at building this identity reflected the growing national concern with civic engagement in the late 1990s. The consolidation of formalized training in civic engagement in the AmeriCorps program during this period reflects the merging of civic engagement discourse with the institutional practices of the AmeriCorps program. This is a history that I discuss in chapter 4. However, the first decade of the twenty-first century provided historical circumstances that cemented much of the identity of the CNCS and of the AmeriCorps program. In the aftermath of September 11, 2001, then-president George W. Bush issued a historic call for Americans to respond to the tragedy in three ways: first, join the military; second, go shopping; and third, do volunteer work. Bush's endorsement of civilian national service as a response to the attack is considered historic by national service advocates, in the sense that for the first time in US history a civilian national service program was not only supported, but expanded by a president that was not responsible for its creation.[41] Bush asked Congress to expand the AmeriCorps program by 50 percent, and he created two corresponding civilian national service initiatives within the executive branch: the USA Freedom Corps and the President's Council on Service and Civic Participation. The USA Freedom Corps worked to engage the not-for-profit and voluntary sectors in key areas of need, including youth, baby boomers, hurricane response and recovery, mentoring, supporting military families, tsunami relief and recovery, and international volunteering.[42] The President's Council was an honorific body composed of supporters of the Bush administration and seemed to have little outputs apart from giving out awards for volunteer service. The overlap between this additional activity promoting public service and the Bush administration's occupation of Iraq and Afghanistan raises questions as to the actual purpose of these two bodies.

While AmeriCorps undoubtedly benefited from the waves of nationalism that followed September 11, it was actually the 2008 fiscal crisis that offered the larger opportunity to expand the program. Barack Obama was already a strong supporter of community service; for example, he celebrated his 2009 inauguration by spending Martin Luther King Day performing community service. In fact, he had declared years prior his intention to make community service a "cause" of his presidency.[43] The American Recovery and Reinvestment Act of 2009 included appropriations for AmeriCorps and VISTA, resulting in an additional 13,000 AmeriCorps positions. This was quickly followed by an extensive reauthorization and expansion of the CNCS and, for the first time, Congress approved the president's proposed national service appropriation in full ($1.149 billion). In Obama's own words, the legislation was successful by "putting partnership over partisanship."[44] In the first half of 2009, the notion of civilian national service began to build as a full-fledge movement, at first organized around the passing of the legislation by national lobbying organizations such as Service Nation, and then continuing with Obama's campaign for a summer of community service, titled United We Serve, and ending on September 11, which Obama deemed a national day of service and remembrance. The Edward Kennedy Serve America Act not only expanded the AmeriCorps program, but also provided new streams of support to the nonprofit sector in general, particularly for the recruitment and management of volunteers. The newest endeavor was the Social Innovation Fund, which Obama visualized as a massive public and private investment in the generation of new approaches to meeting social needs by the not-for-profit sector. The resources accumulated through the Social Innovation Fund were to support "ideas that work," and he further argued that community service represented the "the current of history."[45] This pragmatic perspective on service as a possible strategy to address "gaps" in governance, or perhaps provide innovative solutions to ongoing social problems, demonstrates the integration of discourses of innovation and entrepreneurialism with civic engagement, national service, and volunteerism.

As can be seen in this history, the development and institutionalization of community service as national civilian service has not been solely an altruistic or humanitarian endeavor, although I do not want to discount the intentions of many who are invested in these projects and who believe them to be so. However, the promotion of volunteer service by the federal government has clearly served different political needs at different points in time. This history indicates that the relationship between volunteer labor and the discourse of community service have played a complicated role in consolidating political interests around how to address poverty, on both domestic and international scales. This role has diversified over time, beginning from the humanitarian imperialism of the international development project to an emergent role mediating the dismantling of the social welfare state. However, I believe that this history renders something else visible beyond political interests. It allows us to see the movement of a complex social relation over time. This social relation has been discursively constituted by generations of political leadership as one between the citizen and the state, but it has focused on, and been constituted through, a material relation. The focus of civilian national service has long been material in that is has centered on people's lives within capitalism, whether it be utilizing service to address unemployment or to develop and empower the poor or reduce the reliance of communities on the state. This signifies to me that the merging of community service, national service, and civic engagement can only be understood as a political relation if that relation is understood as not being a material one. This is a paradox, or rather a fragmentation of a social relation.

There are two important pedagogical observations that I want to make about these claims concerning national service as a way for citizens, and in particular young people, to learn democracy. The first is that most of these articulations fall back on an implicit theory of socialization, specifically political socialization. Theories of political socialization, and socialization more broadly, rely on the notion that learning happens in informal and incidental ways; experience can be transformed into meaning and understanding without an explicit pedagogical act. Thus, the learning of democracy does not necessarily require facilitation; the experience itself is sufficient. This claim has been problematized by theorists of service-learning, which I discuss later on, but it speaks to a second pedagogical observation. Socialization, as a theory of learning, does not solely equate experience with learning; it relies on some mechanisms of social rewards and punishments. Socialization works because individuals and institutions utilize rewards and discipline, either through shame or violence, thus cultivating both attachment and fear of stigma on the part of those being socialized. In this way the *meaning* of the experience can be conceptualized as necessarily related to the meaning of another set of experiences; cultural logic then becomes paramount.

This is partially what undergirds an understanding of the meaning-making processes associated with discursive moves at subject formation and I want to flag that this would be one interesting and valid approach to understanding the history and claims of national civilian service advocates. One way to interpret the historical merging of civilian national service and community service as civic engagement is as the neoliberalization of the program, and it is clear that a change in the mode of governing is visible in this history. The logic behind national service during the War on Poverty is not the same logic behind the agenda post-9/11, although there is a deep undercurrent to it. To study civic engagement as a shifting logic through time could be very effectively done using governmentality as a conceptual tool. In fact, a great deal of the scholarship produced to examine the emergence of neoliberal forms of citizenship utilizes the concept of governmentality and draws more broadly from Foucauldian analysis of the state and discursive practices. These conceptual tools are typically located within Foucault's 1978–1979 lectures at the Collège de France in which he sought to understand how the activity of the state is constructed within a particular regime of truth in such a way as to produce new practices and discourses that organize the activity of governing. This method, according to Foucault, is

> a matter of showing by what conjunctions a whole set of practices—from the moment they become coordinated with a regime of truth—was able to make what does not exist (madness, disease, delinquency, sexuality, etcetera), nonetheless become something, something however that continues not to exist. . . . The point of all these investigations concerning madness, disease, delinquency, sexuality, and what I am talking about now, is to show how the coupling of a set of practices and a regime of truth form an apparatus (*dispotif*) of knowledge-power that effectively marks out in reality that which does not exist and legitimately submits it to the division between true and false.[46]

In this way, the method is to determine how particular forms of knowledge (regimes of truth) are able to constitute a set of practices that can then "legislate on these practices in terms of true and false."[47] This approach draws our attention to how people in particular sectors of society begin to talk about people in particular ways, thus creating discourses that are subject-making in that they construct social groups or social processes as objects that can be organized or acted-on, perhaps even disciplined, through instruments of governing. Subject-making, however, is not understood to be solely a discursive process, since this perspective assumes that those discourses are related to actual practices of organizations, institutions, or people, especially in "legislating" forms of conduct and activity.

The interest in Foucault reflects a shift within political science and the study of social policy, which postulates that it is no longer tenable to understand the notion of the state as a structure that imposes itself in singular forms or acts of power. Rather, according to Dean, while the state is still acknowledged as a "body that claims monopoly" on territory and violence, the state is also understood as something more amorphous.[48] For that reason, a conceptual shift in analysis tends toward the activity of governing, which can be thought of as

> more or less calculated and rational activity, undertaken by a multiplicity of authorities and agencies, employing a variety of techniques and forms of knowledge, that seeks to shape conduct by working through the desires, aspirations, interests and beliefs of various actors for definite but shifting ends and with a diverse set of relatively unpredictable consequences, effects and outcomes.[49]

The concern is then how the activity of governing creates subjects who are in need of that very governing or who are articulated to relations of governing in specific ways. In this way, the activity of government becomes less about directly governing subjects and more about the governance of subjectivities, that is, the combining of forms of governance with forms of agency.

This is extremely fruitful ground for the examination of citizenship and political subjectivities. In this tradition, the focus of inquiry is directed toward the active cultivation of political ways of being through "any program, discourse, or strategy that attempts to alter or shape the actions of others or oneself. It includes but is not limited to programs conducted by the liberal state, for governance can also involve internal and voluntary relations of rule, the ways we act upon ourselves."[50] Through this lens, instruments of social policy are examined for their discursive and legislating power, demonstrated in their ability to direct conduct and behavior. For example,

Kwoon has argued for understanding the mobilization of paradoxical state discourses of empowerment and procedures of discipline aimed at youth of color and organized through the depoliticization of the not-for-profit sector as a form of "affirmative governmentality."[51] This mode of subject-making involves busying young people with activities that direct them toward "the exercise of personal empowerment and the building of human development skills, not in the posing of challenges to state power."[52]

I see observations of governmentality theorists as describing, in a much more critical way than in most studies of socialization, the process of political socialization. Their research demonstrates that the process of being socialized into a particular political form is necessarily fraught with relations of power and that it is not simply a matter of learning how to be a good citizen in the active sense. It is at the same time learning that being a passive citizen is unacceptable. It is through the use of dispersed forms of power, such as through devolved funding instruments or policy mechanisms, that individuals can "learn" their relationship to the broader society. This is one way in which we "learn" democracy.

William James's original articulation of civilian national service as a "blood tax" has yet to find real resonance in contemporary discussions of national and community service.[53] Rather, the focus has always been on, to differing degrees, the need to address ongoing social problems in the United States and to regenerate enthusiasm for, and engagement with, democracy for young people. The rhetoric of national civilian service as a place to learn citizenship and civic engagement, rather than a way of demonstrating one's loyalty or "doing your duty," is a more recent argument and is more explicitly linked to the traditions of Addams and Dewey than to James. Despite this claim, there is surprisingly little research interrogating the presuppositions of citizenship within the AmeriCorps program or critical elaboration of what the implications of particular ways of thinking about citizenship and democracy might be. There is plenty of discussion of the civic impact of the program, particularly assessment of the extent to which individuals continue to volunteer as a result of their participation or remain civically engaged, as well as the occasional discussion of how AmeriCorps could be more effective at meeting its civic mandate.[54] Much of the other work on AmeriCorps focuses on the effectiveness of the service methods employed, the vocational and interpersonal skills developed by participants, program models, and effect on organizational program planning.[55] Still others have explored the extent to which participation in AmeriCorps cultivates a commitment to social justice in participants, a position that is marginal within the literature perhaps because of the politically volatile claim that AmeriCorps harbors liberal sympathies and which itself has spurned research demonstrating the neutrality and objectivity of AmeriCorps.[56] Some of the less flattering literature on AmeriCorps has emerged in the context of the effectiveness of the program at the grassroots level and its impact on the provision of public services; many of these studies were conducted soon after the establishment of the program and do not focus on its organization at the federal level.[57]

While these studies move toward questions of the larger social purpose of the program and possibly even its effects on the organization of labor in the nonprofit sector, none approach the question of how AmeriCorps is part of larger shifts in the articulation of citizenship or the relationship of those shifts to the political economy of public life and democratic social relations. For me, this is not just a theoretical exercise. These are questions that have emerged out of my own experience, my own hours of labor and witness to human suffering, as well as my own feelings of a need for growth, the paralysis caused by injustice, and the dissonance of paradoxes within democratic life. I believe strongly, and have seen the evidence many times over, that a kind of learning is possible that can transform everyday people into human beings who are more political, more radicalized, more attuned to social realities and problems of change. However, this anecdotal evidence again begs the questions I have already posed: Under what conditions does this transformation take place and under what conditions is it suppressed?

I will now turn my attention to a second stream that supports the argument that community service is an effective means through which to learn democracy. This stream, however, involves a much more explicit pedagogical assertion than the previously discussed relationship between national service and political socialization. Running parallel to the emergence of civilian national service programs at the federal level, and in the public sector, has been the growth of community service and service-learning as forms of citizenship education, particularly within American higher education.

Stream Two: Community Service, Service-learning, and Civic Engagement

The emergence of volunteer community service and its link to civic engagement is a contested topic. Part of this contestation rests in differing definitions of volunteerism. To begin, there is an important distinction between voluntary and volunteer. Voluntary is often used to refer to free or voluntary association, meaning the ability of individuals to pick and choose with whom they congregate and for what purposes. This voluntary, or free, association is considered a hallmark of liberal democracy and is a long-standing indicator of civic health, particularly to the extent that citizens engage in voluntary association outside of their workplaces and family homes. Many trace this argument back to Alexis de Tocqueville's observation that civic associations "both make individuals better and improve society" by forcing individuals with different interests into spaces of shared concerns and compelling them to work together for the common good.[58]

Volunteerism, however, has long carried an inference of unpaid, and often unskilled, labor. Within a capitalist mode of production, we tend to think of labor and work as paid or unpaid, largely through the mechanisms of the wage. Waged labor is very familiar to us because it is the only manner through which most of us can access the means to subsist; we need wages in order to eat, drink water, shelter and clothe ourselves, have access to education and leisure, and in some places on the planet, breathe clean air. However, much of the labor done to reproduce our society is not paid through a formal wage relationship. Labor can be unwaged in a manner that is normalized by society, such as in the case of reproductive labor in the home done by women. Rendering this labor as "unwaged" or "unproductive" was a crucial aspect of the development of capitalism in Europe.[59] Labor can also be unwaged legally or illegally (such as corvée or slavery), paid in the informal economy (and often not in keeping with employment regulation), or done for free on a voluntary basis, meaning without coercion. Thus, one may "volunteer" by providing any number of different sorts of labor for free, but we typically think of labor done outside the home for no wage on a voluntary basis as volunteer work or charity. I happen to be one of those uniquely American individuals who was, for a good part of my youth, an excellent—and in fact award-winning—volunteer. My extensive volunteerism portfolio earned me a Good Citizens Medal from the Daughters of the American Revolution among other accolades. I pulled weeds, taught preschoolers Spanish, made resource files for parents of sick children, cared for babies during church services, served meals at shelters, provided classroom support at schools, raised money for numerous causes, cleaned up parks, sorted recycling, taught English, and the list could go on for some time. Many of these activities were simply things that needed doing, such as picking up trash in parks or running a recycling program, for which no other entity seemed to be taking responsibility. Some of this labor, however, was directed at providing human services for individuals, such as serving meals and cleaning bathrooms in a homeless shelter. For many individuals, volunteerism reflects the long history of individual acts of kindness or conscience associated with charity. For much of the history of meeting human need, the state has not taken an active role in caring for people, and this burden has fallen to individuals and their associations.[60] For much of this history, good works or charitable acts have been associated with the major religious traditions; people have been motivated to provide their labor and money by their faith, and much of that labor has been directed at caring for the poor or the well-being of the larger community. Some of these traditions have even spawned much more politically radical expressions of charity, such as the Catholic Worker Movement. I, however, had no religious or moral motivation; it seemed to me that it was simply the right thing to do for my community, for my neighbors, and as a citizen. In this way, I am both the subject and object of this research.

This sort of thinking about volunteerism is often traced to the progressive reform era of North America and Western Europe in the late nineteenth and early twentieth century. In fact, while charity and charitable acts have been around for centuries, the concept of community service is thought to have emerged in the United States in the twentieth century and only solidified in common usage after the Great Depression.[61] Morton and Saltmarsh, like many contemporary advocates of community service, trace its roots to what they call the "crisis of community" that emerged in the late nineteenth and early twentieth centuries. This "crisis" was in fact an iteration of a familiar contradiction; abhorrent poverty in the face of massive private accumulation of wealth in conflict with the rhetoric of democratic freedom and equality. These paradoxes, seemingly between the promises of democracy and the worst excesses of unregulated accumulation of capital, drove the emergence of both secular and religious organizations devoted to addressing the needs of the poor. Many of these organizations also demonstrated an interest in reforming social policy and public opinion. They were particularly interested in both addressing problems of fraud and waste within earlier iterations of charitable groups, but also, importantly, in bringing a scientific or technical planning process to the issue of dealing with poverty.[62]

The Settlement House Movement, which began with the building of Toynbee Hall in East London, is famously chronicled in the United States through the history of Hull House in Chicago and the work of Jane Addams. Addams, across her numerous published works, did a great deal to argue that community service was not about providing charity, but should create conditions for the privileged to understand the roots of inequality and for all members of the community to work together to reform unjust systems and provide equal opportunities to all.[63] Based on these texts, Addams's work is largely interpreted today as a reenvisioning of community service not as "service," or something done through charitable and altruistic intentions, but as the necessary work of citizens in a democratic society.[64] John Dewey, who was Addams's contemporary and friend, saw the crisis a bit differently from her; he was concerned with the loss of community and the emergence of a self-interested, consumption-oriented culture that would ultimately pervert the true character and purpose of democracy as a mode of public, collective life.[65] Each of them made a strong case that the work of citizens should be intricately tied to free association across boundaries of class and ethnicity so that citizens could see the tremendous public needs for social reform and press the government to take up policy solutions. These complimentary visions of robust citizen participation in service and advocacy are where we find the roots of the idea that community service should not reflect charitable motivations, but be seen as a way to learn democracy, regardless of whether community service as we understand it today is a faithful reading of their positions.

The contours and parameters of how we define volunteerism and community service have been studied from numerous disciplinary angles, but I am primarily concerned with how community service has evolved as an educational response to perceived problems in democracy. A major caveat is necessary here. It became apparent to many educational theorists early on that community service alone would be an insufficient basis for claims that learning was taking place. To argue that community service is inherently pedagogical, apart from any sort of organized facilitation, is to make an argument for community service as either informal learning (that is, unstructured and not facilitated) or a form of political socialization. To argue for political socialization would mean that the activity itself, done most likely in concert with others, trains one into a particular way of thinking about and orienting the self toward the public realm, particularly through the ritualistic and often prescriptive and punitive way in which learning as socialization takes place. Socialization is a powerful form of learning because it is constant, it comes from many directions, and it is attached to mechanisms of discipline. When you step outside what is normal, the response tends to be emotionally or physically violent. Processes of socialization are embodied in institutions, such as the family, schools, and so on. Much the same way that we learn the cultural necessity of waiting in queues or raising our hand to gain the attention of an authority figure, community service as socialization would teach us a particular axiology or meaning system through repetition and reinforcement of the act and exposure to the community in which the act takes place and among whom the work is done. I have very clear memories of going with my entire family to work in a soup kitchen and of packing sack lunches for distribution at a homeless shelter. It was not something that was done without purpose. My parents intended that my brother and I learn to think about poverty and inequality in a particular way, specifically not to think less of people because they were poor. They wanted us to be compassionate and to recognize peoples' humanity. These activities, however, did not teach me anything about where poverty comes from or why some people have enough to eat and others do not. A structural analysis of poverty was not my parents' aim at the time, and thus any of those lessons learned would have to be incidental to the experience. The incidental, even accidental, character of this form of learning introduces both uncertainty and mysticism into the claim that community service is a means to learn democracy.

In this way, community service alone can be seen as an insufficient means for learning particular lessons about democracy, although that does not preclude the possibility that catalytic incidents or aha moments might emerge; neither does it mean that performing community service could not support the development of a particular disposition toward public or community life. This is precisely the argument that has been made by advocates of a nationalized form of community service as national civilian service. According to these proponents, community service can build an "ethic or personal responsibility or good character."[66] In fact, William James's original call for national civilian service is often interpreted as a call to build national allegiance and character through service. From this perspective, service itself is understood to form at attachment and to lead to the development of civic consciousness.[67]

However, when understood from a pedagogical standpoint, community service as a means to learn democracy requires a more guided hand. This also seems to be the early lessons from experiments in the 1970s and '80s with community service in higher education. As mentioned in the previous section, service and volunteerism began to emerge as popular activities among university students after the Second World War. The popularity of these activities were sharply critiqued by Ivan Illich in 1968 when he argued: "Next to money and guns, the third largest North American export is the U.S. idealist, who turns up in every theater of the world: the teacher, the volunteer, the missionary, the community organizer, the economic developer, and the vacationing do-gooders."[68] The slow movement of these activities from extracurricular to co-curricular and then curricular is part of a larger set of reforms of higher education in the United States, including an emphasis on constructivist approaches to learning, demands from students for more socially relevant education, and movements by faculty and funders to revitalize the democratic mission of higher education.

The result has been a vast body of research and theorization that falls under the banner of service-learning. Service-learning is often distinguished from a "pure" community service by its orientation, intentionality, and institutionalization. Service-learning has the explicit purpose of using community service as a experiential method of teaching and learning curricular or co-curricular subject matter, and is one of several experiential pedagogies popular in secondary and higher education. It is guided or facilitated; it has either implicit or explicit learning goals; and, depending on how it is embedded in an academic content, may be tied to a body of theory or research. Sometimes service-learning that is part of a course is referred to as *academic* service-learning, while the approach in a co-curricular context might be called *community* service-learning. A great deal of effort by a large community of scholars and practitioners has gone into establishing the boundaries of rigor in relation to service-learning, and many of the claims about its possible outcomes are linked to standards of practice.

The literature on service-learning has many different philosophical groundings, drawing from poststructuralist, postmodernism, pragmatist, Marxian, and liberal influences. However, one agreed-on necessity is reflection. Perhaps emerging from the early grounding of service-learning in larger models of experiential learning, a defining characteristic is the requirement that reflection be intentional and organized, not ad-hoc or incidental. In academic service-learning the requirements around reflection must address curricular goals, course texts, and standards of rigor. In community service-learning, there may be some explicit attention to learning goals set out by facilitators or organizers, but the reflection component is often more relaxed. In either case, the pedagogical purposes of reflection are interrelated. The aim is as much to increase the capacity for reflection within the learner and facilitator as it is to reflect on the experience of service and what might be learned from it. In many ways, the literature on service-learning mirrors the same concerns present in discussions of reflective practice among educators and other human service and cultural workers. The quality, scope, extent, depth, and content of reflection are largely pinpointed as the means through which service-learning is able to develop particular outcomes. There are a myriad of aspects of service-learning that have been studied, particularly in the context of the psychosocial development of undergraduate students, but one of the most consistent claims about service-learning is that it is a pedagogical approach with the potential to contribute to the development of good citizenship and democratic dispositions in young people.

While the philosophical influence of John Dewey dominates the literature on service and learning, scholars and pedagogues who diverge from this perspective have provided important insights into the relationship between learning and service as it relates to different ways of conceptualizing justice, social transformation, and even democracy. In fact, early scholarship on service-learning indicated that there were at least four political traditions within the field representing liberal democratic, participatory, social justice, and service-oriented frameworks.[69] Each of these traditions is driven by differing assumptions about democracy, but also different axiologies about the roots of social inequality and the appropriate means to redress such conditions as well as differing epistemologies and ontologies. Thus, service-learning as a body of pedagogical theory involves different and competing models, characterized by possibly incompatible normative claims with important implications for teaching and learning.[70]

However, for the purposes of understanding the claim that service leads to learning civic engagement, particularly within the AmeriCorps program, I want to focus at this point on the tradition grounded in Dewey. I will concentrate here on the arguments made by Giles and Eyler[71] and Saltmarsh[72] that utilize the conceptual universe of Dewey to justify community service as the basis of learning democracy. According to these authors, Dewey's argument begins with the pragmatist position that education is not separate from life, but is rather a means of life. As such, Dewey rejected both a dualism between education and life and the idea of education as an end in itself; rather, education must be related to a purpose. For Dewey, the purpose was democracy and the development of both the self and society. In his early critique, *The School and Society*, Dewey grounded his argument for "new education" in the disjuncture between the organization of the school, the curriculum and pedagogy, and the demands of society or the "active community."[73] He argued:

> A society is a number of people held together because they are working along common lines, in a common spirit, and with reference to common aims. The common needs and aims

demand a growing interchange of thought and growing unity of sympathetic feeling. The radical reason that the present school cannot organize itself as a natural social unit is because just this element of common and productive activity is absent.[74]

This diagnosis is clearly echoed in many of the calls for civic engagement and early calls for service-learning. According to Dewey, the ethical commitment that can reorient education, and schools as institutions, is democracy. Or at least this is the interpretation of Dewey offered by proponents of service-learning. Saltmarsh argues that

> connected knowing treats education not as something separate from "life" but as life itself, and education becomes a lifelong process carried forward by an individual provided with the proficiencies to be a self-directed learner. Education is a means to an end, a way of life delineated by civic engagement. As Dewey wrote, "unless education has some frame of reference it is bound to be aimless, lacking a unified objective. The necessity for a frame of reference must be admitted. There exists in this country such a unified frame. It is called democracy."[75]

The form of education that could stimulate such connection—and one that could ultimately contribute to democracy—is dependent on two positions. First, Dewey, in his opposition to dualisms, insisted that the mind is not separate from action, the body, or activity. Rather, knowledge, or intelligence, involves the reorganization of meaning through experience.[76] This has often been interpreted as the argument that people learn best by "doing." The purpose of education, then, is to attend to and develop the relation between mind and activity in order to develop students as self-directed learners capable of engaging with the broader community, constructing a democratic society, and cultivating their own growth. Dewey concisely discusses this point in the essay "The Need for Philosophy of Education" from 1934.[77] Second, while Dewey dismissed any dualism between education and life, he also argued that experience and education cannot be directly related. They are not the same thing. This position can be seen in his famous claim that experience can be "miseducative," and that in order to be "educative" experience must involve a temporal dimension (principle of continuity) and a social dimension (principle of interaction).[78] This implies not only that learning happens over time and in relation to previous learning, but also that learning involves the interaction between the subjective or individual person and the objective or material situation.

There are two pedagogical implications of this argument that are relevant to the idea of service as a way to learn democracy and are foundational to the service-learning literature as well. The first implication has to do with the relationship between experience and the construction of meaning. In order for a situational interaction to result in learning, and so to not become "miseducative," the learner must have the capacity to engage in reflective thinking or reflective inquiry geared toward particular kinds of experience. Dewey was clear that just as education and experience cannot be conflated, neither can experience and activity. A famous example of his was washing dishes. Such an activity could not be understood as an experience with the potential to be educative unless washing dishes was geared toward addressing a particular problem. Just "doing something" does not constitute the "experience" that he imagines at the center of learning. Rather, human activity should be geared toward problem solving and, in the act of attempting to address objective conditions in need of change, the learner must engage in reflective thought. Reflective thought, in which consideration of previously held or understood fact and belief are brought into relation with the present, was imagined by Dewey as interlinking as a "train, chain, or thread."[79] As a woman who has washed many dishes in her life with little or no explanation of the purpose, I object to his decidedly sexist interpretation of the act, and I would suggest there is much to be learned from the exclusive monotony of being assigned to the kitchen. For me, the doldrums of ironing my father's shirts every week became quite an "educative" experience, especially since my brother never had to do it (nor did my father). Nevertheless, his point leads us toward the perspective that experience is something quite different from everyday tasks and banalities.

Reflective thinking is, for Dewey, the connective tissue between learning and experience. Reflective thought, or reflective inquiry when that thought is directed at overcoming the dualism between mind and activity through problem solving, involves processes of consideration, conjecture, information gathering, processing, and application; and it should, ultimately, evolve into a form of inquiry. This idea that reflection is what mediates the relationship between the individual and the situation, or subject and object, has led to the insistence that reflection is the linchpin that transforms experience into learning. The questions for service-learning pedagogues then become: On what basis does this reflection take place? Should it be facilitated or self-directed? For service-learning scholars, reflection should be facilitated within the context of academic course goals and/or skill-based or attitudinal goals, with the ultimate goal being learners' developing the capacity for individual self-reflection. The need for reflection, however, is nonnegotiable. The basic construction of experiential learning offered by Dewey is ubiquitously present with slight variations in numerous models of experiential learning, including the popularly used framework developed by Kolb,[80] which also iterates forms of reflection, conceptualization, and application as intrinsic to experiential learning.

Taking Dewey's position that education is not opposed to life but rather a means of life, the second pedagogical implication concerns the form in which one experiences society. Saltmarsh's interpretation of Dewey's argument is that free and democratic association is the preferred domain for education.[81] Dewey himself took this point even further to argue that

> democracy is the belief in the ability of human experience to generate the aims and methods by which further experience will grow in ordered richness. . . . Democracy as compared with other ways of life is the sole way of living which believes wholeheartedly in the process of experience as end and as means; as that which is capable of generating the science which is the sole dependable authority for the direction of further experience and which releases emotions, needs and desires so as to call into being the things that have not existed in the past.[82]

To this end, the construction of the democratic community, which is premised on diversity and tolerance, dictates the forms of association that stimulate "educative" experiences. Saltmarsh argued that, for Dewey, association in democratic community is the only way to overcome the dualism of self and society and thus to fully develop as an individual; the individual self finds its realization only through association with others. This association, this connection, Dewey argued, "is that free interaction of individual human beings with surrounding conditions, especially the human surroundings, which develops and satisfies need and desire by increasing knowledge of things as they are."[83] Through this association, the individual comes into contact with interests that diverge from their own narrow perspective, and through such experiences and a practiced capacity of reflection, develops their own interests as part and parcel of the common good. Saltmarsh further argued that while Dewey did not specify community service as a form of this association, he did, through his engagement in the Settlement House movement, come to realize a form of "service association" as ideal for learning democracy. This service association cannot, however, be premised on charitable models. It must be premised on the breaking of social barriers and divisions, the cultivation of reciprocity, the distribution of opportunity, and must reflect an awareness of relationships of privilege grounded in a sense of justice.

This framework grounds the argument that, through community service, people engage in a form of associational life that orients them toward both meeting pressing social needs and solving problems in local communities. The conclusion is that these experiences of community service can, under particular conditions, generate learning about democracy and about the common good, stimulating individual's capacity and engagement to participate in public life. This argument has been widely critiqued on several important bases, including: the problematic notion that community service actually benefits communities; the potential for class, race, and gender power relations to be reinscribed through service activities; the entrenchment of "Band-Aid" or charity models of social change; the pathologizing of poor people; the enforcement of imperialist, colonialist, orientalist, and liberal notions of "others"; and the aiding/abetting of neoliberal reforms of state–civil society relations.[84] While these critiques are deeply important, I want to argue that there is another problem present in this formulation beyond the reproduction of existing inequitable social relations through the politics of community service. I would characterize this additional problem as the violence of abstraction.[85] Such abstraction becomes a problem not just in terms of the outcomes of, or normalization of, community service, but in terms of our ability to conceptualize service as a relation through which people learn in such a way that reproduces exploitative and oppressive social relations and forms of knowledge. In other words, I would argue that Dewey's philosophical mode of abstraction occludes our ability to understand the pedagogical practice of ideology because the particular ontology-epistemology relation on which this argument is built cannot account for the hierarchical organization of our societies, particular along the lines of race, gender, and class.

Absent from this Dewey-inspired articulation of community service as a pedagogy for learning democracy is any substantive engagement with the question of social power. This is despite the fact that Dewey himself professed great concern over issues of inequality, including poverty and militarism. There is little attention to the social relations that compose society, that is, the real people in their historical reality actively creating their social world. Rather, there is a tendency to emphasize the conflation of democracy with commonality and with society as a shared public space. This obscures the reality that civil society, as I discussed in the previous chapter, is composed through real and competing material interests which are in conflict with one another. It further requires ignoring history and the historical development of racist and sexist capitalist relations that have had everything to do with ordering and organizing class relations. For example, racism does not exist because race is a biological reality; it exists because it is an effective means of organizing social power. Racism also exists not just because there are individuals who harbor racial prejudice, or even just because it a cultural phenomenon, but because racism is propagated through institutions that wield power in and over society, institutions such as the state and capital. It is the state, it all its permutations, that is also absent from this conceptualization of society and democracy, as is capital. Without substantive engagement with the state and capital, a framework for learning democracy that prioritizes reciprocity, commonality, equal opportunity, and justice loses its connection to sources of division, inequality, and injustice; it is unable to go "to the roots."

Convergence: A State Politics of Learning Democracy

These parallel and converging movements of advocacy for community service as a form of civic engagement beg the question as to why the pedagogy of service-learning has been incorporated as a project of the state. This is the central concern of the research that follows, asking what exactly this convergence has to do with the teaching and learning of democracy in our historical moment. In the following chapter I examine the ways in which state regulation creates a terrain on which experiential learning through service in the AmeriCorps program takes place as well as influences the pedagogical and epistemological possibilities within more formalized training activities. The purpose moving forward is to try to understand the social relations in which particular conceptualizations of democracy and citizenship arise—and are even made possible—within the AmeriCorps program. This is more than a matter of discourse; it is a matter of the daily activity of service and its relationship to learning and, crucially, how these activities are socially organized.

Chapter Three

The Social Organization of Community Service and Civic Engagement in AmeriCorps

Mike is a twenty-three-year-old white American man. He has a university degree and is a member of an AmeriCorps program, working in public schools to address the achievement gap. Every Monday through Friday, Mike gets up at 6:00 a.m. School starts at 7:45, but he needs to be there by 7:15 in order to get the children off the school buses and into their classrooms. He does not earn enough money to afford a car, and his family is not in the financial position to provide him with one. Gas prices are too high anyway and as a twenty-three-year-old male, the insurance costs are astronomical. He usually rides his bike to school, but if the weather is bad he will have to take the bus and get up at 5:30 a.m. instead of 6:00 a.m. By 7:15, he is dropping his coat and lunch off in the volunteers' office at the school and looking through the calendar to see what his day holds. By 7:30, he is on the sidewalk, waiting for the buses, and ushering hundreds of children into school. The children speak thirty-four different languages, but the sounds of Spanish rise above the crowd, and Mike scans their faces to see if he can spot who among the group has not had breakfast that morning. By 7:45, he is in his first classroom and his day proceeds in a blur: thirty minutes of reading with this kid, twenty-five minutes of math with that one, lunch duty, lesson planning, photocopying for a teacher. In the afternoon he struggles with his math group, three young boys who have no interest in fractions. He wonders if public education is really just a complicated exercise in behavior management.

By 2:45 he is back on the sidewalk, wrangling kids onto buses, watching some wander off into the neighborhood, others peering their heads around the corner waiting for a sight of their parent's car. At 3:00 p.m. he is back in the school, organizing children in afterschool activities, promising that after they do their homework for sixty minutes they can play basketball and soccer. At 4:30, he checks the sidewalks to see who is still waiting for their parents and calls them inside before the "entrepreneurs," as he has come to understand them, of the neighborhood arrive at the playground for their afternoon business transactions. By 6:00 p.m., after a twelve-hour day, he is pacing in the hallway outside his office, starving and exhausted, waiting for a focus group to begin where he can have something to eat and talk about what he has learned by serving in AmeriCorps.

Mike's exhaustion and frustration are in part due to his perception that every day at school is a repetition of the same stressors, anxieties, complications, and struggles as the day before. For Mike, every day in AmeriCorps is experienced as "working in schools," as if the way in which he does his work is the only way one could "work in schools." Mike goes to school each day with his job description in his head, a set of duties he is obliged to perform both out of a commitment to the children he works with and the AmeriCorps program in which he serves. He arrives at school every day with only a vague awareness that his daily experience of service in AmeriCorps is organized somewhere else between federal policy and a local program site, and that what seems like the natural monotony of everyday work is in reality a highly specific form of intervention in school life, theorized and organized to produce particular outcomes. For Mike, this organization disappears as he is presented with the very real struggle of convincing a student to stay in his seat during science class.

In exploring how and under what conditions young people learn democracy within the AmeriCorps program, the question of how could be answered using the traditional theoretical tools of educational research. AmeriCorps members engage in experiential learning through their everyday work experience, most of which could be classified as incidental in that they neither expect nor pursue the new ideas or interpretations generated through their service. They also participate in trainings and workshops and we could assume they learn something in those spaces as well. Educational researchers have developed sophisticated tools for analyzing the experiential and reflective relationships involved in these forms of learning. The tools, however, say nothing about the context of learning in the first place. As Himani Bannerji describes, they arrive at "the experience" as an already "found object"[1] on the terrain of social life and investigate only its interpretive domain, how a learner makes meaning of this experience. While this is an important area of investigation, it is not the kind of inquiry that helps explain why AmeriCorps, as an apparatus of the state, operates in the way that it does and what effect that operation has on learning in the program. This kind of questioning must interrogate *how* the space and practice of learning democracy, or civic engagement, is established in AmeriCorps. How do young people arrive at the experiential base of this democratic learning? How does this experience emerge out of the institutional processes of AmeriCorps?

This sort of analysis is pursued through institutional ethnography, and in what follows in this chapter I will examine the regulations, protocols, and their concretization in institutional texts, all of which coordinate the sites, relations, and conditions under which learning and civic engagement take place within the AmeriCorps program. The sites of learning in AmeriCorps are determined before the arrival of members. By sites of learning, I am referring to the organizational contexts in which AmeriCorps members serve, which are in turn related to the kind of service work they perform. The sites of AmeriCorps work are chosen through a nationally competitive grants process and a Corporation for National and Community Service committee, in theory, selects these because they represent some of the most innovative local-level responses to important social challenges facing Americans today. Each of these sites is created by individuals who work within institutional frameworks and utilize particular ways of knowing to understand the social problem at hand. In this way, each site constitutes a lens, if you will, encompassing an organizational approach to coordinating human activity toward a specific social problem and involving an identified population. In this way each site in fact encompasses a terrain of interconstitutive social relations and ideologies. This, however, is not easily discernible from the immediacy of the AmeriCorps members' standpoint of "working in schools." What constitutes a site of civic engagement and democratic learning in AmeriCorps is a highly regulated process, one produced through the complex interconnections between federal regulations and agency funding priorities.

To begin this process, however, and to attempt to understand how learning is organized within the program, it is important to examine the processes at both the federal and state level that contribute to the shaping and selection of these sites of learning within which civic engagement is expected to be cultivated and learned. I have organized this discussion in two parts, which examine four institutional processes that regulate the creation of AmeriCorps program sites and activities. In the first discussion I examine two processes I call eligibility and sustainability, which emerge through federal legislation and CNCS policy making and determine the selection of AmeriCorps sites. In the second discussion, I examine the third and fourth processes, which stem from CNCS policy and priorities, as well as processes of interpretation of these rules at state and local levels. These processes govern the sorts of activities the members may engage in, those activities deemed permissible, and finally the use of specific organizational development tools, called logic models, which require the use of certain ideological modes of decision making in order to present a coherent and effective program model.

Institutional Regulation of Sites of Civic Engagement

While there are four important processes of institutional regulation that produce a site of learning and civic engagement within AmeriCorps and that determine the experiential terrain for learning democracy within the program, the first two narrow the field of the kind of organizations that are deemed suitable for AmeriCorps. In what follows, I will outline the wandering, and sometimes contradictory, ways in which these regulations are taken up in the social organization of AmeriCorps program sites. In order to do this, I will explore a wide variety of public documentation concerning the program, including federal legislation, codes of regulation, and organizational documentation from the CNCS, such as funding protocols and guidelines.

CRITERIA 1: ELIGIBILITY

It is popularly understood that AmeriCorps grants are restricted to 501(c)(3) not-for-profit, charitable, tax-exempt organizations. The truth of this claim is hard to determine. On the one hand, the 2008 Code of Federal Regulations (CFR) does *not* explicitly limit eligibility to 501(c)(3) organizations; states, tribes, not-for-profit organizations (both public and private), colleges and universities, religious and charitable labor organizations, and in some cases federal government agencies are also eligible to apply. However, the section of the code that lists the prohibited activities of AmeriCorps members includes a prohibition on "providing a direct benefit to (i) a business organized for profit; (ii) a labor union; (iii) a partisan political organization; (iv) a not-for-profit organization that fails to comply with the restrictions contained in section 501(c)(3) of the Internal Revenue Code."[2] Further, the Code of Federal Regulations does not provide a definition of a not-for-profit organization. On the other hand, specific legislative acts governing CNCS, from 1990, 1993, and 2009, prohibit affiliation with organizations that do not comply with the requirements of the 501(c) tax code.[3] The tax code category of 501(c), however, refers to the general category of not-for-profit organizations and not to any specific type within that large, amorphous group. The distinction between groups within the 501c category, as we will see, largely depends on the amount of political involvement of the organization. The language here implies restriction, but lacks specification. Further, the CNCS Notice of Federal Funds Offered (NFFOs) for AmeriCorps funding from 2006 to 2015 include inconsistent directions. From 2006 to 2009, applicants for AmeriCorps grants were required to declare that they were not a registered 501(c)(4) organization in accordance with the Lobby Disclosure Act of 1995. Further, the NFFOs, also called Notices of Funding Availability (NOFAs), state that "any organization described in Section 501(c)(4) of the Internal Revenue Code of 1986, 26 U.S.C. 501(c)(4), that engages in lobbying activities is not eligible to apply, serve as a host site for member placements, or act in any type of supervisory role in AmeriCorps programs."[4] However, between 2010 and 2013, no mention was made, at the national level, of confinement to 501(c)(3). In 2014, the language prohibiting 501(c)(4) organizations returned. A final confounding element is that the 2009 Serve America Act does define a "not-for-profit organization" as follows:

> (3) NONPROFIT.—The term "not-for-profit," used with respect to an entity or organization, means—(A) an entity or organization described in section 501(c)(3) of the Internal Revenue Code of 1986 and exempt from taxation under section 501(a) of such Code; and (B) an entity or organization described in paragraph (1) or (2) of section 170(c) of such Code.[5]

This definition, however, is only provided with reference to the Nonprofit Capacity Building Program (NCBP). The Serve America Act also states that the term not-for-profit can be used interchangeably with the term *community-based entity.*

These regulations paint a confusing picture. Who is eligible for an AmeriCorps grant? While one might be able to make the technical argument that any 501(c) organization is eligible to *apply* for a grant, the regulations are very clear as to what kind of organization is allowed to benefit from the service of AmeriCorps members. Thus, while organizations other than 501(c)(3) are not explicitly excluded from eligibility criteria for funding, they are explicitly prohibited from participation in the program. In this way, non-501(c)(3) organizations are "prohibited" as sites of AmeriCorps engagement, and 501(c)(3) organizations are positioned as the only kind of organizations suitable for AmeriCorps placement. This regulation raises an important question: What is the significance of restricting AmeriCorps programming to 501(c)(3) organizations?

Code 501(c) is used by the Internal Revenue Service (IRS) to recognize entities within the United States that are exempt from federal income taxes. 501(c) literally refers to the listing of these organizations in the tax code, which specifies twenty-eight different kinds of organizations that can be exempt from taxes. These organizations are colloquially known as "not-for-profit" organizations, but in following the intent of the tax code, it is more accurate to refer to them as "tax exempt." Out of the twenty-eight varieties of tax-exempt organizations in the United States, the 501(c)(3) is both the largest and least specific category. According to Title 26, an organization can be designated as a 501(c)(3) if it falls under the following characterization:

> Corporations, and any community chest, fund, or foundation, organized and operated exclusively for religious, charitable, scientific, testing for public safety, literary, or educational purposes, or to foster national or international amateur sports competition (but only if no part of its activities involve the provision of athletic facilities or equipment), or for the prevention of cruelty to children or animals, no part of the net earnings of which inures to the benefit of any private shareholder or individual, no substantial part of the activities of which is carrying on propaganda, or otherwise attempting, to influence legislation (except as otherwise provided in subsection (h)), and which does not participate in, or intervene in (including the publishing or distributing of statements), any political campaign on behalf of (or in opposition to) any candidate for public office.[6]

This definition is widely interpreted as charitable organizations, including religious, labor, human service, or educational organizations. The intent of the code is to reference organizations that work in pursuit of the "social welfare" in such a way that no *individual* gains profit or revenue from the organization's activities.

While organizations listed under designates 501(c)(1) or (2), and (c)(5)–(28) are extremely specific, most organizations in the "not-for-profit" sector are incorporated as either 501(c)(3) or 501(c)(4). In reality, overlap exists between the (c)(3) and (c)(4) statuses in terms of the intent of the exemption from tax liabilities. Both codes designate organizations that serve the social or public welfare. Their core differences arise to the extent to which they engage in political activities as part of their core operations. Categories such as "political activities" and "legislative activities" thus become the characteristics differentiating 501(c)(3) organizations from 501(c)(4) organizations.

What appears to be important to administrators of AmeriCorps is the designation made at the federal level between a 501(c)(3) and a 501(c)(4) organization, specifically in relation to their participation in "political" and "legislative" activities. According to the IRS, a 501(c)(3) organization is

> Absolutely prohibited from directly or indirectly participating in, or intervening in, any political campaign on behalf of (or in opposition to) any candidate for elective public office. Contributions to political campaign funds or public statements of position (verbal or written) made on behalf of the organization in favor of or in opposition to any candidate for public office clearly violate the prohibition against political campaign activity. Violating this prohibition may result in denial or revocation of tax-exempt status and the imposition of certain excise taxes.[7]

But given this, 501(c)(3) organizations are not prohibited from engaging in voter registration, education, or get-out-the vote (GOTV) campaigns as long as these activities are conducted in a "non-partisan" manner. "Partisan" is not explicitly defined by the IRS, but is said to be "activities with evidence of bias that (a) would favor one candidate over another; (b) oppose a candidate in some manner; or (c) have the effect of favoring a candidate or group of candidates, will constitute prohibited participation or intervention."[8] Further, 501(c)(3) organizations are prohibited from lobbying and advocacy.

> In general, no organization may qualify for section 501(c)(3) status if a substantial part of its activities is attempting to influence legislation (commonly known as *lobbying*). . . . An organization will be regarded as attempting to influence legislation if it contacts, or urges the public to contact, members or employees of a legislative body for the purpose of proposing, supporting, or opposing legislation, or if the organization advocates the adoption or rejection of legislation.[9]

However, there are small allowances for this sort of activity.

> Organizations may, however, involve themselves in issues of public policy without the activity being considered as lobbying. For example, organizations may conduct educational meetings, prepare and distribute educational materials, or otherwise consider public policy issues in an educational manner without jeopardizing their tax-exempt status.[10]

501(c)(4) organizations, however, are also understood to be entities that are organized "exclusively for the promotion of social welfare."[11] A 501(c)(4) is differentiated from a 501(c)(3) by allowance for political and legislative activity.

> Seeking legislation germane to the organization's programs is a permissible means of attaining social welfare purposes. Thus, a section 501(c)(4) social welfare organization may further its exempt purposes through lobbying as its primary activity without jeopardizing its exempt status. . . . The promotion of social welfare does not include direct or indirect participation or intervention in political campaigns on behalf of or in opposition to any candidate for public office. However, a section 501(c)(4) social welfare organization may engage in some political activities, so long as that is not its primary activity.[12]

These regulations result in the 501(c)(3) being contrasted to the 501(c)(4) organization as a "non-political" entity that engages in direct human service activity.

In accordance with these regulations, the first institutional organization of learning in the AmeriCorps program takes place by confining the experiential terrain of learning to particular kinds of organizations charged with doing human service work that are explicitly separated from the political domain. This, of course, does not mean that there is no political discourse—specifically electoral discourse—within 501(c)(3) organizations. However, it does mean that this discourse will exist on an informal basis and will not be integrated into the mission, mandates, or officially sanctioned and funded activities of the organization. The *intentional* engagement with politics is removed from daily experience at first through the ways in which the organization directs human labor toward the amelioration of human need. In a 501(c)(3), AmeriCorps members will find themselves working side by side with other individuals doing the same kinds of direct human service activity and, perhaps, the small amount of political activities allowed under 501(c)(3) code. The AmeriCorps members, however, can be disengaged from this work, if it is exists at all, by further restrictions on their labor imposed by the AmeriCorps regulations. It is in this first act of institutional coordination that a central relationship within AmeriCorps arises: *Politics*, meaning the formal electoral and policy domain, and lowercase *politics*, meaning more informal relations of power, are formally separated from one another. While the 501(c)(3) regulations clearly reference Politics in the context of political partisanship, this research reveals that these regulations mean something different in practice.

CRITERIA 2: SUSTAINABILITY

Given the complex of institutional rules and funding protocols that confine AmeriCorps to a particular segment of the not-for-profit sector, the regulations of the program reveal that AmeriCorps sites are further narrowed by a set of program requirements that address their viability. In 2005, the AmeriCorps program issued a new set of regulations called the AmeriCorps Rule. The form of regulation is revamped periodically and reflects amendments to the provisions and regulations of the AmeriCorps program. The 2005 Rule, which went into effect on September 6, 2005, governed the AmeriCorps sites that participated in my research and their most recent grant applications. The revision of AmeriCorps provisions was undertaken in 2004 in response to Executive Order 13331, issued by President George W. Bush, which "aimed at making national and community service programs better able to engage Americans in volunteering, more responsive to State and local needs, more accountable and effective, and more accessible to community organizations, including faith-based organizations."[13] Further, the Consolidated Appropriations Act for 2004, which set the budget for the CNCS,

> directed the Corporation to reduce the Federal cost per participants and to increase the level of matching funds and in-kind contributions provided by the private sector . . . and directed the Corporation to engage in notice and comment rulemaking about the issue of "sustainability."[14]

Again the following year, the Consolidated Appropriations Act for 2005 once again directed the Corporation to "increase significantly the level of matching funds and in-kind contributions provided by the private sector" and "reduce the total Federal costs per participant in all programs."[15] The language of "sustainability" refers explicitly to the ability of an organization to fiscally sustain its program while reducing its reliance on federal support.

In response, the CNCS issued the 2005 Rule, which implemented changes in AmeriCorps practice in four areas of policy: sustainability of programs; grant selection criteria; tutor qualifications; and performance measures and evaluation. Of these four, the emphasis on sustainability and grant selection criteria increased the pressure on organizations to demonstrate their financial efficacy as part of their selection as AmeriCorps sites. Sustainability mandates within AmeriCorps, however, appear in two different places within CNCS regulations. The CNCS enacted measures, under the auspices of the funding match, to make the AmeriCorps program less dependent on federal dollars; the CNCS also introduced grant selection criteria and a new emphasis on capacity building activities in AmeriCorps programming that were focused on the sustainability and expansion of the not-for-profit sector and its funding through private dollars.

In a 2005 internal communication to AmeriCorps program directors announcing the publication of the *AmeriCorps Rule*, Corporation CEO David Eisner and AmeriCorps director Rosie Mauk informed grant recipients that

> Grantees will assume an increasing share of program costs over time. Currently grantees are required to match 15 percent of member support costs and 33 percent of operational costs. The new Rule requires, in addition to the current minimum requirements, an overall match percentage that increases gradually to 50 percent over a period of 10 years. The Rule also specifies that programs that demonstrate they are unable to meet this requirement and operate predominantly in rural or economically depressed areas can apply for a waiver at a lower alternative match schedule.[16]

The "funding match," as it was referred to by research participants, requires that organizations hosting an AmeriCorps program must engage in fundraising activities to support their participation program in addition to their grant writing to the federal government. This requirement poses a significant problem for some AmeriCorps sites.

The problem of funding matches first emerged in interviews with AmeriCorps program directors. In the first round of interviews I asked the program directors, all of whom are referred to with pseudonyms, to describe their responsibilities as AmeriCorps directors and what their job duties encompassed. At the top of each list was the problem of fundraising. Amanda worked as the program director for one of the two AmeriCorps sites that participated in this research. At the time of interviewing, she had worked as an AmeriCorps program director for ten years and was herself an AmeriCorps member in the early 1990s. Amanda's program worked on a model of site fees; her organization, itself a program within a public school district, essentially subcontracted AmeriCorps members to public schools for a fee. In her interviews, she revealed that fundraising was a major challenge for her program. Under the new Rule, her program was required to match 34 percent of the program funding, and this would soon increase to 38 percent. Amanda, however, had her eye on what would happen in the long term when the program was required to raise 50 percent of its funding. Reaching 38 percent would mean, according to Amanda,

> that I have to raise my site fees by two thousand and I'm still thirty thousand short. So if we're going to get a fifty–fifty match, we're probably going to be charging five to six thousand per member. Right now they pay eight thousand for a team of members. So that is going to increase dramatically and it is going to be really prohibitive to some of our sites.

Amanda's problem was clear; in order to maintain her program, she would have to make it more difficult for public schools to access the services of AmeriCorps; in order to reduce federal spending on per member costs, she would have to pass on the expense to the local schools where her members worked as tutors.

> So we have to really think strategically about how we're going to move forward and where else we can augment our budget so that we can minimize the burden to the schools themselves. Because you know their budget cuts are part of the reason we're here to begin with and able to do the work we do. Because they are short staffed and overwhelmed. If it goes up much further they're not going to be able to participate.

Her fear was that some schools, or similar programs in her city, would be priced out of having an AmeriCorps member at their organization. She recounted one morning,

> I got a call today from a site, from another AmeriCorps site for another program. They were trying to get an extra member. And they were just calling around to other programs to see "What are the shots," and you can't blame them; but, you're like, "Your mission doesn't align with us at all." But she had looked somewhere they were charging nine or ten or twelve thousand dollars per member, and she's saying, "We just can't afford that."

The logical next question to ask Amanda was if increasing site fees was her only option to raise the funding necessary to meet her match requirement. Amanda, clearly frustrated with the situation, described the options available to her: foundation grants, fundraising drives, employee contributions from the school district, and private donations. She explained that each activity was time consuming, and that "Right now I just need to do stuff and I'm not supposed to do any fundraising on the clock. As an AmeriCorps program director, fundraising is a prohibited activity for me. I can't even write the grant on the clock." How is it that although she is prohibited from writing the AmeriCorps grant or doing any other fundraising on the clock, she nevertheless found herself in the situation of being responsible for all the fundraising activities of her program? She responded that the CNCS probably assumed "the person above me" was the one responsible for grant writing. In her environment, the only option was to turn to an unnamed person higher up in the organizational hierarchy, who has no real relation to the program, or she would complete the fundraising activities on volunteer time. This problem, she argued, was "one of the reasons it [fundraising] doesn't happen." Despite this problem, Amanda had secured several foundation grants for her program, had collected private donations, and had held a yearly fundraising event. Each activity was accomplished beyond the boundaries of her own very full forty-hour workweek.

The second participating AmeriCorps site did not have the same struggles as Amanda. David was the AmeriCorps program director at a local affiliate of an international not-for-profit organization. This local affiliate was also a long-term AmeriCorps site, and, when we met, David had worked as the program director for the last seven years. David's organization was very different from Amanda's. While Amanda worked within a school district and had access to virtually no institutional resources beyond her AmeriCorps grant, David's organization operated on a budget of approximately $16.5 million. The organization was able to leverage large amounts of resources through charitable contributions due to its reputation, the focus of its work, and long-standing partnerships with corporate and foundation donors. While David was quick to point out that the organization was completely dependent on the labor of AmeriCorps members to accomplish its mission, it did not struggle to meet the fiscal requirements of the AmeriCorps grant program. David described their approach to the match by saying,

> I think it is 38 percent we have to do or maybe its 42 percent this year. But yeah we're at 46 percent; we'll get to 50 percent within the next couple of years. I think we see it as a strategy that we do more than we're asked to as a way to sort of say, "Well, look at us, we're already doing more than we're asked." And we're not having a hard time meeting those numbers either.

All of David's AmeriCorps members worked within the organization, meaning that the members were not contracted to local sites. Thus, David also did not recoup any site fees as revenue to contribute to his funding match requirements. David shared later in the interview that all the money required to make their match was taken from the general operating fund of the organization. While Amanda argued that, "I think there are very few sites that do not charge site fees," there were clearly organizations that do not struggle to meet the fiscal match of the AmeriCorps program. Further, David responded to my questions concerning fundraising by saying that, while at one point he did write the grant, the AmeriCorps grant was now written by the organization's full-time, on-staff grant writer.

This imbalance between well-funded, prosperous, and large organizations and small, underfunded, struggling organizations raises an important question for the organizations that become the sites of learning for AmeriCorps members. One could argue that the AmeriCorps program accounts for this imbalance by providing seed funding, through state commissions, for smaller organizations that are not ready to compete at the national level for an AmeriCorps grant. The purpose of these smaller grants is to expand the capacity of smaller not-for-profits to fully access larger levels of funding. It does not correct, however, the inequality that exists between those organizations that can maintain sustainability within the federal fund matching guidelines and those organizations that barely keep themselves above water. Further, one could point out that underfunded organizations can apply for a waiver from the funding match requirements. When I asked Amanda why she did not take this option, her response was that she had served, and was currently serving, as a peer reviewer for the grant selection process. Applying for the waiver, she argued, made the proposal less competitive.

Regulations around sustainability are built into the grant selection criteria of AmeriCorps Subtitle C programs, which refer to the AmeriCorps State/National program as opposed to VISTA or NCCC. In their announcement of the 2005 Rule, Eisner and Mauk also stated that

> The new rule incorporates elements of sustainability into the grantee selection criteria, and readjusts the "weighting" of criteria the Corporation uses to assess applications. . . . We believe these criteria will more effectively predict program success and ensure a stronger AmeriCorps portfolio.[17]

These grant criteria are infused with sustainability measures in such a way as to suggest that they are in fact presuming, if not encouraging, competition between not-for-profit organizations for private funding. Regardless of intent, which is impossible to discern, the criteria require organizations to engage in relationships with the private sector in order to sustain programs. Beyond the funding match, this requirement appears in three different places in the grant criteria, most explicitly in the categories of organizational capacity and budget effectiveness, but also in the designation of program effectiveness, framed using the language of community outputs.

The criterion of cost effectiveness and budget adequacy is a complicated assessment in which all the program costs are further evaluated against Corporation frameworks for per member program costs and are evaluated as appropriate to the expected outcomes of the program. Most of the criteria have to do with whether or not the grant follows the budget development rules designated in the regulations. As might be expected, budget making is perhaps the second most heavily regulated aspect of the program after recruitment and employment of members. Sustainability enters into this equation when a program submits a recompete grant, or any grant after a previous period of funding. At this point, the program must begin to meet the match criteria and must, in its budget narrative, demonstrate how it has rallied the resources of the private sector to meet its match requirement. In this section, the AmeriCorps program must provide evidence that it is a public-private partnership. This particular regulation was interpreted by AmeriCorps program directors as seemingly innocuous and as logical within the confines of budget-making activities.

However, the extension of funding match requirements into the category of organizational capacity was interpreted as a somewhat harsher introduction. Amanda felt that her difficulty in meeting the match requirements would contribute to the reviewer's judgments of the capacity of the program and thus, technically, would count against her twice in the grants process. At the time Amanda wrote her grant, criteria for organizational capacity included, among other factors, the ability for prior grantees to demonstrate that they had secured matching resources or resources that were expanding in scope or amount, including through evidence of financial and in-kind contributions. The private sector funding requirement is thus iterated in at least two components of the grant review. The push for private support for AmeriCorps programs is most substantially felt at the level of the state commissions. While the state commissions of CNCS serve in a regulatory capacity, one commission employee described their job as "really to bring as much of the funding as we can" to the AmeriCorps program activities in their state. To this end, Rebecca, a state commission executive, described aligning their program areas and implementing accountability measures to secure private funding.

> I'd say a couple years ago, but more and more this year and as it became more of a priority for the corporation, we really pushed our programs because of us raising money; we can really see the value of it. If we can say these are the results we're getting when we tutor these kids to a potential funder, we have a much better chance of securing additional funds from the private sector.

In other words, appealing to private money, or *having* to appeal to private donors, has an impact on the areas of work AmeriCorps takes up. This relation of determination between the not-for-profit sector and foundations or private donors is not new in that there is a substantial history of private money directing the activities of these organizations.[18] State commission employees described developing program areas and state-wide Corps on issue areas that appealed to the private sector, such as education and job training. Further, they described their attempts to integrate support for unpopular programs, such as Head Start, with more corporate-friendly programs, such as reading achievement.

AmeriCorps program sites that will survive in this funding environment will not necessarily be those that run the most effective programs or those whose members go on to serve the nation, but rather those not-for-profits that are able to appeal to private interests and cultivate their entrepreneurial skills despite the fact that there is evidence to suggest that entrepreneurial not-for-profits are actually less effective in meeting their missions.[19] Programs that are effective at raising dollars from the private sector will be able to sustain their work by having the public and private sectors equally bear the cost of meeting humanitarian needs. This cost-bearing goal was further evidenced in the grant selection criteria found in the program design components that assessed program effectiveness. According to the criteria, a successful program,

> (1) is successful in meeting targeted, compelling community needs; (2) has an impact in the community that is sustainable beyond the presence of Federal support; (3) generates and supports volunteers to expand the reach of your program in the community; and (4) enhances capacity-building of other organizations and institutions important to the community.[20]

Much of this focus on sustainability within AmeriCorps program has to do with promoting sustainability in the wider not-for-profit sector through the expansion of volunteer mobilization. However, it also presents a picture of an AmeriCorps program that not only meets a compelling local need in a sufficient manner, but performs this service in such a way as to create a program that spins out of the federal government and into the realm of civil society, charting a path toward privatization. It appears as though the grant-making processes encourages organizations to think like civic entrepreneurs, a popular concept among national service advocates and defined by Alan Khazaei as "taking the entrepreneurial spirit and innovative approaches often found in the private sector to address social problems."[21]

An interesting afterward to this conversation is that Amanda's prediction that the funding match requirements of AmeriCorps would ultimately force her to fundamentally reorganize the focus of her group came true. When I first interviewed Amanda, she was writing (off the clock) the federal recompete grant for her Corp. Her application was denied in part, she suspects, because of a lack of institutional commitment, in the form of dollars, from her school district. On the eve of the program being shut down, a manager from the school district stepped forward with a financial commitment to the program, thus convincing the state commission to extend a one-year operational grant to Amanda's Corp. She no longer had to worry about meeting her match through site fees because, rather than have individual schools find the money to support the AmeriCorps program, the district has decided to do it at a higher level. On the surface this appears as a positive development, but it raises questions as to the nature of sustainability as defined by the federal government. Sustainable for whom? Fifty percent of the cost of this AmeriCorps program has been taken over by an already resource-strapped municipal school district.

Another important element of the puzzle of AmeriCorps emerges in the conversation around financing AmeriCorps programming. In her own exasperation at having to increase her site fees, Amanda referenced her attempts to reorganize her budget as an effort to not "pass the buck" to public schools. She argued, "'Cause you know their budget cuts are part of the reason we're here to begin with and able to do the work we do. Because they are short-staffed and overwhelmed." Here Amanda highlights a central contradiction of AmeriCorps. Amanda spends her days working with a group of young adults who will, in theory and rhetoric, benefit immensely from the opportunity to work for a year in the public schools. Her intentions, as a program director, are that these young people will learn about the challenges of public schools, form important relationships with their students and peers, benefit from vocational skill development, and develop a lifelong commitment to volunteer service, community participation, and youth development. They are provided this fantastic opportunity by the ongoing underfunding of and clawing back of resources from public education. Because public schools in the United States are short staffed and overwhelmed, AmeriCorps volunteers are "able to do the work" that they do, while children continue to learn in unsafe buildings with outdated texts in too-large classrooms, and while volunteers replace previously paid staff.

The Coordination of Work in AmeriCorps

As part of my research, I attended a statewide AmeriCorps conference held during the annual AmeriCorps Week of activities. This conference was held at a local college and was attended by an estimated 600 AmeriCorps members. The agenda for the daylong conference was open-ended and organizers used a model of facilitation whereby attendees organized their own discussion groups over the course of a morning session. The facilitator of the conference, who was a professor at another local university, took suggestions from the floor for sessions that were to be held throughout the day. The sessions would focus on whatever conversations AmeriCorps members wanted to have with one another. The assertion was made that there were no experts or professionals, only peers. Each session was structured as an informal conversation; one attendee would volunteer to facilitate while another typed notes directly into an online forum. During the opening session to set the agenda, an interesting pattern emerged in how AmeriCorps members introduced themselves. Each was asked to state their name, designate their AmeriCorps program membership, and where they performed their service. In their introductions, the members began to mirror each other in their language as one after another introduced themselves by saying, "My name is X and I work, I mean, I serve at Y organization." I was struck by this impulsive self-correction—or perhaps self-censoring—and urge to replace the verb *work* with *serve*. When I informally polled some attendees at lunch, the answer I received was quite simple: AmeriCorps members do not *work* anywhere, neither are they employees. They *serve* the community.

It is an ideological mystification to rename work as service, and I will explore this in the next chapter in a discussion of service, citizenship, and democracy. What I want to focus on here is the work that AmeriCorps members do, or rather, the activities that comprise their everyday service in the program. These activities organize the core experiential components of their learning and, as this research has uncovered, shape the nature of their interaction with the communities that they serve. Within the approach of institutional ethnography, the work done by AmeriCorps members and their supervisors constitutes the primary source of data in this research. Work is understood quite broadly within institutional ethnography. It is not necessarily bounded by relations of employment, labor, or the production of surplus value, which constitute our normative understanding of work within capitalist social relations. Work in this sense is more akin to the relations of production and reproduction explored by Marx. In this way, work can be unpaid, unacknowledged, unseen, or even not known to others. Work simply describes, "anything done by people that takes time and effort, that they mean to do, that is done under definite conditions and with whatever means and tools, and that they may have to think about."[22] What is important to institutional ethnography are individuals' knowledge of this work; how they understand their own activity, its purposes, its outcomes, and its formation. This notion of "work knowledge" for Smith has a dual character: "one is a person's experience of and in their own work, what they do, how they do it, including what they think and feel; a second is the implicit or explicit coordination of his or her work with the work of others."[23] This second dynamic, the coordination of the work of AmeriCorps' members, is my focus here.

PERMISSIBILITY AND PROHIBITION IN SERVICE ACTIVITIES

In the daily experience of AmeriCorps members, their supervisors, and their program directors, the most significant and most discussed regulations are those that govern permissible and prohibited activities. These regulations are first encountered by the program site in the grant-writing process and are then passed on to members through both the employment and the orientation processes in which they participate. The regulations are also a source of tension in the program because they raise questions about the intent of their content as well as their purpose. Interpretations of the regulations differ across sites, within sites, and between state commissions. The state commissions are ultimately responsible for ensuring that prohibited activities are not taking place, and in interviews with state commission staff it was reported that the majority of questions they receive from sites have to do with the permissibility of particular activities. In this section, I want to introduce these regulations in the context of how they coordinate the daily work of AmeriCorps members. The direct exclusionary effects of prohibited or "unsanctioned" activities are the most apparent and visible aspects of the regulations in the program. However, this research revealed that the regulation of activities has a much more profound effect on the program, and so I will return to these regulations in subsequent chapters in both my discussion of organized training activities as well as the civic engagement components of the program.

Each of the NOFAs released by the CNCS over the last five years has advised applicants to closely examine the restrictions on permissible program activities for AmeriCorps Subtitle C grants within the Code of Federal Regulations. These restrictions begin by confining the work of AmeriCorps members to two broad categories: direct human service and organizational capacity building. These two kinds of work must be undertaken pursuant to the larger goal of expanding the capacity or ability of the organization to provide public services or respond to unmet needs.[24] This regulation forms the basis of what will become the program model, or program design in the language of Corporation grant making. It is essentially a logic model, a frequently used tool in not-for-profit program planning. I will return to the importance of logic models in the next section, but want to acknowledge here that AmeriCorps logic models can only emerge out of the context of the regulations around permissible activity. The restriction of service activities to direct service and capacity building are further described in detail in the Code of Federal Relations (CFR) (2008).

At this point it is important to pursue a definition of what is meant by the concept of direct service, the original mandate of the AmeriCorps program. Permissible direct service activities are further described by their outcomes, rather than by their content. For example, as outlined in the CFR, direct service activities will "advance the goals of the program," "result in specific identifiable service or improvement," "address local environmental, educational, public safety, or other human needs," and "provide a direct, measurable benefit."[25] The activities of AmeriCorps members are equally regulated by what does and does not count as service within the program. In many ways, this relation between permissible and prohibited defines the nature of service activities and direct service. The prohibited activities can be understood as having a relationship with not only the exclusion of certain activities from the daily experience of AmeriCorps members, but also as having a role in defining what is deemed permissible. As the CFR states, AmeriCorps members are expressly forbidden from the following:

> (1) Attempting to influence legislation; (2) organizing or engaging in protests, boycotts, or strikes; (3) assisting, promoting, or deterring union organizing; (4) impairing existing contracts for services or collective bargaining agreements; (5) engaging in partisan political activities, or other activities designed to influence the outcome of an election to any public office; (6) participating in, or endorsing, events or activities that are likely to include advocacy for or against political parties, political platforms, political candidates, proposed legislation, or elected officials; (7) engaging in religious instructions . . . ; (8) providing a direct benefit to . . . (i) a business organized for profit; (ii) a labor union; (iii) a partisan political organization; (iv) a not-for-profit organization that fails to comply with the restrictions contained in section 501(c)(3) of the Internal Revenue Code of 1986 except that nothing in this section shall be construed to prevent participants from engaging in advocacy activities undertaken at their own initiative; and (v) an organization engaged in the religious activities described in paragraph (g); (9) conducting a

voter registration drive or using Corporation funds to conduct a voter registration drive.[26]

The Serve America Act amends this list by adding the provision that AmeriCorps members are also prohibited from "providing abortion services or referrals for receipt of such services,"[27] while additional rules regulate the consumption of alcohol at AmeriCorps events and further affiliation with religious organizations. The broad interpretation of this regulation is that, similar to the restriction of AmeriCorps programs to "non-political" organizations labeled 501(c)(3), the service activities of AmeriCorps members cannot take on the political dimensions described above while AmeriCorps members are accruing service hours, wearing AmeriCorps gear, or perceived to be AmeriCorps members who are accruing hours—in other words, "on the clock" as it was described by AmeriCorps members. The extent and intent of the regulations is a source of great confusion among members, and even as they approached the end of their year of service, many AmeriCorps members were deeply unsure of what exactly was covered in these prohibited activities and what the implications of the regulation might be. As I will argue in the next chapter, the implications are far reaching. The pertinent issue at this point, however, is to explore what dynamics of the prohibited activities are important to the coordination of work and learning in AmeriCorps.

Crucial to understanding the coordination of work is how those within the AmeriCorps program interpret the regulations. This is a difficult question to answer because, as one state commission employee put it, there are as many interpretations as there are members of AmeriCorps. In attempting to dissect the interpretations, I encountered an effort by various parties to pass the buck, for lack of a better term. By this I mean that at each level of the hierarchy of AmeriCorps, interviewees were emphatic to point out that their working interpretation of the regulations came from somewhere else. For members, they gleaned their interpretations from their program directors. Program directors deferred to the interpretations of state commission employees. State commission employees followed directions from the Corporation. However, this official interpretation breaks down when it comes to how various components of the program are organized at the local level. Interpretations of regulations that program directors argue are resolute end up taking on a differentiated character within local programs.

This effect can in part be explained by the existence of a culture around the interpretation of the regulations. In one instance, this culture appears haphazard or piecemeal, with state commission employees admitting that much of the interpretation happens on a case-by-case basis in the analysis of actual activities rather than in the abstract. Robert, a state commission employee who conducts site visits to AmeriCorps programs, commented,

> Programs will ask questions, like, a big one is the "not lobbying" requirement. And so what is allowed, whether they can write a letter to a newspaper about a certain bill that's happening, you know, what they can and can't do. So we'll provide a lot of interpreting. . . . A lot of times I ask for the specific, you know, what are they looking to do, what does the letter say that they're writing. And just helping them interpret and walk through.

If the case given appears to be a "gray" area to state commission employees, they defer to the interpretation at the federal level. In this case, individual employees' interpretations are subjective and are based on their reaction to the specifics of cases rather than general categories of activities. Robert attributed much of the interpretive activity to the program directors, arguing the following:

> In their [program directors'] level of nervousness about the regulations, I think for lack of a better term, some will do everything and anything to avoid coming anywhere near that line. Where others will say, "You know, I'll come right up to that line, and I know pretty much where it is, and I'm happy to be there." So I think it comes down to program directors more than any kind of Corporation guidance or us [state commission] guidance.

In this instance, the interpretation of the regulations appears as decentralized and on a continuum. In reality, this continuum most likely exists, although program directors who come up to and possibly straddle the line of the prohibited activities are said to fly under the radar for the sake of their own program's viability. However, comments from state commission employees indicate that the process of interpreting and applying the regulations cannot be understood as a closed process in which each director works in isolation.

These interpretive processes take place within a larger framework concerning not just what the regulations mean, but also what interpreting them in too lenient a fashion *could* mean to the continuation of the AmeriCorps program. Michelle, a former AmeriCorps program director, and Susan, a community member and not-for-profit employee, described their CNCS state commission executive director as "a figurehead of risk averseness who impeded anybody who wasn't brave on their own" and as having established a culture in which the interpretation of regulations should tend toward the conservative for the purposes of preserving the appearance of neutrality within the program. Michelle argued,

> When I was an AmeriCorps director, it was very frustrating to me how most Corps ways of dealing with—there feels like there's some grey area here—was just to, like, not go anywhere near it. Which then denies people the opportunity to engage with elected officials. I mean, anything that people have thought was anywhere near [this].

Susan continued, arguing "the ED [executive director] of the state commission, I remember being *very* frustrated with her interpretations, which were often overturned by others who actually knew better, that were so risk averse that it was impeding folks ability to engage."

What emerges here is the notion that interpretive processes of the regulation are taking place in an environment of threat. What exactly is this threat? Simply, defunding of the program. As one male AmeriCorps member explains it,

> I remember way back when we had our orientation, they told us there was something going on at the capitol, like a protest. And there was a guy there, who was in AmeriCorps, but he wasn't part of the protest, but he was carrying something or wearing his AmeriCorps shirt and his picture got taken and put in the newspaper about this protest and there was an AmeriCorps there. And a bunch of people wrote in, our taxes fund AmeriCorps, why is there an AmeriCorps at protests. I just kind of remember that.

This picture of the environment surrounding the prohibited activities is one of fear, threat, instability, and arbitrariness. Interpreting the programs in an open way requires program directors to be brave. Others, who are nervous about the consequences, will tend toward a conservative interpretation. Why would program directors be nervous about violating regulations and threatening the stability of their programs? As most are employed by the same AmeriCorps grants that fund members, their own livelihood is implicated in the compliance of their program. Although they may feel empowered by the vagueness of the regulations to stretch their interpretations, that same vagueness can be the cause for punitive action. As Rebecca explained it,

> There are lots of grey areas. This and this and this, but you can't use your AmeriCorps status to do any lobbying or influence legislation unless it's on your own time. There's all this variation. What does that mean? Can you do it on your lunch break? Is that really your own time? It's up to the interpretation of whoever would be doing your audit, inspector general or whoever.

In the case of the resubmission of a grant, those doing the interpreting could extend to peer reviewers, corporation employees at the federal level, and so on. Taking all of these possibilities into account, program directors clearly work in an environment where the stakes for their interpretations of the regulations have high consequences.

It is perhaps counterintuitive to argue that coercion might exist in this environment given that there is no ironclad interpretation of the regulations. In an environment where ambiguity and subjectivity in decision making are the rule, it is entirely likely that the most logical and defensive position is to drift toward the center. This is exactly what program directors expressed; their purpose is to make sure that there is no room in which to subjectively judge that their members are engaging in unsanctioned activities on AmeriCorps time. However, program directors also engage in self-monitoring to different extents. Some are quite diligent and exert effort to reiterate to their members what they can and cannot do within the program. For Amanda, the issue was crucial.

> It is revisited. And it comes up, especially in a year like this, in a politically heavy year like an election year, it gets revisited in individual emails, as things come up, you know you can do this, can't do this, this event is sanctioned, this one is not.

Others, however, find that they do not need to police members. For these program directors, this lack of policing had everything to do with how they themselves understand the purpose of the regulations and how they convey that interpretation to their members.

How do AmeriCorps program directors and members interpret the purposes of the regulations? The members who participated in this research had not read the regulations beyond what was provided in their member contract. The program directors had read the regulations and explained the existence of the regulations to their members using a complex of two separate logics. The first logic presents the prohibited regulations as logical within the context of publicly funded programs. David described his approach to this in these terms: "The way I explain it is that the government doesn't— how I interpret the government—want to be giving people money that would be like engaging and like disputing their decisions." Further, "It's me looking at the regulations, me trying to figure out like, you know, with most regulations, what's the spirit of the regulation and what is it they're exactly—I mean I'm not going to look at the letter of the law; I'm not a lawyer. What is it they're trying to prevent, and I think it's exactly that, like you promoting your own political agenda."

Within this framework, it is presented as common sense that the government would not fund activities aimed at contesting public policy decisions. Members echoed this framework back in focus groups by arguing that the regulations make sense within the larger framework of 501(c)(3) organizations. When pressed to explain why the government should not support so-called political activities, members often reverted to the second logic. This second logic returned to the notion of threat and marshaled the notion of bipartisanship to explain why these activities had to be excluded from the program. As one male AmeriCorps member recalls,

> That was the message I got. That we have these strict rules about political activities and drinking and not even being able to register people to vote because the Republicans tried to shut down AmeriCorps in the '90s, and we don't want that to happen so now we have these rules. I think national service has bipartisan support, but AmeriCorps is still seen as a leftist project by a lot of members of the right.

This history is indeed the case; there were many attempts by Congressional Republicans to defund the VISTA program, and there have been many efforts since to do the same. The threat is not imagined. Beyond the reality of the threat to the program, the fact that those involved with the program can see the regulations as common sense and logical has important implications. At one level, it tells us something about how the state is positioned within the program, which gives us clues as to how the program articulates a politics of democracy and citizenship. This point will be pursued in the lengthier discussion of civic engagement that is to come. On another level, it has important implications for the coordination of work and learning. Within the apparent logical exclusion of political activities from the program lies the formation of direct service as something other than political.

The regulated activities are drawn along lines labeled permissible and prohibited. The category of prohibited activities is further labeled partisan, political, and as having an "agenda," including not just politics but religious proselytizing. You may recall that permissible activities are vaguely defined by their outcome; following these definitions the regulations provide examples.

> (d) Examples of the types of direct service activities AmeriCorps members may perform include, but are not limited to, the following: (1) tutoring children in reading; (2) helping to run an after-school program; (3) engaging in community clean-up projects; (4) providing health information to a vulnerable population; (5) teaching as part of a professional corps; (6) providing relief services to a community affected by a disaster; and (7) conducting a neighborhood watch program as part of a public safety effort.[28]

Direct service is defined in the AmeriCorps program by both its contribution to meeting community needs and by the fact that it is not prohibited. Rather than clearly defining "direct service," the regulations are prescriptive about what *cannot* be considered service. Direct service, or service more generally, is articulated as mutually exclusive with partisan activity. In this process, AmeriCorps regulations construct direct service as nonpolitical in character and postulates that "meeting unmet needs" can take place in a similarly nonpolitical fashion. The effect is that work activities are bifurcated: some of these activities are considered political while other activities are not. This bifurcation is clear for activities such as attending a protest or organizing a union. This fragmentation is not easy to see within the most vague of the prohibitions, which forbids "participating in, or endorsing, events or activities that are likely to include advocacy for or against political parties, political platforms, political candidates, proposed legislation, or elected officials."[29] This regulation and the articulation of "political" and "partisan" in regards to training sessions proved to have tremendous effects on the organization of civic engagement within the program.

This bifurcation of activities is mirrored in the daily lives of Ameri-Corps members and how they make sense of organizational imperatives such as civic engagement and active citizenship. However, it is also plays out in how the daily work activities of AmeriCorps members are defined. Each member receives a service description as part of his or her work contract. These service descriptions are generated through a program planning process that begins with the separation of permissible from prohibited. However, AmeriCorps members further feel the ambiguity of the regulations in their daily lives, and this ambiguity drives them to invoke and avoid the regulations in different ways. For some, the ambiguity in what is permissible drives them to abstain from prohibited activities on their own time, despite the fact that they are allowed to conduct these activities as a private citizen. One member reminded her focus group that they had a Corp member who had left the program under unclear circumstances after he was arrested at a protest. Another female AmeriCorps member commented on that situation, saying: "That kind of puts a damper on the idea that you can do whatever the hell you want in your private time. It's not one-hundred-percent true. If you get arrested while protesting in some way, shape, or form, you could get asked to leave." Other members expressed the difficulties that emerge from having to have a dual persona vis-à-vis the community in which they work. Michelle, who observed this bifurcation during her period as a program director, commented on the prohibitions of AmeriCorps by saying, "Yeah, well, the reality is that it is difficult to really be 'off the clock' if you're living and working in the same community."

These prohibitions are extremely important in the organization of learning in AmeriCorps, and they serve as another institutional organization of experience and learning. Clearly, they confine the experiential terrain of learning to a particular set of activities from which anything that could be interpreted as partisan is excluded and, at the same time, postulate the permissible activities as nonpolitical in character. While the idea that humanitarian service work is nonpolitical is deeply contested,[30] the AmeriCorps program postulates to its members, its staff, the United States Congress, and the American public that politics does not happen in the provision of human services. Politics is not only something that happens elsewhere, but it is appropriate that it should happen elsewhere, the converse being that it is inappropriate for those working on the public dollar to engage in the inherently political nature of public problems such as school achievement gaps, affordable housing provision, public safety, or environmental degradation. The staffs of not-for-profits around the country enter into this framework when they sit down to write an AmeriCorps Subtitle C grant. They must plan an AmeriCorps program in such a way as to justify the logical and measurable impact of nonpolitical direct service activities on the community need that they identify. This process, the most explicit process coordinating the everyday experience of AmeriCorps members, is the focus of the next section of this chapter.

The "Logical" Organization of Service Work

I want to explore how program design is organized within the grants processes, using the participating AmeriCorps sites as examples of how program design plays out in actual, successful federally competitive grants. This analysis requires two activities. First, I will explore the "logic" embedded in AmeriCorps program design that establishes a particular relationship between service work and social problems. Second, I will explore how this articulation of "community needs" affects the character of work in the program. The instruments used to design AmeriCorps programming, primarily logic models and performance measures of outcomes, are the final form of institutional organization of the sites of learning within the program. I have written extensively about logic models elsewhere,[31] so I will only briefly reference the program planning theory from which logic models are derived.

Member activities are organized in AmeriCorps grants and program planning through both the explicit and implicit use of logic models. A logic model is a "graphic display or 'map' of the relationship between a program's resources, activities, and intended results."[32] Logic models, however, serve the additional purpose of attempting to surface the assumptions and preconditions of the relationships within a program by making "the implicit theory explicit."[33] Logic models emerged in the late 1980s in not-for-profit and public sector program planning and evaluation in response to a funding environment, in both the public and private sectors, which emphasized accountability and measurable results. According to Renger, in 2005 President Bush's Office of Management and Budget (OMB) undertook a program review project aimed at eliminating programs that cannot "get results."[34] The OMB developed the PART (Performance Assessment Rating Tool), which scores programs on purpose and design, strategic planning, program results and accountability, and program management. Logic models became a bulwark against this kind of criticism because "logic modeling provides a mechanism to ensure that the important dots between underlying assumptions, strategies, and outcomes are meaningfully connected."[35]

There are a variety of versions of logic models floating around in the world of program planning, although all include the same basic components.

These components, however, often have different terms to describe similar functions. The most basic components of a logic model include activities, populations, and outcomes.

> Activities are the things the program does to work toward its desired outcomes. Target groups are the individuals, groups, or communities at whom the program's activities are directed. Outcomes are the changes the program hopes to achieve. These are differentiated between short-term and long-term outcomes.[36]

The logic model postulates a theoretical relationship of effect between the various components of the model. The theory that is established in a logic model is often called a theory of change or sometimes a program theory. A theory of change establishes a series of *if-then* relationships between various factors; *if* event X happens, *then* event Y will occur. We can use as an example the most basic theory of change postulated by the CNCS. The assertion found in the legislation establishing the CNCS is that *if* young adults participate in civil society through community service, *then* they will become more engaged citizens. The population or target group in this example is young adults, specifically AmeriCorps members. Their activities are their community service activities and trainings. The outputs define the quantifiable, measurable components of their work, for example 1,700 hours of full-time service in one year. Finally, the outcomes of the program will be various levels of civic engagement on a short- to long-term continuum.

The difficulty with logic models, and the way they conceptually organize information, has to do with the type of implicit theory that is made explicit. As Bickman argued,

> Every program has a theory. Unfortunately, it may be implicit, fragmented, and not well conceptualized. These theories are composed of a number of important assumptions that can include basic constructs such as human nature, assumptions about the nature of the problem and of the population, and the boundary, or limiting conditions, of the effects of the program. These assumptions are in addition to assumptions about the causal linkages within the program.[37]

Logic models can establish relationships between variables that exist on a continuum of oversimplification to radical complexity. They are conceptual models that are limited by the theoretical and analytical tools available to the individuals who design them. Renger's research questioned how deeply practitioners reflect on the nature of the problems identified in the model prior to the development of activities and expected outcomes. Renger argued that logic modeling "begins by defining the problem of interest. Most problems are influenced by behavioral, environmental, social, and biological conditions; these factors, or antecedent conditions, must be identified and understood to focus intervention efforts."[38] He claims that in this process, planners should map various answers to the question of why the condition occurs. And yet, popular logic model design tools do not push practitioners to engage in this reflective process. The use of logic models can be further complicated by the funder's own agenda.

> Often when funders require the development of a program logic model, the emphasis is on laying out the activities and expected outcomes. Although articulating the underlying rationale for a program is critical to its success, it is frequently a second generation or post hoc activity—one that is never quite completed.[39]

Renger's research demonstrates that when exploration into antecedent conditions is not undertaken, a chain reaction of abstractions can result, including the incorrect identification of the nature of the problem, targeting aspects of the problem that may not have strong relevance to the actual problem, the separation of programs from one another, and the development of activities that do not target antecedent conditions.[40]

However, the errors found by Renger are largely errors in the logical claims of the relationships established. They do not necessarily recognize that the interpretation of antecedent conditions—that is, the definition of the problem at hand—is a theoretical, political, and ideological activity. Theory, within the logic model notion, refers to program theory. Although Bickman defined program theory in such a way as to include basic assumptions, within the activity of a logic model, this theory becomes pragmatic in nature, meaning that its focus becomes the claim to effect. This is the theoretical relationship of interest to funders, because it results in the articulation of measurable outcomes to which program planners can be held accountable.[41] As Kaplan and Garrett have pointed out,

> In its essence, use of the logic model guides program participants in applying the scientific method—the articulation of a clear

hypothesis or objective to be tested—to their project development, implementation, and monitoring.[42]

To see underneath this process requires that the components of the logic model be interrogated for their organization of social relations. Through this process, it is possible to see the ideological construction of the notion of "community needs" at the center of AmeriCorps programming.

An examination of the supporting documents for AmeriCorps Subtitle C grants provides evidence of how community needs come to be defined through the logic of program planning. Ironically, the entirety of the program rationale and approach, which contains the theory of change of each AmeriCorps program, is seen from the Corporation's perspective as the least significant part of the grant and counts as only ten percent of the overall selection criteria, despite the fact that the relationships depicted in this section dictate all other logics employed in the grant. The CNCS designates the criteria for the rationale and approach section as follows, in addition to the criteria around sustainability already mentioned:

> (1) Whether your proposal describes and adequately documents a compelling need within the target community, including a description of how you identified the need; (2) Whether your proposal includes well-designed activities that address the compelling need, with ambitious performance measures, and a plan or system for continuous program self-assessment and improvement; (3) Whether your proposal described well-defined roles for participants that are aligned with the identified needs and that lead to measurable outputs and outcomes.[43]

The structure of the grant and the evaluation criteria ask grant writers to conceptualize AmeriCorps programs in a particular way. After identifying a social problem and articulating it as a community need, planners must then identify permissible service activities that can address the need in a quantifiable, measurable way. This is of course an ideal, if unique, arrangement for program planning, one that asks practitioners to first consider the problem at hand before developing activities and performance mechanisms. Within AmeriCorps, the logical relationship around change is thus confined to these parameters.

In interviews with AmeriCorps program directors and state commission employees, the portions of the grant application that are of the most concern are the performance measures that conclude the grant and which are distributed between member outcomes and community outcomes. Rebecca, the state commission executive, pointed to a more recent, post-2005, emphasis on measurable outcomes as part of the overall plan to ensure effectiveness in programs, emphasizing that the insistence on sustainability and capacity building are not separate from the emphasis on measurable outcomes.

> There's a new way of thinking about AmeriCorps and how we use those resources. The focus is really on measurable results. If you can show that because you tutor these 300 kids they're staying in school or whatever the outcomes are—there's a lot more focus on outcomes. So we really push our programs in their performance measures to make sure you have something measurable and that you can point to the AmeriCorps members as making a difference.

Grant writers build performance measures through the use of the Performance Measure Worksheet, a tool available in the online grant submission system (eGrants). In the section of the worksheet titled Needs and Activities, the relation established between the community need and the service activities is phrased as results. Specifically, after briefly describing the need, the grant writer is asked to describe how they "will achieve this result." They substantiate this claim by detailing how many members will perform the activity, how often the activity will occur, and what the duration of the activity will be. In order to accomplish this logical articulation, the performance measures must articulate the need through the logic of the activity rather than vice versa. For example, in Amanda's program, a performance measure on academic support for K–12 students, the need is paradoxically defined as a solution; the grant reads, "students who are below grade level in reading and/or math will receive tutoring by an AmeriCorps member." The need to engage in this kind of articulation emerges from the climate of regulation, threat, and accountability already seen in other aspects of program regulation. As Rebecca argued,

> I think congress and everyone is saying "show me the results"—you can't just say you're doing good work. They want to know how many kids we are impacting, how many have jobs, how many houses built. We can submit stories, but what we report to the Corporation is hard data. They want to know how many kids

across the country increased their test scores, as they basically have to roll it all up to congress.

This emphasis on outcomes dictates the kinds of service activities that will be designed for AmeriCorps members, and thus the logic through which members will engage with the community they serve and the need they address. In many ways, the emphasis on outcomes forces AmeriCorps program planners to work backward from the logic model described above, asking first what can be achieved and measured. Increasingly, institutional ethnographers are uncovering the pervasive logic of the imposition of performance measures and accountability practices embodied in endless paperwork. These activities have multiple effects in organizational settings; importantly, they work to impose an extra-local set of priorities within local organizational contexts, tie staff promotion and professional enhancement to compliance measures, reproduce particular social relations of need and deviance, and obscure the actual root and functioning of particular program policies and practices.[44] In this way, the logic model is the very definition of an ideological process.

The best way to unpack this process is to walk through what these grant selection criteria actually look like after they are processed and interpreted by AmeriCorps directors and articulated in their grants. Whereas logic models posit the relationship between activities and outcomes as linear or causal, what emerges in the grant writing is a process of defining community needs not only through an explicit rationale, but also through the identification of activities and outcomes as well. Ultimately, a speculative process emerges in which a set of guiding, abstract assumptions about the nature of the problem direct the generation of a set of activities which in turn become part of the definition of the problem.

Moving from the grant-writing process to program implementation, the definition of need is the first step in defining the nature of the problem that faces the AmeriCorps member as they step into their service work. It also has a compelling effect on how AmeriCorps members are trained to understand and go about meeting this need. In their recommendations on how to interpret the selection criteria, the state corporation advises grant writers to include four points: (1) a description of the need; (2) why the need was selected; (3) how the need was identified; and (4) provision of documentation of the need. For the organizations participating in this research, the grant writers took two divergent but equally successful approaches to establishing need. In their grant application, Amanda's organization provided a list of statistics with very little narrative explanation or development. The list of statistics stated that in the organization's school district, 67 percent of students receive free or reduced lunch, 72 percent are students of color, and 23 percent are English Language Learners. The statement of need then lists that around 50 percent of students read below grade level at the fifth-, seventh-, and tenth-grade levels and that between 62 percent and 84 percent of students are below grade level on math scores, while graduate rates are around 60 percent. This need is further supplemented by the $120 million dollars cut from the district budget in the preceding five years. Amanda's need statement comprised about 80 percent of one page, double-spaced.

David's organization took a different approach, crafting a need statement that first and foremost focused on the credibility of his organization in terms of its ability to address the problem of affordable housing and to stabilize low-income families. This need statement continued by arguing that stable housing is the "foundation for family success" and that the "development and preservation of affordable housing is imperative as the gap grows between wages and housing costs." David provided some statistics around low-income households and housing costs for the local area, as well as federal definitions of the categories. David's organization went on to support this claim by arguing that children with stable housing have greater academic success and that evidence exists linking the achievement gap to income inequality. The need statement also argued that poor families lack social capital and that this deficit must be addressed in order for poor families to maintain self-sufficiency and stability.

On a first read, Amanda's need statement establishes the frank reality of disparities in educational outcomes. Amanda was confident that the numbers "speak for themselves" and are not in need of any further elaboration. In David's application, however, the need for affordable housing is not treated as a self-evident need. Rather, it is linked to other social problems such as academic achievement, self-sufficiency, and family stability. David takes the approach, in part, of justifying his identification of need on housing, rather than for example on job skills, by referencing the interrelated nature of social problems. However, despite their apparent differences, when the next section of the grant, activities and outcomes, is included, it becomes clear that Amanda and David have both taken the same approach to defining need. Amanda has used her need statement to describe the need that exists (inequalities in educational outcomes) and to document the need through statistics. David has accomplished the same thing. However, as each describes the necessary activities, they further define community need by describing the activities that will address the need. They in effect *explain* where the problem comes from by delineating the activities that will ameliorate the community need. Amanda's grant proposes five activities for AmeriCorps members, each of which in turn addresses one aspect of the achievement gap. The service activities for members are to include tutoring to address academic support, service-learning projects to foster leadership development in students, out-of-school programming to foster the development of social skills, mentoring to improve self-esteem, and volunteer recruitment to provide positive role models. David's program proposes that affordable housing needs can be met by mobilizing volunteers to help stabilize low-income families by developing the affordable housing stock, helping low-income youth improve academic performance, and finally organizing social networks and fostering a sense of community in low-income neighborhoods.

How should we interpret the fact that each of these grants focuses its explanation of a community need largely on individual deficits? In the case of Amanda's program, all the designed interventions focus on the individual dysfunctions of young people. They are behind academically, they have low self-esteem, and they need to develop their social skills. In the case of David's program, lack of affordable housing and the instability of poverty become functions of a lack of social capital among poor people. These definitions of community needs become more clear when we examine how students are trained to address these problems and how they understand the relation between their service activities and the community need they are working to solve. The impulse present in these programs, to frame social problems as matters of individual or cultural deficit, is a long-standing ideological practice, enshrined in works such as *The Negro Family* written in 1965 by Daniel Patrick Moynihan.[45] Such impulses constitute not only a redefinition of poverty in a manner after Moynihan's "tangle of pathologies,"[46] but also work to reinscribe particular notions of race and its relation to social inequality. In this way, the "logic" of an AmeriCorps program reflects an ideological framing of the nature of social inequality in that we can see the activity of AmeriCorps volunteers, while they build social capital in poor communities or struggle to increase individual engagement in schools, as processes that reproduce a certain way of understanding a social problem and acting in relation to that problem—that is, by organizing social interventions at the level of individual behavioral change.

AmeriCorps as New Public Management?

Thus far I have argued that the daily experiential reality of AmeriCorps members is organized through four regulatory processes that establish what the sites of AmeriCorps work will be, that is, four processes that establish where members will conduct their service and that coordinate the kind of work AmeriCorps members will do at these sites. These regulatory processes work together to confine AmeriCorps activity to a particular set of activities defined by the Corporation as direct service and capacity building. The terrain of these activities, and thus the terrain of experiential learning in the program, is increasingly narrowed in the program through these regulatory acts. Thus, while it may appear as though AmeriCorps members are hard at work in diverse areas of civil society, they are in reality confined to a very narrow arena of citizen activity, one which is premised on the *necessary* separation of meeting human need from both relations of power (politics) and state intervention or reproduction of these conditions (Politics).

This experiential terrain is important to an exploration of learning about democracy and citizenship in the AmeriCorps program for several reasons. First, the daily experiences of AmeriCorps members are the ground on which praxis develops. For the AmeriCorps members who participated in this research, their most profound learning activities involved making sense of their daily experience through informal conversation with their peers. Second, in their attempts to process their learning around and assumptions concerning the concept of civic engagement, their daily experience in service work served as their first point of interpretive departure. Third, the bifurcation of work activities into political and nonpolitical activities has some influence on the learning of AmeriCorps members regarding democracy and civic engagement. Finally, and most importantly, the same regulatory processes that explicitly organize daily work practices in AmeriCorps also implicitly organize formalized training practices within the research sites. This effect on learning has serious implications for how democracy and citizenship are framed within the program. These processes will be explored in the following chapter, which focuses on how learning about civic engagement is intentionally organized within the program and what other aspects of training and service activities have unintentional effects on the learning of members.

What is evident is that the sites of AmeriCorps learning are crafted in the contemporary context of the defunding of public and human services; this inherently political context forms the backdrop of the program and attention to this provides additional depth in analysis to the notions of sustainability and need advanced in the program. Although the advocates of national service have taken steps to ensure that the sites of AmeriCorps programs are written up and organized as nonpolitical spheres, they are unable to contain the external pressures of shifts in the larger political economy of public policy that craft these sites as inherently political and subject to ongoing struggle and contestation. At the same time, the very steps taken to downsize public welfare provision and download these services onto both the private sector and civil society are clearly discernible hallmarks of neoliberal public policy. The technologies of this process, found in grants, protocols, performance measures, outcomes accountability, permissible activities, and so on, are now well established facets of new public management.[47] I think utilizing the concept of new public management would be a very valid interpretation of the current state of the AmeriCorps organization and could possibly lead us to understand how the program is enmeshed in a broader neoliberal shift in our conceptualizations of the state, citizenship, and democracy.

However, in the following chapter, I want to suggest that by looking at the relations between human labor and learning about democracy, citizenship, and social inequality that emerge within these institutionally organized sites, we can begin to examine the limits of the concept of neoliberalism as a means of explaining the ideology of civic engagement. It would be insufficient to only examine this social organization aspect of the program. The voices and experiences of AmeriCorps members must be situated and understood within in this context. Thus, in the following chapter I explore the emergence and consolidation of civic engagement as a mandate within the program and what the implementation of this mandate meant in the context of the programs I studied.

Chapter Four

The Actualities and Vacuities of Civic Engagement in AmeriCorps

In the previous chapter, I described the institutional and bureaucratic organization of the AmeriCorps program through the various federal legislations, codes of regulation, and funding mechanisms that coordinate its practical activities in local sites of service. I want to continue by examining the ways in which these various instruments not only organize the practical daily activity of AmeriCorps programs and members, but also create the space in which different forms of consciousness emerge in relation to the activity of service and are challenged through the language of civic engagement. In what follows, I expand on the ways in which civic engagement was taken up in the AmeriCorps sites I examined.

I want to explore the contours of what "learning democracy" looks like within the parameters of AmeriCorps and understand how civic engagement is taken up by staff and participants as a particular politics of democracy, one that is inextricable from questions of social inequality and injustice, but one in which the material needs that drive the existence of AmeriCorps are obscured. It is for this reason that I have chosen the concept of vacuity to describe this appearance of civic engagement. The common definition evokes emptiness, idleness, and thoughtlessness. To work from this definition would denigrate the efforts of those involved in AmeriCorps, people whom I believe to be sincerely expressing a desire to better our collective social life. I am not implying that civic engagement is an empty project; rather, I am making the argument that civic engagement is full of meaning. I choose the term vacuity because its more technical definition refers to the absence of matter. While the term may refer to an artificial vacuous state, it serves as an important and grounding metaphor for the findings of this research; there is literally, and pedagogically, an absence of matter within the civic engagement activities of AmeriCorps. In what follows I discuss first the history behind the CNCS's adoption of civic engagement as an institutional mandate and specifically in the form of a performance measure. I then examine the ways in which civic engagement as a performance measure is translated and transformed into pedagogical acts and choices within the program sites I studied as well as within the broader state-level interpretation of federal mandates. I end by returning to the question of the relation between ideology and pedagogy before continuing this discussion in the following chapter.

The Emergence and Consolidation of Civic Engagement in AmeriCorps

The National and Community Service Acts of 1990 and 1993 include congressional mandates for all national service programs, including AmeriCorps. Both documents state that the purpose of national service, second only to meeting unmet public needs, is to "renew the ethic of civic responsibility and the spirit of community throughout the United States."[1] Throughout the document, national service programs are described repeatedly using the phrase *civic responsibility*. In Waldeman's account of the legislative process that established the CNCS, he depicts Bill Clinton, Eli Segal, and other founding advocates of national service as seeing a very explicit relationship between volunteer service and service to the nation.[2] They envisioned community service as part of a larger project of civic engagement that would develop a commitment to the local community and, by extension, the national community. In this way, civic engagement is a foundational concept within AmeriCorps, but its appearance within the program has developed in different ways at different times.

There is little public documentation of early efforts to promote civic engagement among AmeriCorps members in the first four to five years of the program. Research participants with long institutional connections to the AmeriCorps program referred to early efforts as "top-down" and "prescriptive," but could only muster vague memories of early curricula or mandates provided by the CNCS for the purposes of promoting civic engagement. It appears as though there was little organized or concerted effort to promote civic engagement in a systematic way prior to 1998. It is clear from various

CNCS civic engagement studies and curricula that the 1998 report from the National Commission on Civic Renewal had a strong influence on the renewed emphasis the CNCS placed on civic engagement within national service programs.

Following the publication of the National Commission on Civic Renewal report, the CNCS commissioned the production of two curricula on active citizenship and civic engagement for use in all national service programs, but specifically in AmeriCorps programs. One curriculum, titled *By the People*, was produced in 2001 by the Center for Democracy and Citizenship at the University of Minnesota and was edited by Harry Boyte, an international advocate for citizenship in the public work and civic republican tradition. The other curriculum, entitled *A Guide to Effective Citizenship through AmeriCorps*, was also produced in 2001 by the Constitutional Rights Foundation, a 501(c)(3) organization devoted to producing and distributing curricular materials focused on the US Constitution, the Bill of Rights, and other materials that place special emphasis on the American judicial system. The curricula were initially distributed to a sample population of AmeriCorps sites, and the CNCS later hired the consulting firm CHP International to produce facilitator guides for the curricula. Not long after the curricula were "piloted" at various AmeriCorps sites, the CNCS commissioned a research project, through the National Service Fellows program, which examined how national service programs responded to the process of civic disengagement through trainings and the use of the two nationally sanctioned curricula.

In 2001, the CNCS released the findings of that study, titled *Citizens in Service: The Challenge of Delivering Civic Engagement Training to National Service Programs*. Known as "The Diller Report," after its author, it demonstrated a large incongruence between the civic ideals of AmeriCorps participants and the effort and intentionality to address these ideals on the part of state commission offices overseeing AmeriCorps programs. Diller argued that the young people participating in AmeriCorps were interested in civic engagement, were involved in their communities, and were demonstrating leadership skills in the public domain. However, she often found substantial evidence that state commissions were ambivalent about addressing civic engagement, with these commissions frequently arguing that it was best accomplished at the program level while at the same time Diller found program directors ill equipped to deliver civic engagement training to their corps. Based on her findings, Diller recommended that the CNCS should incorporate high quality and challenging civic engagement programs into the member-training curriculum; develop guidance or a definition of civic engagement for commissions and programs . . . program staff could be encouraged to include civic engagement training as part of member development objectives.[3]

It is difficult to know to what extent Diller's recommendations affected decision making at the highest levels of the CNCS. However, Diller's report was published on July 27, 2001, and the events of September 11th fundamentally altered the national conversation around volunteerism and thrust national service programs into a new rhetorical position in public life.

In his 2002 State of the Union address, President George Bush introduced a new effort to organize the federal government's support of volunteer community service initiatives. After detailing the "successful" occupation of Afghanistan, the long road that would become the War on Terror, and the necessity of vigilance and surveillance by every level of government as well as individual citizens, Bush moved on to remind us that citizens of the United States had many freedoms, but many obligations as well. He outlined the agenda of the new USA Freedom Corps: to mobilize volunteers in the service of rebuilding communities, responding to domestic crisis, and "extending American compassion throughout the world."[4] He called on every American to commit to 4,000 hours, or two years of full-time work, to community service. Before continuing to discuss why the occupation of Afghanistan was not only necessary, but also desired by Afghans themselves, Bush offered the following summary comments on the importance of volunteerism:

> This time of adversity offers a unique moment of opportunity—a moment we must seize to change our culture. Through the gathering momentum of millions of acts of service and decency and kindness, I know we can overcome evil with greater good. And we have a great opportunity during this time of war to lead the world toward the values that will bring lasting peace.[5]

Throughout the spring of 2002, Bush and his congressional allies struggled to pass the Citizen Service Act, which reauthorized the CNCS and its programs but with several important changes to policy. The events of September 11, 2001 remained central to the arguments for the legislation.

> The spirit of community service in our country is stronger than ever because of the tragedy our Nation has endured. Since so

many Americans are looking for a sense of community and looking for ways to contribute constructively to their communities, we must take this opportunity to reform our Nation's service laws. The principles outlined by President Bush and included in the Citizen Service Act of 2002 seek to build on this spirit and will help to sustain it in the future.[6]

Although the Citizen Service Act ultimately failed to pass Congress, and in fact never left conference committee, the influence of Bush's emphasis on the relationship between service and citizenship was felt at the CNCS. For the 2003 grants cycle, the CNCS released new guidelines for AmeriCorps programs and new grant applicants. These guidelines, referred to by research participants as the 2003 Guidelines, took the furthest steps yet in mandating AmeriCorps programs to include civic engagement programming as part of their member development efforts.

The 2003 Guidelines included a specific recommendation for the inclusion of civic engagement in AmeriCorps program plans. As described by then-CNCS CEO Leslie Lenkowsky, the Guidelines were designed to put the principles of the Citizen Service Act "into practice as much as possible within existing legislative authority."[7] While unable to force AmeriCorps programs to implement civic engagement training, the guidelines "clarified" the CNCS's goals in this regard, "while leaving to the programs themselves considerable flexibility in the methods they use to attain them."[8] The 2003 Guidelines are infused with what could be described as persuasive arguments concerning the inclusion of civic engagement training. For example, one section on member development says that "successful applicants will provide training and use the service experience to help members acquire the knowledge, skills, and attitudes needed to be active citizens of communities—local, state, and national."[9] The knowledge, skills, and attitudes of active citizens were further detailed in the appendix to the guidelines. To support the learning of these skills, the CNCS launched several efforts to support member development in active citizenship including the redistribution of the two curricula described above, the development of several other smaller online curricula, and an online resource library to develop member training around citizenship "priorities." The CNCS announced its intention to distribute copies of historical American documents, such as the Declaration of Independence, to all AmeriCorps members with the argument that these documents "invite us to reflect on who we are as a nation and why service is vital to our communities and to our nation."[10]

There is scant documentation concerning the effect of the CNCS's attempt to implement widespread civic engagement trainings in the

AmeriCorps program. While the program had a very specific effect in the locality where this research occurred, such as the development of a statewide performance measure for civic engagement, the efforts appear to have elicited a negative reaction from local level AmeriCorps directors. Years later, Laura, a state commission employee, described the imposition as "top-down," saying,

> I mean it's definitely a CNCS priority, that members are engaged in civic engagement. . . . I think they were probably going in the way of direct recommendations when they came up with the two competing curricula that they actually paid for people to develop, and I think programs were just like, "No, that's way too strict," and they backed off on prescribing, so now they let programs kind of determine what civic engagement is on their own.

The experience of new layers of requirements within program had mixed reaction among research participants who had worked for AmeriCorps during this period. Some were excited that the CNCS was putting an explicit emphasis on the citizenship components of AmeriCorps. Others were frustrated by what Michelle, a training consultant, described as "the decentralized world of AmeriCorps where everyone can do whatever they want, except you all have to do X, Y, and Z, and we're not going to tell you how." The curricula also led to concerns about their appropriateness for differing AmeriCorps programs. Michelle, who was also a former program director, remembered,

> What was really great was when they were trying to introduce those curricula to the tribal communities, who were going, "I'm not doing this with my Indian Nation members. This is completely culturally and politically inappropriate."

This anecdote is telling, as it gives another point of reference for how the regulations and the nature of the concepts "partisan" and "political" are interpreted in the program. While it may be considered "political" to discuss treaty claims made by First Nations peoples, it is not "political" to suggest to tribal communities that they need to learn about American citizenship and incorporate themselves into the national body.

Despite the ambiguity and ambivalence among state commissions surrounding the entire project of citizenship education in AmeriCorps, as detailed in the Diller Report, the CNCS in this period pushed forward a list of goals for citizenship learning in AmeriCorps that remain influential within the programs. The 2003 Guidelines state that

> By the end of their term of service, AmeriCorps members should: understand and be able to participate effectively in American democracy; discuss and explore their community and the people, processes, and institutions most effective in improving community conditions; help plan effective service projects that respond to real community needs and emergencies; foster within themselves and others positive attitudes regarding the value of lifelong citizenship and service for the common good; have new or increased existing life and/or employment skills; and gain a greater appreciation and understanding of what it means to be an American, including an appreciation and understanding of those of different backgrounds.[11]

It is clear from these goals that the CNCS's intentions for AmeriCorps programs not only transcend "active citizenship" defined solely as some vague form of democratic participation, but that they also strain toward the values and virtues of citizenship. These values and virtues contain seeds of national identity, a particular work ethic, and a myriad of self-improvement goals, all of which have been interpreted by educators as the neoliberalization of the "entrepreneurial self."[12]

In some spaces, these interests consolidated in the emergence of performance measures around civic engagement with the AmeriCorps apparatus. When performance measures were introduced in AmeriCorps program planning, the CNCS required every state commission to have common or aligned performance measures, which every local corps had to meet. In their individual grant-writing process, AmeriCorps programs had to include not only their program-specific performance measures, which I discussed in the previous chapter, but their state-mandated ones as well, and they were required to incorporate these performance measures into any other applicable component of the grant. In the case of civic engagement, this meant introducing civic engagement into the member development sections of the grant. In the state where this research was conducted, there were two aligned performance measures: civic engagement and volunteer mobilization. The choice of these performance measures was not made in a political vacuum; rather, state commission employees recalled their strategic choice to align their performance measures within the priorities of CNCS. At the time of my conversations with them, interviewees remembered their efforts to directly respond to the guidance that emerged in the post-9/11 national service context. This does not discount the possibility that civic engagement was, and remains, authentically a programmatic goal for many AmeriCorps programs. However, the performance measure created the space in which programmatic civic engagement activities emerge in a *compulsory* form.

Just as with the local AmeriCorps program sites, the state commission was required to produce a logic model for its aligned performance measures. Their civic engagement logic model employs the basic components of all logic models in that it attempts to establish a logical relationship between the activities of civic engagement and the outcomes defined by the CNCS. In the logic model, the performance measure dictates that sites will organize three primary civic engagement activities: structured service projects, member training curricula, and civic engagement action plans. Program directors reported that their understanding was that each program site had to provide a minimum of three civic engagement trainings, although the state commission never confirmed the number to them. Further, they understood that each member had to complete five civic engagement action goals (although some sites thought it was three), and that there was no specified quantity on the number of structured service projects. The outputs of these activities, according to the logic model, were that members would be trained in the designated civic engagement skill areas while their capacity in this regard would be measured through a civic engagement survey and by completion of their civic engagement action plan. Said more plainly, AmeriCorps members would be deemed civically engaged if they evaluated *themselves* as such on an end-of-the-year survey and if they completed the mandatory civic engagement components of the program. The state set a high bar for the performance measure, as it said that the measure would be reached if 90 percent of members across the state reported that, as a result of their participation in AmeriCorps, they acquired the skills, attitudes, and knowledge for effective civic engagement.

The presence of the performance measure and the CNCS goals could not ensure that civic engagement activities were conducted uniformly across the state. Rather, these parameters set the context in which civic engagement activities had to be organized. This point is key, because it is in the interpretation of the performance measure that a second key organizational process occurred within the AmeriCorps program. It was clear that there was little oversight by the state commission into the content and form of civic engagement activities. However, all research participants concurred that the performance measure could only be interpreted through the preexisting logic of AmeriCorps regulations prohibiting unsanctioned, political, and, by some interpretations, controversial issues and activities. The lack of oversight may have allowed some program directors to flex the boundaries of what was permissible and sanctioned within the program, but it posed a significant challenge to other program directors. While both the program directors interviewed in this research have a long-term affiliation (ten or more years) with AmeriCorps, and each has their own sense of what is encompassed within civic engagement, state commission employees did acknowledge that there is a steep learning curve for new program directors when it comes to civic engagement. When I asked in interviews if there was any required content for civic engagement trainings, I was told that it depended on what individual programs wanted to do and how involved they wanted to be. I asked if there was any training, consultation, professional development, or peer support on facilitating civic engagement activities, and again the answer was no. The only support structures to implement the civic engagement performance measure were what was available in national online resource centers, the two CNCS-sponsored curricula, and whatever email messages happened to emerge on the program listservs.

The performance measure thus appears to program directors as an external condition that was compulsory for their funding. While some program directors took on the project with gusto, state commission employees admitted that others do not. Thus the uniformity or generalizability of the civic engagement curriculum is not the issue at hand; rather, it is important to consider what kind of space within AmeriCorps programs can be filled with civic engagement activities and how that space will influence the meaning of civic engagement. From the vantage point of administrators, the program appeared open and fluid. Laura, a state commission employee, argued the following:

> I think it has become a little more flexible, but what we've learned, well, the CNCS had put out a couple of curricula that were very—not boring, but didn't engage the members' creative side. It was so general, and "This is how a bill becomes a law, this is the three branches of government" kind of thing. Versus now how we have it set up is that programs can be a little more flexible and they can determine what civic engagement means to them. So it might be attending a school board meeting or

maybe they want to create a service-learning project in their community, and that's civic engagement. So it's up to them to determine; they could read an article and write about how their community reacted to a flood or something like that. It just depends on how programs want to have their members interpret civic engagement.

This flexibility hinged on the notion that the category of civic engagement is open to collective interpretation at the program level and individual interpretation at the member level. The apparent openness appears as the primary way in which members understood the concept of civic engagement, but was nevertheless in contradiction with the other forces articulating a particularly closed approach to the concept.

From Performance Measure to Pedagogy

The civic engagement performance measure allowed for the creation of a kind of pedagogical space within the AmeriCorps program. I would not go so far as to argue that there was a curriculum in our traditional understanding of that concept; there was no planned content with aligned teaching activities and assessment strategies. Nevertheless, there was a coherent set of activities linked to learning goals and with some kind of facilitated structure on a program-by-program basis and designed by the staff of AmeriCorps programs. The activities surrounding civic engagement were not haphazard, incidental, or spontaneous. They largely took place in the context of Corps training days, with expectations that members completed their action plans individually and largely on their own time. As something of a preface, I would argue that the members did not experience the civic engagement components of the program as meaningful learning opportunities. However, the intent of promoting a particular *vision* of civic participation was apparent to the volunteers. In this way, the civic engagement activities were largely experienced as directive, fragmented, and arbitrary. The division and abstraction between the concept of civic engagement and the members' daily service work emerged as a key contextualizing factor in understanding what it was about democracy that was learned through their participation in these activities. This lack of any material ground or social relations in the learning of democracy in the program constitutes the vacuity of civic engagement within AmeriCorps. It is manifested through the pedagogical and epistemological relations that are developed within the program and emerged within the contradiction of "learning democracy" on the terms set by the state through the program regulations.

Perhaps the first instance in which important contradictions between the rhetoric and practice of civic engagement began to emerge was within those Corps training days designated as civic engagement trainings. Each site engaged had at least three, beginning with an introduction to the civic engagement activities of the program. Each program took a different approach; one focused on the value and importance of national service while the other focused on the importance of community service and volunteerism. Within the context of these trainings, each program director introduced the program requirements related to civic engagement, including mandatory participation in structured service activities and the completion of the civic engagement action plan.

Each of these training activities were characterized by the belief of the program directors, based on long-term participation in AmeriCorps, that both meaningful national service and the cultivation of a continued commitment to community volunteerism were key aspects of civic engagement within the larger AmeriCorps vision, a position that echoed the assumptions of CNCS reflected in the Diller Report and other internal documents. Each program director facilitated a conversation during a civic engagement training about what service meant to the participants. The participants were encouraged to engage with each other's conceptualizations of service and civic engagement. Through facilitation, they were required to interact with each other's perspectives, but, as David points out, they were discouraged from engaging in debate with one another. David characterized the role of the facilitator, sometimes himself or another staff member, as

> We're just sharing opinions. It's not like "You're right and I'm wrong, I don't really agree with you or let me tell you why I'm right." You can share your opinion, but I don't want it to become combative or you try to persuade someone else.

The emphasis on sharing opinions emerged as a major motif of AmeriCorps trainings, and it appeared in many forms. Sometimes sharing opinions came to mean, and serve, as reflection. Most often, however, sharing opinions was offered as a pedagogical technique to hold space for self-expression and to share one's opinion represented meaningful participation in learning activities. AmeriCorps members themselves later challenged this approach as a shallow opportunity to exercise their own voices.

The foundational trainings on civic engagement focused on members generating the variety of activities that could fall under the category of civic engagement as well as exploring various levels of government. One activity asked members to evaluate their own past levels of civic engagement and speculate on their levels of commitment in the future; the activity was extremely unpopular with AmeriCorps members, I believe in part because of some of the qualifying rejoinders placed on the concept itself. I will return to this point later. Nevertheless, each took a similar track for explaining the concept. Amanda described the process in this way.

> We just ask them to discuss it. . . . We put it all up on a list, and then our bottom line summary would be that in AmeriCorps, we want them to find a definition that fits for them. And they can see just by having this conversation that there are a lot of different ways to define it and different people think about it in different ways.

To say it another way, the process of defining the concept civic engagement began in the program with the introduction of the concept as a category imposed on members as a *thing*, presupposing the existence of something called "civic engagement." Members were then asked to say what they think the term meant. I asked AmeriCorps members if they remembered the kinds of activities or ideas that surfaced as part of the discussion in their first civic engagement training. It would be accurate to describe their recall of these trainings as hazy; many admitted the experience did not make a strong impact. For example, in detailed lists generated by a focus group of AmeriCorps members, they remembered the following as elements of civic engagement: buying a U2 CD; adopting a highway; going to a neighborhood council meeting; any sort of volunteering, lobbying, or writing letters; international adoption; city councils; welcoming immigrants into the country; sponsoring a child in another country; and "self-education stuff." Based on the activities the members were able to generate, the trainings then proceeded to emphasize the ability of the members to get involved in civic engagement activities before turning to the requirements of the performance measure and the civic engagement plans.

In reflecting on their first civic engagement training, the members expressed two major concerns. First, they experienced a feeling of judgment concerning the amount or extent of commitment to service that one was able to make. In response to one activity in which members discussed their current level of engagement and the possibility of future engagement, one AmeriCorps member argued the following:

> They were putting values judgments on what they thought we should be thinking. Because like when we did the future thing and I thought, "If I want approval, I should move towards this end of the spectrum." But Audrey went backwards, and they went after her and asked her why. And she said, "I want to have kids and a family and I probably won't be as engaged as I am now." She was upset, like life is sometimes more than civic engagement, and sometimes just living can be civic engagement. Sometimes the best thing you have to offer the world is being a happy, fulfilled participant in it.

For many, it was impossible to envision a future in which they would be more civically engaged than during their time in AmeriCorps, since during this time they were serving forty hours a week. This association of civic engagement with time, however, was not exclusive to this group. I encountered the same concerns in other groups and in the state-wide AmeriCorps conference, where members also noted that as they age and have families and full-time jobs, they will necessarily become *less* civically engaged. The second concern focused on the public and private dimensions of civic engagement. As one member described,

> The debate was, if you went around your block, by yourself, and picked up the garbage on the side of the streets, is that civic engagement? And there were people who said, "Yes that is," and there were people who said, "No, it is only civic engagement if you go through your neighborhood organization." Or if you and your neighbors form a litter pick-up club.

This conversation was recalled by many participants, and it clearly had some impact on their thinking, as it resurfaced at several other points in discussions. The members, however, were troubled by the resolution of the conversation, which they felt was a return to the "sharing opinions" position. There were, it seemed, no answers or fixed definitions, only their own definitions of the concept. Amanda argued the case to her Corps in this way.

> We give them a little bit of a historical piece—this is an AmeriCorps performance measure and all AmeriCorps programs have to address it in some way. And in the past they've had these curriculums and kind of a top-down approach to telling you what you need to learn about it and in what way. And we don't buy that. We think you have some sense of what civic engagement means and how it fits into your life and what's important about it. So we're going to do things this way. So that way they can find something that fits for them, and they can find something that's much more meaningful. So that's kind of our bottom line. Pick something that works for you.

The openness and flexibility that state commission employees described as part of the intent of the performance measure appears in the program through a lack of conceptual clarity around the concept of civic engagement. As one AmeriCorps member argued, "I think the point was that everybody had a different definition of civic engagement. And we didn't really debate it, but we, like, argued our points versus other definitions and in that process everyone made up their own definition."

The combination of the trainings on service and civic engagement composed the conceptual apparatus for civic engagement in the AmeriCorps program vis-à-vis the members. When pressed to discuss what impact the trainings had on their understanding of civic engagement, a variety of responses emerged. For some, the intent of the message, as understood by the program directors, was received in that they took from the trainings a reinforcement of the value of service and participation. Others were turned off by what they saw as the conceptual weakness of the notion of civic engagement. As one member argued, "I would say I had not put much thought into civic engagement before, but hearing their definition, you consider civic engagement to be anything 'good.' It's not useful." Still others were upset by what they perceived as the imposition of a program requirement that was redundant with the experience of serving in AmeriCorps and which expressed a value judgment on their own participation. One AmeriCorps member summed up the feeling by saying, "I was frustrated with the message, which was like, 'You need to be civically engaged,' and

I was like, 'I'm in AmeriCorps.' Not to be selfish about it, but I am civically engaged." Although there was much frustration expressed in the focus groups around the topic of civic engagement, there was also appreciation, at times begrudgingly, of the value of the trainings. Many expressed the idea that they now had a "better appreciation" of how to get involved in their neighborhood or city; however, this appreciation of the capacity and value of their participation was restricted to a local level.

Despite the confusion surrounding the purpose and content of the trainings, the civic engagement activity that most embodied the ambiguity of the concept of civic engagement within the AmeriCorps program was the civic engagement action plan. The "plan," as members referred to it, was a list of civic engagement activities that they committed to completing during the course of their service. The plan was based on several assumptions. First, rather than offer a curriculum in civic engagement, the plan allowed AmeriCorps members to engage in a personal way with the concept. The intention was that through the plan they were able to set their own goals and follow through of their own accord. Second, the action plans were meant to be more flexible than traditional curricular models. Instead of a required series of trainings on predetermined models, the plan allowed members to move at their own pace. Third, the plans were open-ended, meaning that they set no official lines around what would or would not count as civic engagement, apart from the agreed-on definition within the program. As long as what the member wrote down on the action plan corresponded to the definition of civic engagement discussed in their Corps trainings, it counted as a civic engagement goal. This included activities that would technically be not sanctioned within the AmeriCorps program. As such, some programs did not allow members to count any civic engagement action plan activities as hours of service, while some allowed members to count hours *if* the activity fell within the parameters of the program. Full-time AmeriCorps members were required to complete a minimum of five civic engagement goals, set forth at the beginning of the year, and part-time members completed at least three. Program directors expressed how they encouraged their members to write down more than five items on the plan in case something happened that prohibited their completion of one of the goals. This is key, because being able to say they had completed the five goals was an indicator of the performance measure, which argues that *if* members completed the plan, *then* they may be described as civically engaged.

The action plans were introduced during initial civic engagement trainings. For many members, it was their first introduction to the concept of civic engagement, although not to notions such as volunteerism, community participation, or activism. Given member reflections on the content and experience of these trainings, it is not surprising that what they wrote on their action plans reflected their ambivalence about the concept of civic engagement. The most frequent activities on the action plans were to volunteer, live a green lifestyle, vote, learn about another culture, and go to a public meeting. Less frequently included activities were broad in range, but all the activities can be organized in four major categories: community building (e.g., community clean-ups or block parties), learning activities (e.g., learning more about a public issue), electoral activities (e.g., vote or go to a public meeting), and personal lifestyle choices (e.g., consume less). The most popular activities were those associated with electoral politics or elected officials, but when we remove voting, which most were planning to do since it was an election year, and attending a public meeting, an event required and facilitated by both of the Corps participating in the research, the frequency of engaging with elected officials drops significantly. Electoral activity then became the third most popular activity after learning activities and personal lifestyle choices. I make this point because the act of voting was indicated by most participants as something they were already going to do and would count toward completion of the civic engagement performance goal, while attending a public meeting was something that was happening through the auspices of Corps training days. These members disclosed that their approach was to tread as easily as possible through the requirements of the civic engagement curricula. In this way, learning activities and personal lifestyle choices become significant as they lead us to conclude that they indicate what members are willing to do external to the program and on the basis of their own energy. In discussing the plans, members often expressed concerns about time, priorities with families and friends, conflicts with their part-time jobs, and being "overcommitted."

Member reflections on the experience of writing up their civic engagement action plans were largely negative, perhaps influenced by the increasing pressure, as the year wore on, to complete the goals. The civic engagement action plans present themselves as the most visible form in which civic engagement is experienced as an external imposition on the learner. This was described by some through the language of *force*, which was perceived by members on a scale from minimally invasive to bordering on coercion. One member argued, "It was so forced. It was not a training that empowered us to be civically engaged. It demanded civic engagement and made us fill out a worksheet." Perceived as an extra requirement on top of the 1,700-

hour service commitment they had already made, some members expressed resentment at the requirement while others were ambivalent, seeing both positive and negative aspects of the experience. This ambivalence may have led many members to express a lack of enthusiasm for the assignment or unwillingness to fully commit to the intentions of the work. One AmeriCorps member argued the following:

> For me it was the path of least resistance, so a lot of it is a reinforcement of good behavior. I mean, of course I could do more to be civically engaged, but I feel like I'm doing pretty well right now and didn't want to resent the idea of civic engagement by taking on too much.

For most of the members, the action plan was interpreted as one of many program requirements, and it did not carry special meaning particular to the goal of becoming a more civically engaged person. For many, the experience of writing and fulfilling their civic engagement plans was an extension of their overall lack of engagement with the civic engagement requirements and brought to the surface feelings of incoherence, indecision, and confusion in association with what was being asked of them. One member reflected,

> I got a little overwhelmed. There is so much to do, and what can I do and how do I decide what is important and what I should work on. . . . You get all these thoughts going and then I have to get them organized and put them to action and see what I can do. But, there is already so much going on that I sometimes forget to stay on top of my goals.

Some of this discomfort could have been dealt with pedagogically, but it also reflects the lack of conceptual coherence identified by the members. When *anything* can be civic engagement, than anything *can* be civic engagement. Perhaps the most interesting version of the "anything goes" notion of civic engagement is to be found in the civic engagement goals of a previous year's members, which included flamenco dancing among other endeavors such as voting and recycling.

The vision of the civic engagement trainings and action plans that emerged from the members' perceptions is one of an external requirement that is engaged in a perfunctory manner. Program directors admitted as much, one going so far as to say that the action plans are a larger symptom of a "ridiculous" performance measure. Despite the lack of validity conferred by participants, these two pedagogical activities reveal a telling component of the way in which civic engagement is actually conceptualized within the hierarchy of AmeriCorps. Pedagogically, these activities construct civic engagement as something that can be learned in individual ways, in isolation from one another and the program, with no coherent conceptual framework but an implied and felt axiology and in a way in which accountability to learning is demonstrated through checking a box marked completed.

The civic engagement trainings, however, cannot be sealed off from the overall pedagogical approach to Corps training days within the program sites; rather, they embody pedagogical relations that emerge within the overall structure and regulation of the AmeriCorps program. This approach is premised on particular epistemological relations that have significant impacts on all the pedagogical acts within the program. These relations are characterized by: (1) a reliance on "expert" knowledge; (2) a conflation of "expert" knowledge with "neutral" knowledge; (3) a technocratic interpretation of social problems; (4) depoliticization of the subject matter; and (5) an abstraction from the experiential base of knowledge and the members' ongoing service work. Let me provide a few examples of the complexity of these relations as they appear in actual pedagogical work within the program.

The first training I went to as part of my fieldwork was with the tutoring program and was facilitated by a diversity officer from the school district. It began with a lecture explaining what the diversity officer's role was within the school district. The man was a lawyer, and his job was to make sure the equal opportunity standards were upheld in employment practices. The major activity of the training was to watch a video containing a series of images of people of color. The members were instructed by the facilitator to take notes on "who they thought these people were." After watching the video, the facilitator asked the group to volunteer their responses to his question. For example, when shown an image of a middle-aged man and asked to describe his race, participants guessed Latino, and were then asked to speculate as to his job or his name. After several rounds of this, we watched the video a second time. This version of the video revealed the names of the individuals and their occupation, many of which upset prevailing stereotypes of various racial groups. Yes, the facilitator told us, the man in the video identifies as Latino, but his name is Andrew and he does not work in food or cleaning services. The lesson of the activity was that "everyone has stereotypes," and we apply them on a daily basis. The members felt betrayed by the trainer; he solicited stereotypes from them and then scolded them for acknowledging them. He amended his claim, arguing that we all have stereotypes, but the problem lies in not acknowledging that we have them. As long as we make this acknowledgment, he argued, we might be able to have a productive conversation around diversity. Despite his insistence on the necessity of productive conversation, at no point were the members asked for their own opinions on the subject at hand or asked to think about their experience in the context of their AmeriCorps service.

The training shocked me. Despite the numerous multiculturalism, diversity, and antiracism trainings, workshops, forums, events, and facilitations I had attended over the course of my education and career, I had never been to one that lacked any acknowledgment of the reason why we undertake such training in the first place. There was an active avoidance of the idea of racism as a social problem in the United States. In my field notes for the training, I took note that the facilitator never used the word *racism*. I was surprised, given that the tutoring volunteers were charged with bridging the achievement gap. I later asked the program director and her support staff what perspectives or frameworks they used to introduce their Corps to politically charged topics such as No Child Left Behind (NCLB), racism within schools, the achievement gap, special education programs, English as a second language (ESL) programs, and homophobia in schools. Their frameworks, she argued, were professional experts. She invited experts in to discuss the issues in factual and descriptive terms. For example, the discussion of No Child Left Behind involved a compliance officer from the district. The woman reviewed the mandates and the current performance standards. Someone from the school district facilitated a discussion of the achievement gap and provided statistical information on the nature of the gap and which social groups were disproportionately represented. The presentations tended to be technical, oriented toward practical interventions, and focused on developing the skills of AmeriCorps members.

For the program director, relying on experts from the school district precluded the possibility of delivering ideological, biased, political, or partisan trainings to AmeriCorps members. Amanda asserted that they used no frameworks for analysis; their purpose was just to give the members the information and let them decide on their own perspective. It hardly takes much attention, however, to acknowledge that the claim to neutrality is no such thing; the expert who chooses to discuss "diversity" within a context in which history and power are not acknowledged has firmly situated her- or himself within a particular framework. This became a pattern; the absence of an explicit, or explicitly politicized, framework for understanding an issue pertinent to service in AmeriCorps repeatedly gave way to an implicit approach to learning about the issues at hand.

I had multiple experiences in trainings in which problems of political difference were quickly swept away in favor of conversations that focused on technical interventions in social problems. For example, I attended a county commissioner's meeting with the housing Corps. Serendipitously, the commissioners were set to debate a proposal for county funding of affordable housing development. Despite their nearly eight months of service in affordable housing development work, the members were not prepared for the discussion at all; most of them had no idea what was being discussed. They knew nothing about the public policy conversation around housing, even to the extent that one of them asked me what *foreclosures* meant. They were fidgety and bored. At one point two of them turned to me and asked what the commissioners were discussing. When I replied "affordable housing," they quickly whispered it to each other, settled down, and tried to follow the debate. When the conversation turned to strategies for dealing with wide-scale home foreclosures, a Republican member of the commission stated that he thought the commission should "let the market handle it." A Democratic member quickly countered that they had already had that conversation in a previous meeting but had agreed to move forward with a policy proposal. It was a palpably tense moment in the meeting. After the meeting, the members had the opportunity to meet with one of the commissioners, who kept the conversation solidly on the responsibilities and jurisdiction of the county commission. When one member asked what the argument between the commissioners had been about, the commissioner replied, it was "just a discussion we've been having for a while," and quickly returned to his description of the relationship between county and municipal governance. Members later asked me for further clarification, visibly frustrated at the lack of direct response from their program director or the county commissioner. Not wanting to intervene too strongly, I simply stated that there are differing political perspectives on how to address human needs through social policy and service delivery, like affordable housing, and that the comment to "let the market handle it" was a nod to this philosophical division.

The Corps members had strong, and often polarizing, feelings about the trainings. Many felt they were useful for their emphasis on practical skills. They would often complain that the skills were not particular enough to their situation, but they appreciated the ongoing effort to train them in their service work. Many others, however, were vocally frustrated by what they felt was a truncated experience. In one focus group, members discussed their experience completing the civic engagement survey. They narrowed in on a question that asked them if they felt prepared to address the underlying causes of community issues. The conversation began with an AmeriCorps member arguing, "Absolutely not. I feel like we've been prohibited from discussing the underlying causes of community issues." Another participant replied that she agreed with him before another young woman jumped into the conversation to say,

> I don't know. I feel like sometimes the discussions we've had in a cultural sensitivity training are ones that certainly no one that I know is having outside of a college. But also, like, why can't we fund education, specifically political issues. We've talked about that race matters, class matters; I still think about our training on No Child Left Behind, not that it's an underlying cause, but it is tied up.

A second AmeriCorps member responded that

> I feel like we've spoken a lot about some of those things, but I feel like I would have gotten more value talking about the underlying issues in our schools or those neighborhoods. But yeah, I don't feel like we've discussed it.

I asked them to reflect further on training they received on No Child Left Behind. The young man who began the conversation said,

> I mean, talking about the achievement gap is inherently political and bridging it is our meaning. And when we were having orientation, we were trying to talk about what is the achievement gap and why does it exist. And there were definitely issues that were introduced, like, we had someone talk about multiculturalism and the disparity between minority and Caucasian students, and sometimes it would veer into the why, but mostly it was, "This is what it is." I mean, there were moments where it would shift; we read one article where the woman wrote about education in the segregated South and how important those schools were in the Black community even though they were dangerous as well, so that was an example of us crossing into thinking about those issues on a more substantive level; but I think mostly we

stuck to this is what NCLB is, this is what the law is, this is the statistics that outline what the differences in achievement are.

The members indicated that the ways in which the trainings dealt with social problems contained several important dynamics. First, the trainings naturalize the "community need" to some extent by dehistoricizing it and not acknowledging contested political conceptualizations of the problem. Second, the emphasis on practical intervention demonstrates that the trainings relied on largely technocratic interpretations of the social problems, following from the first articulation of "need" in the logic model. Third, the trainings emphasize a description of community issues as needs or problems and did not endeavor to explore various explanations of the problems, only their surface appearances.

The fact that some AmeriCorps members were aware that they were only engaging partial or fragmented understandings of the social problems at hand indicates that their consciousness is more politicized than the parameters of AmeriCorps allows. For these members, the AmeriCorps trainings were a frustrating experience, both because they were unable to substantively explore any issue and further because the members were actively discouraged from engaging their own experience through processes of reflection. One member characterized the trainings by saying, "We listened to speakers, but didn't engage." The format was overwhelmingly based on lectures, with some divergence into small group activities. The members indicated that when reflection activities were included, they were organized in an ineffectual way. One female member argued as follows:

> Well, it wasn't stuff that needed reflection, and it was always framed as stupid activities. Or it would be in really big groups. Like, I'm sick of sitting in a huge circle and going around the circle and everyone gets two minutes to talk. It is really hard to pay attention when there are 45 of us. But I feel like something like civic engagement, stuff that we don't really know a lot about, there should have been reflection.

Program directors explained their lack of emphasis on reflection by saying that if they were to open the discussion to people's "opinions" and "personal experiences," they believed the conversations would become too chaotic and difficult to manage; the tone of the conversations would change, become "too personal," or diverge into an unintended direction. This justification conflicted with their earlier description of civic engagement trainings as a space to "share opinions." Despite these concerns, AmeriCorps members in every focus group expressed their opinion that the trainings were "boring," in part because they were being lectured at and unable to reflect on their experience in their service activities. For some, this lack of reflection was experienced as a curtailing of their own voice within the program. One AmeriCorps member, in reflecting on how her best learning experiences in the program happened outside of formal activities, argued that only in the research focus groups did she feel open to really reflect on her experiences in the program because she could "let her guard down." She went on to say,

> I also feel like this [the focus group] is discussion for the sake of processing, and some of them [corps training days] are discussion for a purpose only. Like, we're going to make something fit into AmeriCorps scheme. I don't feel like I've been truly invited at Corps Day to do this kind of reflection.

One male AmeriCorps member, reacting to a question on the civic engagement survey, said, "I feel like those questions were really to monitor what we were supposed to do. I don't feel like we touched on a lot of those things. Like, 'Express myself?' Were we really given the chance to express ourselves?"

What is the pedagogical effect of training organized in this way? Learners experienced subject matter as external bodies of knowledge purposefully disconnected from their own experience. In the context of a program such as AmeriCorps, in which experiential learning is the primary mode of engagement, learners make connections informally between daily experience and the theoretical context of that experience. Without structured reflection, which is emphasized in the best practices of many forms of service-learning and experiential education, learning becomes incidental and can have an effect opposite to what is intended by program directors. On the one hand, this can be interpreted as the miseducative experience described by Dewey that can inadvertently reinforce existing stereotypes or forms of knowledge rather than challenging previously held beliefs.[13] On the other hand, there is a deeper and most disconcerting relationship with knowledge established within the pedagogical parameters of the program. While certain types of learning, such as changed perspectives or growth in bodies of knowledge, can certainly come from the kind of epistemological and pedagogical relations expressed in the program, the pedagogical activities also alienate learners as they experience the source of epistemic authority as external to themselves or their experience. While this can be disempowering for some learners, the more typical outcome is disengagement, frustration, and exasperation, particularly among individuals who are accustomed to hearing their own voices. The Corps members provided ample evidence of this in their discussions of these activities. However, the alienation of learners from their own experience within AmeriCorps programs is likely to have different effects on different members, based on their previous experience with classroom-based learning and their positionality within social relations of power. For some members, these relations can be experienced as an active avoidance of a truth they know existentially or through the history of their own communities.

The effect of this kind of learning is aptly demonstrated in an experience I had with the housing Corps during a structured service experience, another pedagogical aspect of the civic engagement performance measure. The Corps completed one service project per month. For the first few months of the year, the program director and other organizational staff organized the service projects. However, after several examples, the program director organized the members in small groups and asked them to coordinate a service activity for the whole group. He described his purposes in this way.

> I kind of explain to them what the goals are, that we want members to be busy. We want them to have a project that is appropriate for 30 to 40 people. Our goal there is to get things done, but it's also tuned to learn about the organization and figure out what role they play in the community. So, what is the need they are trying to address, how are they addressing it.

His goal in the service projects was for members to go through the work of planning a quality service project, organizing it, and facilitating it. Through this work, he hoped that his members would learn more about what agencies are working in the community, what kinds of issues not-for-profits address, and what the components of a good volunteer experience are. It also addressed the state performance measure on volunteer mobilization. He did not provide any research materials or training on how to go about investigating a community "need" or the organizations that meet such needs. His best guess was that the members worked with connections they already had in the community, although he was sure many simply went with large organizations that already have developed volunteer programs. David acknowledged that it is difficult for an organization to coordinate a volunteer activity for thirty to forty people that is a "good" use of their time. David was not sure that the members remembered the argument he used to introduce the service projects at the beginning of the year. For this reason, and because of best practices in service-learning, each member "reflected" on the project at its completion by filling in a half-page form. The questions provided on the form asked members to evaluate the utility of the service project (to themselves as well as the community), to briefly discuss their learning, and then to recommend whether the experience should be replicated for another group. Among the members, these reflections were understood as evaluations; they understood that the purpose of the service projects was to learn the difference between a good volunteer experience and a bad one. This understanding was reinforced by some of their own service activities that involved coordinating volunteers; the members felt that their organization put strong emphasis on the quality of volunteer experience and on retention of volunteers.

From the program director's perspective, a large number of AmeriCorps members remaining civically engaged after their year of service was demonstrated through their continued commitment to service, which, again, is a priority for CNCS as well and has been the subject of several longitudinal studies. For this reason, he felt it was important that they developed, through civic engagement activities, a commitment to serving outside of the AmeriCorps program and additionally an understanding of how to facilitate service experiences for themselves and others. This way, in the future they would be able to pursue further volunteer activities elsewhere. While philosophically he argued that service is only one component of civic engagement, the other components did not materialize in his program with anywhere near the amount of emphasis as community service. Within the housing program, service projects were organized under the framework of the civic engagement activities, meaning he reported them as part of the performance measure. A significant result of his effort, and the most problematic outcome of the service projects, has to do with the extent to which civic engagement and volunteer mobilization became conflated within the logic of the program. AmeriCorps members' demonstrated this conflation in their reaction to one particular service project. This experience, and several others, provides insight into why the civic engagement activities of these AmeriCorps program are met with such a lukewarm reception by AmeriCorps members.

I participated in several of the service projects organized by the housing Corps members. All had a similar structure. We converged at the given location, listened to a ten- to fifteen-minute presentation from a staff person about the structure, mission, and programs of the organization, engaged in two to three hours of service work, gathered for final questions, filled out reflection forms, and departed. One service project had a decidedly different rhythm to it, and it turned out to be an incredibly telling experience. A few Corps members had made arrangements with an organization on the northeast side of the city to engage in what they described as an "act of neighborly kindness." The organization was a loose association of neighbors who assisted anyone in the neighborhood with household projects they could not accomplish on their own. They did housework and property maintenance for elderly residents and those without the income to employ others to do so. As such, they described their work as doing odd jobs around the house for people. The Corps members had informed the organization that they would have thirty volunteers at their disposal for three hours on a Friday morning, and that we could be assigned to any task. The day before the scheduled activity, a staff member called to say that we would be helping a neighborhood resident move and asked us to meet them at a residential address. We assembled at 9:00 a.m. in the street and waited approximately thirty minutes for the woman to return to her house with a moving truck. The AmeriCorps members were frustrated by their idleness. After the truck arrived, the staff organized us into a long line of people winding from her attic apartment down to the moving truck, and we proceeded to pass objects down the stairs. Several times the procession of objects stopped for ten- to fifteen-minute stretches, at which point the members grumbled and complained about the disorganization of the process.

When the truck was packed, nine or ten vehicles caravanned to a storage unit center on the east side of the city. The woman led us to her unit, which she opened and revealed to be completely full. She asked several volunteers to begin pulling items out so she could get to some objects that were in the back. Ultimately she had more to move than room in her rented truck, so several members began packing her belongings into their cars. When the packing was completed, she dropped the keys off at the office, her storage unit still two-thirds full, and we drove her and her possessions to a third storage center on the south side of the city. At this point, we had reached the three-hour marker, and about half of the AmeriCorps members began leaving to return to their afternoon commitments. Those with either no pressing engagements or a desire to complete the project remained. We unloaded all of the trucks and packed her things into a new storage unit. When the project was complete, those who remained filled out their evaluation forms and then left; the woman remained at the storage center waiting for someone to pick her up.

Throughout the entire morning, the AmeriCorps members vocally expressed their irritation at the "lack of organization" of their service experience. They were upset that the woman was not organized enough to fully utilize the "free" services. They were frustrated that she had arrived late, that she was not finished packing, and that she did not have clear directions on how to get to either storage center, and they complained that she was frazzled and "ungrateful." Some AmeriCorps members remained quiet during the morning; however, all of those who participated in the focus groups later joined the chorus of complaints.

My experience of the service project was quite different, in part because I offered to drive the woman from site to site. She was indeed frazzled, a bit disoriented, and appeared disorganized. On our first car trip, we made small talk and she felt the need to apologize to me multiple times for her level of disorganization. She told me she had lost her housing forty-eight hours before and had only had a short time to pack. She explained that the relationship with the people who owned the house had become "untenable," and she alluded to both a problem with violence in the home and an inability to pay her rent as her son had recently been involved in a workplace accident that resulted in extensive medical costs. On our car ride between the two storage centers, I asked her why she was moving her things to a different storage center. She told me that she could no longer afford the larger unit and needed to consolidate her things into a smaller unit. I asked her when she would be moving into new housing. She told me she had been approved for a senior unit in public housing, but that it would not be open for five months. In the meantime, she would "crash" with friends. When the move was complete, I offered her a ride to wherever she needed to go, but she was unsure where she would be sleeping that night.

The next week, I met with the AmeriCorps members. I had not seen them since the service project. I asked them for their thoughts on the experience, and the entire reflection, in both groups, revolved around the "quality" of the service experience. They rehashed their frustrations about the level of disorganization, the inefficiency of the work, the poor use of time, and even the seemingly irrational nature of their entire project. Why get things from one storage unit, they asked, to just move them to another? They discussed ways in which the "volunteer experience" could have been improved, with a focus on time management. As one member reflected, "We spend our time thinking, 'How are we being effective as volunteers?' That's how we were coming at it. What it effective? Was I utilized?" They reflected that if they were just regular volunteers and not AmeriCorps, they might have left the project because they were not being "properly utilized." The important outcome of the experience was that "You feel as though you've contributed during the day, not just sitting around. If you've taken a day off of work, so you feel like you've done something." One member complained that the entire experience at the first storage unit was a waste of time because all she had pulled out were "personal items" like children's drawings and baseball trophies.

I found the situation extremely difficult from an ethical standpoint. I was sitting with groups of young adults who had been working full-time in an affordable housing organization for nine months. They worked with families moving into affordable housing projects. They worked with volunteers to develop the housing. They did maintenance in the homes of people who did not have the money for basic home repair. They were confronted, on that drizzly morning, with a person in crisis; someone who was not in control of her housing and who was, in reality, homeless. They treated her with disdain. Only a few of them talked with her or inquired about her situation. She had revealed to me in the car that she felt uncomfortable talking about her "situation" with a group of "college kids." They were completely unaware of the dynamics of the situation they were confronting on the ground, and their AmeriCorps program directors did nothing to try and problematize their reaction to the experience or intervene in their behavior. They merely evaluated the quality of the experience and moved on. They were faced with a visceral opportunity to understand the suffering in the "community need" they were charged with alleviating and toward which they had committed to "getting things done," and yet there was no conversation. The approach of the program had left them utterly ill equipped to recognize, let alone understand, the social reality before them. I asked one group whether only people who can afford housing should be allowed to accumulate mementos of childhood. Was she not allowed to keep her son's baseball trophy? Was it not telling that she had abandoned all her possessions in the storage unit except her children's school-age artwork? Why would she have her possessions in three different parts of the city? Did we not see that morning what it means, in very real organizational terms, to not have control over where you live? Was this not the "community need" they were here to understand?

I asked the program director the same set of questions. He regretted deeply the way the morning had developed and realized that an opportunity had been missed. However, his initial reaction was in keeping with his original learning goal for the service: How to organize a good volunteer experience. Both the program director and his members worked within their own logic of the experience; their purpose was to learn about "doing community service" and "being civically engaged." Their purpose collided, violently, with the reality of why their "service" was needed in the first place, and they were at a loss to recognize the paradox.

This experience demonstrated the ways to which civic engagement activities reproduce the relations found in other member development trainings *and* are substantially impacted by what happens, and does not happen, in those trainings. The abstraction and fragmentation in learning runs across all relations of the program; it is not possible to separate out the civic engagement activities from the overall epistemological and pedagogical relations within the program. What I came to understand, however, was that the civic engagement activities were further complicated by an additional relationship to the prohibited activity regulations. Regular training activities avoided politics in so far as they circumvented discussions of the underlying or root causes of the "community need" they address. However, on the terrain of civic engagement, they had to not only avoid the political nature of the problem, but the political nature of possible solutions as well.

A particularly awkward example of this reality emerged during visits to the state capitol as part of the planned civic engagement activities of the programs. Both groups had similarly structured visits. Each began with a training session from a local not-for-profit umbrella group. The agency was charged with advocating for the interests of the not-for-profit sector within government. The training focused on the structures of government, the differences between the various legislative bodies at the state level, and the difference between lobbying and advocacy work. The training concluded with a tour of the capitol building and session chambers, which in the case of the tutoring group were empty as it was a Friday and most lawmakers had returned to their constituencies. By my observations, the AmeriCorps members were distracted and disinterested throughout the training. Many had stressful mornings trying to find parking at the capitol building and then locating the correct room, getting lost in the vast complex of state buildings. They were uncomfortable in their official AmeriCorps gear, which was not weather appropriate, and they were constantly adjusting their layers of clothing to accommodate the different temperatures in the building.

The general atmosphere of disengagement and tedium was broken by a few significant events throughout each of the two visits. The tutoring group had a fairly uneventful training and then proceeded to meet with a group of elected officials from the metropolitan area. Prior to meeting with the lawmakers, a staff member of the program reviewed with the group the kinds of questions they were prohibited from discussing with lawmakers. Reminding them that they could not tread toward anything that was "political" or "partisan," she emphasized that their questions should remain vocational in nature. She told the group they could ask the senators and representatives why they ran for the legislature, what they liked or disliked about the work, or how they interacted with their constituencies. Their purpose was to understand what working in state government is like and how citizens get involved in the process. What followed was an extremely awkward conversation. From my perspective, the lawmakers acted exactly how they always act when placed in front of a group of voters, particularly young people; they asked the group of almost fifty young adults what issues they cared about, to which the AmeriCorps members responded that they were not allowed to talk about "the issues."

In their discussions reflecting on the experience, every focus group responded by commenting on several characteristics of the experience. First, it was awkward; they were unsure of what they could discuss with the representatives or if they could respond to questions or prompts. The conversation was thus very stilted, and they acknowledged that the session was not participatory in part because they were unsure of how to participate. This is related to the second characteristic, which is that they felt monitored by the AmeriCorps program staff who were there. Third, they remained deeply confused about how to discuss their service work or their "community need" in public contexts where questions of "permissibility" were paramount. Fourth, they identified that the elephant in the room was not only the avoidance of legislation or mandates, but also "controversial" topics more broadly, which they discussed as "the issues."

I asked the members what they thought it meant for something to "be controversial." The response from one AmeriCorps member was that it if is politically partisan, then they cannot talk about it. Another responded that issues are only considered partisan because the parties disagree. I asked if they could think of an issue in a democracy where there is not partisan disagreement. One responded, rather facetiously, with "babies and flags." One frustrated AmeriCorps member described the situation in this way.

> It was very, very general. Like, about their job and how they got into it. Nothing about what they are working on, just about the process. Personally, I didn't really like that day. I don't think I've

ever been to the capitol, so it was nice to see it, but if I want to know what a legislator does, I can google that and see the job description. The whole point of getting to meet those people is the issues. It didn't have to be in an attacking way. Like, "Why did you vote that way?" But just to talk, "What issues are you working on, where do you stand and why." That would have been way more interesting than what or how do you do what you do. Or how did you get into it.

Despite many negative reactions to the day, several focus group participants reported that they left feeling as though they could more easily interact with state government, such as writing their elected officials or visiting them at the capitol. I observed a few key dynamics. First, they were confused about the regulations, even nine months into their service. Second, the experience was "hollow" for them in that they could only talk about "the process" or "the vocation," but not about a key feature of democracy, which is public debate over issues of public concern. Third, the conversations were not "conversations" because they are necessarily one-sided; AmeriCorps members were restricted from accessing their own knowledge or experience and from participating in the conversation as an exchange of positions. It was a telling opportunity; the lawmakers could have learned a great deal from the members experiences of service at the community level, but to discuss the service would require discussing "the issues."

The housing group also experienced their own regulation-bounded moments at the capitol. In their morning training with the not-for-profit advocate, they were joined by the government-relations staff person from their organization. Remembering that the housing organization was large and well funded compared to tutoring group in the school district, they had recently employed a lobbyist to promote their interests at the capitol; her role was to both support a progressive agenda around affordable housing and, indirectly, to secure funding for not-for-profit affordable housing development. When she began detailing this agenda, AmeriCorps members in the room became visibly uncomfortable, looking at each other with concern and looking to their program director to see his reaction. At one point, a member interrupted her and asked, "I'm not from this state. Why does everyone in the not-for-profit sector hate the governor?" Both of the women facilitating the session, in my opinion, did a decent job of providing as "permissible" an answer to this question as possible. They explained why some felt the governor made harsh cuts to not-for-profit funding while others felt the cuts were justified and necessary. They then swiftly diverted the conversation back to the agenda for the day and left to take the group on their tour of the capitol. As we were walking, the program director asked me if I thought the conversation had crossed the line. I responded that I thought it had not, that it had remained focused on why the organization felt the need to have a presence at the capitol. He agreed, but felt that if the conversation had not crossed the line, it had at least come "right up to it." In a focus group following the incident, AmeriCorps members expressed that they felt it has been one of the only times "real" issues had been discussed. One female member observed,

> They did try and explain why some people feel that way, so, on the one hand it was a governor-bash fest. I was glad she asked the question because sometimes people are being partisan when they feel like they aren't. It was a good question, I sensed this, but I can't explain it. I thought it was highly entertaining, 'cause we talked about a lot of hard stuff.

In other focus groups, participants described the situation as "dicey," and that it made them "uncomfortable." The situation demonstrates a paradox within the program; on the one hand, AmeriCorps members expressed frustration at not being able to "talk about issues," but they then self-policed the environment by retreating from such "dicey" conversations and activities.

Pedagogy or Ideology?

How should we explain these kinds of experiences? If we accept the prohibited activities and regulations as common sense, then we are unable to explain why AmeriCorps members experience the dissonance they described and why the situation both made sense and did not make sense at the same time. Michele, a former program director, directly correlated this experience, and my previous description of the diversity training, to program director anxiety concerning the regulations and their lack of preparation for the role.

> So civic engagement to me, that and diversity, are two areas where people aren't comfortable or people don't have—the people who

are supposed to be doing it, don't even know. And I just think that that's a disservice ultimately to the members. And in both areas people are scared of either emotions or going over a legal line or whatever it might be, so they do as little as they can to meet the requirements and not get in trouble. And it's perfectly understandable why that's where they end up.

In this context an interesting problem arises. While I am arguing that the regulations exert a strong influence on not just the service work of AmeriCorps members, but also on the pedagogical activities within the program as well, we do have to be careful not to reify the regulations. By this I mean that we cannot interpret the regulations as some kind of independent agent, acting within the program and driven by their own inertia. The regulations are an expression of a larger process at work; however, they are not the ideology of citizenship within the program as much as they are the fixing of that ideology in a particular institutional frame through the ways in which they are interpreted by and direct the work of both AmeriCorps staff and members. If we give the regulations that kind of power, we obscure the actual relations of praxis and consciousness within the program. For example, one member of the housing Corps approached this problem in his analysis of the experience at the capitol.

> But then you could say I'm in favor of vouchers or merit pay or whatever as long as you don't say I'm in favor of House File 3, which is in favor of vouchers, for example. That would still be advocacy, not lobbying. I mean, our working definition of advocacy is being as vague as possible. Advocacy is saying, "I think schools are good." And lobbying is saying, "You should hire more AmeriCorps members to work in schools." But that's not really what it is. I think we are just being told that you're not supposed to say you support a specific plan of action because of prohibited activities.

This member is confronting the contradiction embedded in his experience of AmeriCorps; he is being asked to learn a certain way of thinking about democracy, conceptualized as civic engagement, that he recognizes as inauthentic and inaccurate. The necessity of being vague, which is embodied in the ambivalence to the action plans, also emerged in the focus group discussions when members were given the opportunity to discuss the validity of the civic engagement project within AmeriCorps. A particularly insightful conversation between three members is excerpted below.

> Member 1: I feel like it is hard to teach someone civic engagement without being political. It's like saying, "Recycling does help the environment if you choose to do it," instead of, "This is what happens to the environment if you don't recycle." "You should probably vote," but don't tell them how or why to vote. That doesn't help us know about the politicians. You could tell us equally what each one thinks, but we can't be political. So I think civic engagement trainings themselves fall short, but I think it's because of our inability to have political trainings.
>
> Member 2: I don't know if I quite agree. I don't know if you have to involve politics in civic engagement.
>
> Member 3: I think you can separate politics, I mean I do. You can, you said, say, "It's good to vote." I can't tell you who to vote for, but you can educate them.
>
> Member 1: I feel like it's generalities.
>
> Member 2: But it gives people the tools to learn themselves. It's not putting a bias in their heads.
>
> Member 3: Like, I'm not choosing to recycle because I fall under a certain political party [implied sarcasm].
>
> Member 2: For me, when I was sitting through those trainings I felt like it was a lot of generalities or vague statements. And if it is something I'm going to act on, I'm going to need more. . . . You're not telling me anything but "Voting is important." I already know that. You're not actually talking about anything but voting. At that point the civic engagement trainings are wasteful. Yes I vote, yes I recycle. We aren't talking about any issues right now. Are you trying to get me to go out mobilize other voters? I can't do that either. I felt like I didn't get a lot out of it.

The Diller Report made a substantial claim about the potentiality for civic learning in AmeriCorps when Diller argued that political socialization can be, and should be, separated from politicization.[14] What she meant by this is that people can be socialized into democratic values and practices without being inculcated into a particular way of thinking about specific issues. Clearly, AmeriCorps members disputed this claim when faced with the reality of what this means; in theory, they understand the point, but in practice, such as at the capitol, the assertion begins to lose its cohesion, and it felt "weird."

But can you separate learning about the substance of democracy (issues) from learning about democracy as a structure? Or does learning about democracy in this way constitute its own form of politicization? An important addition to this discussion is that in the final focus group meetings, I asked the members to reflect on a significant learning experience. My intention was to get them to think about times in their lives when they had noticed themselves learning, had changed their mind, or had felt a shift in their thinking. When I asked them to elaborate on what made these experiences so significant, they described the experiences as emotional and reflective. In these experiences they learned to see patterns over time, engaged with cognitive dissonance and contradiction, discovered they were wrong about something, connected an idea to their personal experience, and came to understand that the "thing" was more complicated than it seemed. They described processes of theoretical abstraction, philosophical ambiguity, and ethical conflict. These are the kinds of processes that are implicit in critical reflection and which are absent in the AmeriCorps program. The opportunities for this kind of learning are endless in the AmeriCorps program. One female AmeriCorps member described a particularly powerful experience she had when she encountered firsthand the fear and anxiety children experience when they live without legal immigration status.

> I mean, I've never had to think twice about going home and my parents not being there. And here's a kid that I know who is terrified to go home because his parents might not be there. So, I knew about it, but never knew people who, you know . . . it made me think a little bit more about policies that exist about immigration.

This member was quick to point out that this kind of experience could not be discussed during Corps day training. She felt that only in the focus group discussion was she allowed to broach the subject. Ultimately, she felt cut off from the opportunity to understand where the problem actually came from and what kind of political imagination could fix it. As an educator, I found it difficult to listen to these young people recount their experiences and then watch them grasp helplessly for meaning, offered little opportunity beyond informal conversation to process or make meaning. One member said, "It feels like there are a million answers swimming beneath the surface and I can't grab at one." The daily experience of AmeriCorps members is a rich and contradictory milieu of power and privilege, ongoing confrontations with racism, classism, and sexism, and ultimately, a powerful opportunity to examine the scope and interrelations of social problems. In what I observed, these opportunities are purposefully, and forcefully, suppressed within the program in the name of compliance.

The claim to the dichotomizing of political learning and politics needs to be further examined in its implications. It raises the question as to what the relationship between pedagogy and ideology is within the AmeriCorps program. In reviewing the challenges I have raised to the efficacy of civic engagement work within AmeriCorps, it would be easy to claim that the solution to these problems could be found in new pedagogies, better adherence to the best practices of service-learning, or even a firmer hand in oversight and implementation. I do not doubt that pedagogical innovation within the program would result in an improved and more meaningful experience for AmeriCorps members. I do believe there is space within the AmeriCorps program for a more progressive and critical engagement with democracy and community problems then what I observed in my case studies.

However, in the next chapter, I want to make the case that the types of vacuity emerging in the AmeriCorps program are not the result of a lack of expertise or pedagogical know-how on the part of program directors. Rather, the ideological frame of democracy and citizenship within the AmeriCorps program expresses the limits of the forms that democratic learning can take. If this ideological frame is taken to its logical extensions, it has important implications for the kind of democracy AmeriCorps members will be prepared to engage with as well as the ways in which educators understand the terrains of learning democracy through community service.

Chapter Five

Civic Engagement and Community Service as Ideological Frame and Practice

> In the end, when it comes to the challenges we face, the need for action always exceeds the limits of government. While there's plenty that government can do and must do to keep our families safe, and our planet clean, and our markets free and fair, there's a lot that government can't—and shouldn't—do. And that's where active, engaged citizens come in. That's the purpose of service in this nation.
>
> —President Barack Obama

In the previous two chapters I have explored the social organization and coordination of community service work and the pedagogical practice of civic engagement in the AmeriCorps program. I've conducted this examination using the analytical framework of institutional ethnography, which I discussed in detail in the chapter 1. Exploring democratic learning in AmeriCorps through an institutional ethnography of the program presents an important paradox in understanding civic engagement. On the one hand, as I discussed in the chapter 4, there is an appearance within the program of openness, flexibility, and hermeneutic freedom associated with the category of civic engagement. There is no official definition of civic engagement, and at each point in the hierarchy of the organization, the duty to name and claim such a conceptual apparatus is passed down to those below in an attempt to maintain the appearance of a populist and democratic nature within the concept itself. The pattern of passing the buck, so to speak, continues all the way to the federal level as, according to the CNCS, state commissions must set the mandate for explicit attention to democratic learning. According to the state commission, each of the programs must decide for itself how it will activate the concept. According to program directors, the members will decide what the category means to them, and each permutation of the notion is considered equally valid. One AmeriCorps member summed up her civic engagement training, a bit cheekily, by reflecting, "The definition was that there wasn't one. My group compared it to porn; you'll know it when you see it. That's what they said: Civic engagement is whatever you think it is." On the other hand, from the standpoint of members, the project of civic engagement is transparent to AmeriCorps volunteers as an explicit interest of the Corporation. Phrased in different ways by different groups, a thread wove through the focus groups discussions that left participants grappling with the extent to which civic engagement is imposed within the program. Members were not in agreement; many supported the project of civic engagement, while others resented its imposition as a requirement within the program, and still others were more critical of the apparent depoliticization of the trainings.

These uneasy and multifaceted orientations toward the concept of civic engagement within the program raise the question as to the origin, content, and function of ideology within the program, which is what I want to focus on in this chapter. Understanding ideology as process of knowledge production grounded in the material and social activity of people is the ultimate goal of institutional ethnography as an approach to research. Similarly, critical education theory has a long history of critical engagement with ideologies of both liberal democracy and capitalism. In these conceptions, scholars have drawn from diverse theoretical traditions ranging from Gramscian-inspired cultural studies to the works of Freire, Marx's various articulations, and, more recently, work in psychoanalytic thought. How we conceptualize ideology itself will determine how we understand what is happening in the program, both in terms of epistemology and pedagogy. I want to avoid two frequent modes of analysis with the concept of ideology. The first is a pull toward some kind of correspondence position where AmeriCorps members are depicted as uncritically consuming state ideology, which is imposed on and passed down to them as if they were plugged into a local electrical socket of an ideological state apparatus. The second is to posit the experience and ideas surrounding citizenship and democracy that circulate with the program as illusory, fantastical, or unreal. This aligns with two popular ideas in critical education theory. The first is the reductive argument around false consciousness, which has been around for decades. There is nothing false about the forms of consciousness that are circulating in the AmeriCorps program, which I will discuss further in chapter 6. The second idea is the line of ideology critique stemming from Žižek's work, which has been taken up robustly by contemporary critical education scholars.[1] I will discuss the differences between this argument and my own further in this chapter.

Thus far I have used the approach of institutional ethnography to demonstrate how "learning democracy" is organized within the confines of the program and through the conceptual apparatus of civic engagement. I have argued that civic engagement emerges within the broad social organization of the program, which is characterized by a depoliticization of direct service work in narrowly defined types of organizations and with a heavy dose of rational-technical social planning processes aimed at individual behavioral change. I have also demonstrated that the civic engagement curriculum within the program takes on the particular characteristic of *vacuity*—that is, learning is violently abstracted from its experiential base formed in both the daily activities of AmeriCorps members and their already existing forms of knowledge. This vacuity constitutes an abstraction from materiality in knowledge production. At this point, I want to articulate the ideological components of the institutional discourse of civic engagement in AmeriCorps and demonstrate how this form of praxis operates throughout the program and organizes learning. To say that ideology is a form of praxis is to argue for the inner relation of knowing and being; it is to say that the ways in which we think and the ways in which we act are mutually determining. Paula Allman has already implied the conceptualization of "ideology as praxis" through the concept of uncritical or reproductive praxis, which occurs when we "simply partake in the relations and conditions that we find already existing in the world and assume that these are natural and inevitable—that this is the way things are, always, or at least for a considerable amount of time, have been, and always will be."[2] How and why an ideological praxis of democracy emerges is something I will explore further in the following chapter. However, here I want to focus on fully describing this ideology, using institutional ethnographic concepts of ideological frame, practice, and socially objectified forms of consciousness. The purpose is to demonstrate how civic engagement functions as an ideological practice within the program; that is, both how the notion of civic engagement is taken up by participants and how it is used to coordinate and organize the conceptualization of learning democracy within the AmeriCorps program. In this way, I hope to push our conceptualization of the relation between ideology and learning beyond its appearance as a form of thought and into the epistemological and pedagogical relations that organize ideology as a social practice and relation.

AmeriCorps members enter into a variety of institutional relationships when they enroll in the program. Seen from their daily experience, most of these relationships exist at the local level, for example, with the people they serve, their Corps members, their supervisors, and their coworkers. Much like Mike, in chapter 3, the relationships in their immediate view are confined to their daily experience, although many AmeriCorps members I met were actively working to understand some of the social context of their experiences. These relationships are also, however, implicated in a set of institutional relationships that are organized outside of their local experience; this organization is driven by an agenda set at the federal level and, in the case of the civic engagement movement, by interested parties beyond government, including think tanks, corporations, academics, and lobbyists. These relationships are coordinated translocally as part of a national initiative to organize young people's participation in civil society in a particular way and for particular purposes. These purposes, repeatedly emphasized by the CNCS, are "to get things done" and support "the American culture of citizenship, service, and responsibility."[3]

A central purpose of institutional ethnography is to explore the extralocal organization of experience in its translocal practice. What I mean by this is that through institutional ethnography we attempt to illuminate the ways in which human activity becomes coordinated across multiple sites through institutional processes that do not arise out of the daily experience of those individuals engaged in local practice. Further, by utilizing a dialectical conceptualization of praxis, we understand that the organization of human activity has an inner relation to the forms of consciousness that make meaning of this activity. The way that individuals think and work cannot be artificially separated. Ideology, in institutional ethnography, refers to the very specific processes associated with the production and deployment of knowledge and its use to coordinate practice. It is characterized by George Smith as "the imposition of objective, textually-mediated, conceptual practices on a local setting in the interest of ruling it."[4] Clearly, the processes of imposition within AmeriCorps have taken a central focus in this research. However, I now contend with the question of what *exactly* is being imposed. In this way, we should be better able to see the complications of mutually determining relations between the individual and the forms of social cooperation concretized in civil society.

To do this, I utilize Dorothy Smith's notion of ideological frame, which differs from other popular approaches to analyzing ideology in educational research in that its focus is not only thought content, but epistemological function. Smith explains her notion of ideological frame as not a "thing" or a discourse, but as a process and a social relation. She describes an ideological frame as an "interpretive schema" that

> is used to assemble and provide coherence for an array of particulars, thus selected and assembled, will intend, and will be interpretable by, the schema used to assemble them. The effect is peculiarly circular, for although questions of truth and falsity, accuracy and inaccuracy about the particulars may certainly be raised, the schema in itself is not called into question as a method of providing for the coherence of the collection of particulars as a whole.[5]

This is a fitting characterization of what I have observed in the AmeriCorps programs. Although there may be some complaining about civic engagement in terms of logistics or content or outcomes, there is little contention around civic engagement itself. This articulation also raises the conundrum I pointed to in the introduction to this book; in learning about democracy, we are free to be critical of everything except the premises of democracy itself. We can debate what civic engagement means, how to do it, and how to teach it, but "civic engagement," as a virtue and form of democratic engagement, stands undisturbed.

However, if there is no official content for civic engagement, how can I make the claim that civic engagement constitutes an ideological frame within the program? I argue that civic engagement is not the ideological frame itself, but rather that the category operates as the conceptual orchestration of a collection of ideas about democracy and participation, which in turn drive the operationalization of civic engagement within AmeriCorps. Said differently, the category of civic engagement comes to stand for an ensemble of ideas about democracy and participation. In this way, the variety and form of participation can change, but the driving logic of the frame remains constant. For this reason, I find it more productive to relate this notion of ideological frame back to Smith's articulation of the link between power and ideology as objectified forms of social consciousness that reproduce the social relations that constitute our material and cultural existence.[6]

Based on data gathered from interviews, focus groups, and textual analysis as well as the findings I have thus far presented, I argue that the particular ways in which consciousness around democracy, citizenship, and participation are organized within the AmeriCorps program are key to understanding how civic engagement works as an ideological praxis. That is, within the institutional apparatus of the program, its regulatory structure, and its methods of promoting civic engagement, certain ways of thinking about democracy emerge. These forms of consciousness are engaged and activated by those participating at all levels of the AmeriCorps program, including the members themselves. These forms of consciousness penetrate one another, creating for AmeriCorps members tensions and contradictions in thought and experience which, given the regulatory structures of the program, were left formally unengaged outside of focus groups. They do not always fit easily together, creating a blissfully uncomplicated ideological form. Sometimes they contradict one another and crack under the pressure of experience. Nevertheless, they persist.

It is not difficult to discern that one of the primary purposes for the existence of the Corporation for National and Community Service and its programs, including AmeriCorps, is to promote volunteer service; that is clearly stated on the organization's website. With only a little bit of cursory research, it is equally as easy to establish that the federal government imagines this volunteer service to be an important component of meeting human needs at the local level within the United States. To argue that promoting service is thus the institutional agenda of AmeriCorps is an oversimplification of the ideological project at hand. It is a complicated task to unravel a narrative of what this notion of community service actually means and how it operates within a vision of democracy. This requires examining the ways in which community service and democracy emerge in particular forms within the program and take on objective characteristics, which appear in program activities and confront the consciousness of AmeriCorps members as objective realities. In what follows, I want to explore the emergence of these forms of consciousness in the program in two different ways. First, I will examine how the operation of civic engagement suggests a particular relationship between community service, citizenship, and the state. Second, I will explore the localization and privatization of forms of social inequality and the articulation of political imaginations related to social change.

Service, Citizenship, and the State

In the discussions with AmeriCorps members, community service and service to the nation emerged as a central component of their consciousness around democracy and citizenship. In our second meeting, I asked the members to reflect on and discuss the difference between citizenship and *good* citizenship. Their general organization of these categories does not differentiate substantially from the kind of public rhetoric we are all familiar with, although it was interesting to note that many had a hard time drawing a line between the two categories. For many, citizenship meant simply being a good citizen in that both have the same defining characteristics, such as obeying laws and cultural norms, voting, and participating in the community. Others recognized that citizenship is a legal category that affords a citizen rights and protections based on their membership in a nation-state; one could, theoretically, never engage with the community or the government and yet one would remain a citizen. The dominant position among the members was that being a "good citizen," however, had several key dimensions. Voting, obeying laws, and paying taxes were the bare minimum, but participation was the singular defining characteristic and community service the most salient example. This notion of participation was then reconnected to the idea of civic responsibility and being "active." Good citizens are not passive or consumptive in their orientation toward public life; they are engaged, not necessarily with the state, but within civil society and with "the community" writ large. Emerging in their explanations was a general orientation toward the communitarian critiques staged against the liberal emphasis on rights consumption; "good citizenship" has an active component to it and transcends simply abiding by laws and paying taxes. What I saw in the focus group discussions largely corresponds with various studies on citizenship that demonstrate that learning democracy and citizenship, at least in schools, exists along a philosophical continuum that moves between the classically liberal, personally responsible citizen through to a care-oriented communitarian vision to a more socially democratic, activist orientation.[7] AmeriCorps members, in all their diversity, embody and enact this continuum in their beliefs and forms of engagement, although I argue that these philosophical paradigms alone do not explain how such notions come to the forefront of consciousness. Rather, these categories demonstrate how forms of consciousness function; they describe the appearance of a particular democratic consciousness rather than explain its emergence. Nevertheless, their participation in AmeriCorps has an important impact on their beliefs in the practice of volunteer service. Their participation in AmeriCorps either confirmed their perspective that community service was an important aspect of citizen participation, or it reintroduced the notion. I say "reintroduced" because many described that they had always known they should be volunteering because, very similar to me, that is "just what people should do"; their paths, however, had led them away from service and AmeriCorps reinscribed the notion of its importance within their idea of not just good community, but good citizenship as well.

In the spring of 2009 former House Representative Michelle Bachman, a Republican from Minnesota, made a series of comments on a talk radio show about the AmeriCorps program. She referred to AmeriCorps as either a socialist or a communist "reeducation camp," according to various media outlets.[8] She argued that the AmeriCorps program was a front for the Democratic Party and for the spreading of Obama-style socialist values. When I raised her comments with the AmeriCorps members, they caused much concern. I asked the members to reflect on the Corporation's commitment to volunteer service. As a reflective prompt, I used the Corporation's claim that their purpose was "to activate a culture of citizenship through service." What exactly did this mean? My intention in provoking the conversation was to flesh out the way in which AmeriCorps members understand the concept of service; it was an attempt to continue the conversation that had woven through our previous sessions. Instead, the members brought to light the larger project of promoting service through AmeriCorps. One AmeriCorps member took this position.

> I thought of what Michelle Bachman was saying about AmeriCorps and how it could be viewed as a communist re-education camp. There are broader cultural values as stake here, and I think that's fine. I think that is what this is about. They [the CNCS] have this idea of what a healthy society looks like, what a good public is, and however they have arrived at that they are going to pursue it by making AmeriCorps members and other people under the Corporation this critical mass who have learned to experience the values of service, the value of engaging in community and then carrying that with you and going into the communities that you become a part of. Not indoctrinating, but sharing those values with the people around you. So, I don't know, maybe she is onto something, although it is far less sinister.

Michelle Bachman's comments had an interesting effect on the group. On the one hand, they moved into a defensive position vis-à-vis the value of volunteer service. On the other hand, they were forced to confront the notion that community service might involve a political platform. A tremendous tension arose for the groups concerning whether service could be both political and apolitical at the same time. There was general agreement among AmeriCorps members that the Corporation does have an agenda. But what is this agenda, and is it permissible for the CNCS to have an agenda? This was less clear, in part because stepping back from the assumption that their service was politically neutral came into conflict with other previously held assumptions.

The notion that service is a universal good contradicts the position of the state within AmeriCorps. As I argued in the previous chapter, the state is discussed in a vague and technical manner within the program. The regulations are legitimated through a logic that claims the state as neutral; the state would never pay for something that was partisan or political, which is why AmeriCorps members are prohibited from those arenas while serving. What emerged in these conversations was fascinating. Members appeared stuck between the claim that the CNCS, the "they" of these conversations, was an agenda-less or neutral entity and the opposing perspective that citizenship based on service is only one possible vision of citizenship. One AmeriCorps member argued,

> They're trying to foster a particular kind of citizenship that is service-based. And what if this was, "activate a culture of citizenship that celebrates individual achievement." That would be a different statement; or a culture of citizenship through service to god. I like how he put it; there are broader cultural values tied up here with the AmeriCorps mission. Like the projects they identify as being worth putting money towards and the problems they think are worth solving.

This members' position was echoed in another group when an AmeriCorps member asked, "What if it was citizenship based on human rights?" Each group of AmeriCorps members demonstrated an awareness of and debated the implications of the possibility that service is not the only component of good citizenship.

However, there was little evidence that the implications of this argument, such as why actors within the state would select service as the kind of citizenship they would want to promote, were an easy analytical step for the groups. The position of service as a universal good was evidenced by the fact that they remained stuck in the service conversation. From their perspective, they could see that the state was promoting service, but because service was assumed to be normatively good, it ceased to be an agenda vis-à-vis the state. The following text is excerpted from a focus group conversation on this problem:

> Member 1: One thing about AmeriCorps that I think in some ways doesn't facilitate learning, or perhaps a different kind of learning, is that they aren't really supposed to have an agenda for what we're supposed to learn. And I think a lot of the things that people talked about [at the beginning of the conversation] were opinionated videos or essays or classes that influenced moments of learning. And the fact that AmeriCorps is not supposed to take a particular opinion about something or have an agenda about what were supposed to learn or come out with, in any sense that anyone could define, that doesn't facilitate learning but also does leave open [the possibility] to not have to come to the conclusions that are held by the program director, which I guess is better for the whole grant federal money thing.
>
> Member 2: But it's a socialist reeducation camp!
>
> Member 1: Yeah, there are all sorts of reasons for why AmeriCorps doesn't have an agenda for what you're supposed to learn.
>
> *Sara: Do you all agree that AmeriCorps doesn't have an agenda for what you're supposed to learn?*
>
> Member 3: Yeah they are teaching national service.
>
> Member 2: But, there's not a perspective that exists besides national service is good. The only official AmeriCorps perspective is that service is valuable.
>
> Member 3: But that's an agenda.
>
> Member 1: I just think the perspectives are so vague, for good reason to be careful about political things, but I think it cuts us off from a certain kind of learning that could potentially happen in a national service program if we were a socialist re-education camp.

Member 2: I don't mean that's not a philosophy. It's just so close to a platitude that it doesn't really count.

Sara: What doesn't count?

Member 3: That national service is good. Yes they are teaching it, but that's a platitude.

Member 1: It's not really offensive to anyone. And that's part of the point.

Member 2: Exactly; it's something that everyone agrees on even if they have different conceptions of what it means.

Member 3: On the Corporation's website, they had this thing, to create a generation of civically engaged people. If you're creating a generation of somebody, that's kind of an agenda.

Member 2: Just the idea of civically engaged doesn't mean anything other than civically engaged. Because there is no definition of what civic engagement is; officially, everybody agrees with it. That's all.

Member 3: I just think our country had an era of apathy, so it's positive.

Member 4: They might be apathetic, but that doesn't mean their opposed to being civically engaged.

Member 2: That's because we are at a point where everybody accepts it. Everyone is all about this national service. That's why I don't think you see that there is an agenda to the point where the whole country likes it right now, not to where it's a good or bad thing. I don't know.

In having this conversation, the AmeriCorps members struggled with a few contradictions happening at the same time. First, the members arrived on the topic of a service agenda through a discussion of what makes a meaningful learning experience. In discussing AmeriCorps as an example of learning that did not share the "meaningful" characteristics the group had discussed, they acknowledged that the good learning experiences they had discussed involved some sort of agenda on the part of the teacher or the curriculum. They then had to grapple with the idea that "having an agenda" or rejecting neutrality or objectivity might not be completely negative. The group then identified that the CNCS has a dual character: it positions itself as nonpolitical and as not having an agenda at the same time that it clearly states that it does have an agenda. How is this paradox resolved? For the members, it was not. I argue that the contradiction between having and not having an agenda was left unresolved because the agenda itself is not the source of the contradiction; rather, the notion of service is what is important. If the member above is correct, if service is a platitude, then the CNCS can assume its dual character without such apparent contradiction; they can have an agenda that is agenda-less.

The stability of this arrangement depends on how the notion of service is defined by the Corporation and how it is, or is not, positioned in relation to politics. As articulated by the CNCS, it is the kind of category that, as AmeriCorps members pointed out, does not need to be defined. It can be held in the position of common sense; everyone knows what it means to serve and, as four successive presidents of the United States argued, from George H. W. Bush to Barack Obama, everyone can and should do it. However, there are some contours to this definition that emerge when we pay close attention to the rhetoric used by the CNCS, by presidents, and by AmeriCorps members. Remembering the analysis in chapter 3 in which I argued that service takes on a distinctly apolitical character in the program, a further distinction is drawn within the confines of the idea of national service. According to its proponents, we can talk about two kinds of national service: military and civilian. Beginning with James's original argument, those advocating civilian national service make the case that it is analogous to, or morally equivalent to, military service. As such, one dimension of this service is that we are not talking about going to war, at least not against a militarized enemy. We might go to war against poverty, homelessness, hurricanes, drugs, or illiteracy, but service to the community does not involve the domain of violence in terms of conventional understandings of violence. The target of such service is not a foreign army, but the relations of inequality that exist within and between communities and are discussed within AmeriCorps as social problems and community needs. Another distinction is that service can be paid or unpaid. This is made by the constant evocation of great public "servants" to the nation, such as Edward Kennedy or George H. W. Bush, and the constant emphasis on the aspiration of public service as vocation. Edward Kennedy and George H. W. Bush, however, were monetarily rewarded for their service, and while young people can aspire to these positions, the majority of us will not, nor should we have to. As Obama argued in his address at the twentieth anniversary of the Points of Light Foundation,

> You don't have to devote your entire career to service—though I hope that many of the students here will. But I'm asking you to have a public service mindset. I'm asking that no matter where you live, or what job you do, or what obstacles you face, you're always looking for ways to make service part of your life.[9]

Thus, service can be done on a part-time basis without fiscal compensation. More importantly, service *should* be done in this way. As the CNCS draft strategic plan for 2011–2015 argues, "service is a cost effective investment in community solutions."[10]

The contours of the *kind* of service we are talking about within AmeriCorps and within the CNCS are now emerging: It will take place within community settings, it will be aimed at social needs, it will take place on a part-time basis, and it will not be remunerated. As President Obama argued in the quote opening this chapter, where the government cannot—or should not—provide for the public welfare, citizens will through service. This "agenda-less" agenda begins to take shape as a particular strategy to organize citizen participation. This position, however, is difficult to discern from the standpoint of daily service in the AmeriCorps program.

Local People with Private Politics Faced with Public Problems

Service emerged within the program as such a powerful expression of participation not only because it is the "agenda-less" agenda of the Corporation, but because its privileged position within the program was reinforced by other dynamics of the civic engagement activities. The clearest of these is the emphasis within the program on the local domain of action. Within the AmeriCorps program, this imagined citizen is active and engaged on the local terrain. While notions of community can be defined from diverse standpoints, "the local" is reinforced by the corporation in numerous ways. Throughout organizational literature, including strategic plans, guiding principles, the Code of Federal Regulations, the Notice of Funds Available, and even legislation, the refrains of local needs, local communities, and local organizations are constantly sounded. If service is a central feature of how AmeriCorps members understand their participation in the community, the local emerged as a core component of how AmeriCorps members understand their relation to democratic processes.

In the early sessions of the focus groups, I structured our discussions in such a way as to gather the perspectives of the members as to what constituted good democracy and good citizenship. My purpose in pursuing this line of questioning was to discern their own understanding of democracy and the role of a program such as AmeriCorps. Their descriptions of democracy vacillated in such a way that it was clear they were working through a central organizing feature: the relationship between the individual and the social in democracy. For some, democracy was strictly a macro-level ensemble of institutions and structures that organize a society. In other words, the concept of democracy is conflated with that of the state. For others, democracy is understood through the aggregate of individual democratic behaviors, such as voting, exercising their rights, and so on. For the majority, democracy lies in some mediation of these two positions, acknowledging that within a democracy the most salient tension is between what is good for individual citizens and what is good for society as a whole. These conversations very quickly morphed into discussions of the present challenges to and within democracy in the United States. Again, their evaluations followed the same individual-social logic. Many argued that the root of democratic dysfunction was individual pathology; people are lazy, selfish, apathetic, ignorant, or just plain bad citizens. Equal numbers agreed that the problems of democracy were systemic in nature; people are excluded from centers of power, government is bureaucratic and inefficient, or the size and scale of the nation, particularly at the level of federal government, is prohibitive to "true" democracy.

Nearly every member of the focus groups expressed the opinion that in the United States democracy is not working, at the federal or state levels, because the size and scope are unmanageable. Something about size and scope creates inefficient institutions, including "rules" that members see as slowing the process down. The plurality of public interests, issues of access, and concentrations of power were seen as further barriers to the creation of effective democracy. Government was seen as impossible to access, or even in some cases, understand. Two AmeriCorps members engaged in this exchange when discussing their perspectives on government.

> Member 1: A lot of people might be apathetic or don't care or they just don't know or they hear a sound bite and think it's awesome, but they don't realize the intricacies of the issue. I feel like a lot of us, like how many of us read the stimulus bill? It is hard to be that active, involved, informed citizen. Where there is so much out there, you can't have an informed opinion.

> Member 2: Like, when we went to the county commissioner's office, I was so confused. So many things I did not understand, and I was so overwhelmed and not able to follow because they don't put it in layman's terms for those of us who aren't involved in the government. I'm all about personal accountability; I think people are ultimately responsible for their own outcomes, but it is difficult to learn about tax levies and bond revenue. I don't know what bond revenue is!

While many AmeriCorps members reported that their trips to the public bodies made the processes of government appear more accessible, many of their reasons for this accessibility were because of a previous dearth of participation. Issues of inaccessibility and inefficiency in government strongly influenced members in their opinion that the local level of engagement was the optimum location for the efforts. Components of the civic engagement curricula that were designed to influence members' engagement with government often had the opposite effect; members felt as though in these activities the game of politics was revealed for the distasteful and corrupt process that it truly was. As one AmeriCorps member argued,

> I mean anytime we go to a training that is supposed to get us more involved, like going to the capitol, is that supposed to inspire me? Hell no. More shadiness. The process of getting a bill passed, it is just a game, not helping anyone. Is it about anyone but themselves?

Others felt as though the program activities directed their gaze towards the arenas in which engagement with government can be effective, the assumption being that engagement with anything beyond the 'local' was ineffective. One member described her learning in this way:

> I feel like I learned about which politics are important. It seems like your local folks, city council, local reps are way more important than the president even though people put all their emphasis on the president. 'Cause your city council people affect your life directly, fix the pothole on my street, or keep Trader Joe's from moving in across the street.

An effect of this kind of consciousness around the state is to position "the local" as accessible and the "extra-local" as inaccessible. In this form, the state becomes an effective entity only at small levels of government and with extremely limited scope. Susan, an AmeriCorps consultant, described the emphasis on the "local" within AmeriCorps as the limitation of impact. She argued that it is very difficult to talk with AmeriCorps members about the impact of their actions beyond the local level in part because this requires moving into the terrain of policy, which many regard as off limits within the regulatory structure of the program. The local and service emerge as reinforcing one another at this point; the local is the preferred terrain of participation while community service is structurally produced to be confined to local impact.

The AmeriCorps members' commitment to the local is further emphasized in their understanding of civic engagement as something that requires a particular arrangement of local factors. I asked the members if they saw civic engagement as something they would continue to participate in after they completed their year of service. Almost uniformly they reported that they imagined that they would continue to volunteer, but beyond community service they could not speculate. The conditions of their life held too strong a sway over their ability to participate. For many the issue was time; from their perspective, civic engagement required a huge commitment of time and the importance of jobs or families might supersede community involvement. For others the issue was their connection to place. From this view, civic engagement was something that required local rootedness. Many saw themselves as transient, as renters, as students, as precarious workers; to be engaged beyond volunteerism would require being fixed in time and space. Their discussions indicate that geographical communities rise to the forefront of their perception of community but further suggest that the extra-local terrain, which is not in conflict with transient or unstable lifestyles, was beyond their conception of being "civically engaged." One caveat that may explain why AmeriCorps members have such focus on the local terrain is that many involved with AmeriCorps suggest that the young people attracted to the program are less likely to have participated in social movements. Susan, the AmeriCorps consultant, described AmeriCorps members as "square." Thus, their consciousness of the translocal terrain of political participation may not be as sophisticated as other young adults engaged in activist politics. In my group of research participants, there were only two or three AmeriCorps members who identified themselves as politically active beyond the local scale.

Within AmeriCorps, the local emerges as the preferred terrain of citizen engagement within a context in which extra-local relations are purposefully obscured. However, AmeriCorps is not the only organization emphasizing a focus on local needs and interests. In fact a key hallmark of recent policy reform is to reject the notion of big government and instead to emphasize the local as a necessarily more efficient and effective, and often more moral, scale for policy development, citizen engagement, and decision-making. It is worth noting that some policy makers are not the only parties with a particular interest in preferring the local. The so-called postmodern or cultural turn in social and cultural theory has similarly directed the rejection of the translocal and emphasized the local as the only legitimate terrain of knowledge production. Similarly, the post-socialist left has been divided among and against itself by various articulations of the local as a rejection of the translocal, by an emphasis on particularity, and by a reified conceptualization of the social that is unable to see its way to an even more complex articulation of the particularity and universality of the social and material relations of capitalism. The power associated with the local has caused tremendous problems for any actors trying to construct a transnational, let alone international, political project, including such diverse efforts as human rights, transnational feminist organization, and even the development of working-class solidarity or solidarity among the colonized and/or displaced. I say this only to note that while the local is a particularly problem within AmeriCorps, there are other political imaginations that suffer from similar political limits.

Nevertheless, the confinement of democracy to the local is a specific challenge. Mark Purcell has argued that the concept is used uncritically by many within the social sciences and constitutes something of a conceptual trap, which expresses "the tendency of researchers and activists to assume something inherent about the local scale. The local trap equates the local with 'the good'; it is preferred presumptively over non-local scales."[11] Through its use the notion that the global reach of capitalism is an uncontestable terrain is, perhaps unintentionally, reinforced. There is much to take from Purcell's formulation that resembles the AmeriCorps members' articulations. Purcell argues that "the local trap" includes a conflation of democratization with localization, allowing for the notion that "local people" equates with popular sovereignty. Purcell also argues that community is then defined by its geographic expression, despite the fact that community can be named and drawn in a multiplicity of ways, many of which are often paradoxical.[12] Finally, "the local trap" reaches its zenith in the equation of local with participation. Purcell observes that the local stands in for populations who either demand popular sovereignty or who are constructed as the objects of regulation and intervention from those who hold power over political and financial forms of governance. In this way, the emphasis on the local can express a complex theoretical mish-mash of both neoliberal thinking and more participatory forms of political theory. From a governmentality perspective, this kind of emphasis on the local is seen as part of a broader reorganization of political life under neoliberalism and under the diffusion of late capitalist modes of economic organization that advocate "new entrepreneurial approaches to local economic development as well as diverse programs of institutional restructuring intended to enhance labor market flexibility, territorial competitiveness, and place-specific locational assets."[13]

An important thing to remember here is the relation of state, citizen, and democracy that emerges in the local. If citizens myopically focus on the local terrain, then they could have more power over their local domain, but they could also have less power over regional, federal, and international levels of organization. They could have more access to particular systems and centers of power, but less impact on the ways in which those systems relate to one another and to macro-level processes. They could grow more connected locally and more disconnected translocally. Local struggles could transform an understanding of the state into an emphasis on local organization, without dismantling or transforming existing state apparatuses, leaving them to do their work in their existing, hegemonic forms. Each of these risks associated with too much emphasis on the local comes with a corollary risk associated with too much emphasis on the global or universal. I think that the experience of AmeriCorps, from the perspective of institutional ethnography, is instructive in this regard.

I have argued elsewhere that one way to understand the problem of the local in the AmeriCorps program is through the concept of fetish.[14] A fetish, in Marx's critique of the forms of consciousness associated with

Enlightenment political economy, is described as a form of thought that "attaches" to the products of human labor as soon as they become commodities. Paula Allman argues that fetishism is the ultimate form of reification, "a form of distortion where the attributes and powers, the essence, of the person or social relation appear as natural, intrinsic, attributes of powers of the 'thing.'"[15] While Purcell argues that the "local trap" is geographically represented, the concept also implies that the local becomes objectified in our thinking, which is itself a form of reification. For AmeriCorps members, the local is similarly fixed; it constitutes a political field they are able to act on whereas the trans- or extra-local is too far beyond the control of democracy. We could argue that fetishism "attaches" itself to many concepts in democratic, and capitalist, social relations, but we must recognize that this fetishism is always the outcome of processes of abstraction, both from history and from material relations.

The emphasis on time and lifestyle choices indicates something further beyond a commitment to the local scale; they bring up the question of the relation between the public and the private within AmeriCorps. This tension emerged many times throughout the focus group discussions; AmeriCorps members, for example, were aware that a notion of the public or common good was difficult to establish. They demonstrated a commitment to the idea that the social problems they engage with in the AmeriCorps program are public problems, in that they are vast, complex, pervasive, and systemic. Affordable housing, poverty, racism, achievement gaps, and failing public schools were all understood as problems of democracy. However, a significant contradiction emerges when AmeriCorps members attempted to reconcile these public problems with their service work. After lengthy discussions on good citizenship, I asked them to reflect on the relationship between their service work and democracy. My question was, what did working on the achievement gap or trying to increase access to affordable housing have to do with democracy? To answer this question, AmeriCorps members were unable to move out of the individual-behavior dimensions of service work. They argued that through their service work they are helping others to "help themselves" and to become individuals who are able to surmount the inequality of American society in order to succeed. They acknowledged that inequality is a threat to democracy and that in order for communities to remain stable, or achieve stability, inequality had to be transformed. This transformation, however, was an individual act of self and hard work.

I argued, in chapter 3, that one of the effects of the logic models used to plan AmeriCorps programming is an institutional push toward rational technical means of understanding social problems. The "achievement gap" can be attributed to institutionalized racism, the historical legacies of segregation, poverty, political neglect, and many other macro-level social factors, but within the regulatory apparatus of the AmeriCorps program its solution can only be articulated in terms of helping kids to better comply with the existing function of schools. Policy-level solutions are largely off the table, as are questions about why there is so little political will to address the root causes of the achievement gap, despite the fact that AmeriCorps members have much to say on this matter. This perspective is echoed in the Corporation strategic plan for 2011–2015, in which the educational and behavioral outcomes of school-age children are a major strategic objective.[16] This introduced a different dimension to the emphasis on capacity within the universe of AmeriCorps; we were not only talking about the capacity of organizations, but the capacity of individuals to subsist and thrive as well.

Combined with an emphasis on "private politics" in the program, the relations between social inequality and democracy began to wear on the AmeriCorps members, and they struggled, profoundly, to reconcile a vision of citizenship based on substantive participation and access to resources, such as time, with the reality of persistent, structural inequality. The tension between these positions finally broke as they explored what it means to be a good citizen. In one focus group, an AmeriCorps member was the first to raise the issue, saying,

> I was thinking about some of the students I work with and their family situations. For them being a citizen, because of the family situation and just being in poverty—their outlook on how to be a citizen is maybe a lot different than someone who has a college education and all this other knowledge, just because of their circumstances and where they are at and what role, what part they can do, physically and emotionally and mindfully do. 'Cause if someone is thinking about what they can feed their kids for dinner, it is a little more difficult to think about what I can do to be involved in my communities.

A second member responded to him by saying,

> I want to add on to that. I think that for someone who is like that, who doesn't have time to think about anything else but putting food on the table for their family, like that's good citizenship for them. 'Cause they always have the choice not to put food on

> the table, or neglect their kids. So that is what . . . um . . . not to like excuse the fact of poverty in our nation, but that is an acceptable form of citizenship in that one realm that people have power over and can actively do.

In a different focus group, another member raised the issue in a slightly different, more individualized way.

> I had trouble with the good citizen/good person distinction too. It was iffy for me. I wrote [in a reflection activity] informed, vote, care what goes on, concerned, involved, and responsible. But then I added "to an appropriate extent," 'cause I can't really begrudge someone who is working three jobs and can't find time to read the stimulus bill. I guess they can find time to vote once every four years. And it is very subjective as to what's an appropriate level of involvement.

These AmeriCorps members raised an extremely important issue; not everyone can participate in equal ways. This is to say nothing of the realities of settler colonialism and white supremacy, which may mean that not everyone wants to participate or sees themselves reflected in the nation at all. In fact, some may understand their role, perhaps even their very existence, as a form of resistance and opposition to a colonizing force. But their point is well taken. Many in the United States struggle to eat every day; going to PTA meetings or reading the stimulus bill cannot take priority. The corporation's response to this sort of tension would likely be that even the most disadvantaged can be empowered through service, which it seems is not only a universal good, but an emancipator as well. This has been a consistent component of the rhetoric of AmeriCorps since its inception and is implicated in the debates concerning "maximum feasible participation" of the poor in their own development.[17]

However, the AmeriCorps members were moving in a complicated direction. The tension they raised has many dimensions: surviving versus thriving, acting versus being acted on, independence versus dependence. What the AmeriCorps members evoked in these conversations was the tension between the idea that part of being a "good citizen" is being a "good worker." Some of their earliest memories of lessons of good citizenship involve working hard, providing for their families, paying taxes, and being self-sufficient. In the United States, being independent, either of the state or a male partner, is a historical component of the construction of good citizenship, with the position that those who are dependent do not have the capacity to participate in an effective manner and are more of a burden than an empowered, self-sufficient, independent, and autonomous member of a democratic community. This historical and social relation has led to strong feminist critique of the patriarchal dimensions of citizenship and the discursive equation of productive labor with participation and value.[18] The AmeriCorps members were ultimately unable to reconcile the possibility that good citizenship may not look the same for those who are unable or unwilling to serve in the way described by the CNCS. In this way, choosing not to neglect one's family, to be a good worker and provider, becomes an expression of good citizenship. It is worth noting that nowhere in these conversations or in the rhetoric of community service writ large do the survival mechanisms or forms of social capital within poor communities become apparent as modes of participation.

Some AmeriCorps members struggled extensively with the relationships between power and privilege within the program, and race was often present as a subtext in conversation, although often masked through abstract characterizations of "poor people." They saw service as an example of "leveraging privilege" and "providing access" to communities socially different from their own in a "legitimate way." Others came into the program with a much more politicized understanding of the social problem at hand than what they encountered within the mechanisms of the program. These AmeriCorps members, paradoxically, struggled deeply with what working with individuals in crisis on a daily basis means. While I observed that more conservative AmeriCorps members had insights into the reality of structural inequalities and the organization of those inequalities along the lines of race and gender, those for whom that reality was already evident, either theoretically or in practice, struggled to make sense of the dialectical relation between structure and agency. One AmeriCorps member, in an extremely exasperated moment, argued,

> I feel white guilt, but my parents weren't wealthy, and they got divorced and my Dad's not the greatest guy. But my mom pulled it together, and she had two jobs. And I find myself getting angry at the parents of my students. And I know it is systemic, but on a more like gut level, I'm like how can you over sleep four days a week and not get your kid to school on time! Why can't you get your shit together? And these are actual emotions that I

have, and I can always talk myself down, but they've definitely popped into my head.

This young man, who I came to know as an extremely conscientious and ethical individual, summarized the position of many AmeriCorps members who were struggling in their experience of AmeriCorps to hold these multiple threads of experience in tension with one another. Their debates moved quickly, with single individuals occupying several positions within the length of thirty-minute conversation. Yes, good citizens should participate, serve, get their kids to school on time, and hold down jobs. Yes, poverty throws up barriers to this kind of participation, but wait, people make choices, although some people have different sets of choices to choose between. It was apparent that the analysis of social inequality within AmeriCorps—that social problems can be solved through individual behavioral modifications—was a source of great discomfort and unresolved questions for many.

Citizenship as Relations of Ruling

In chapter 4, I demonstrated the ways in which the organization of the AmeriCorps program created a particular context in which democratic learning emerged as the form "civic engagement." I argued that within the AmeriCorps program, the spaces of democratic learning are narrowed by institutional regulations and protocols, in both de jure and de facto forms, that create a space for learning that is characterized by the depoliticization of service work, social problems, nonprofit agencies, the state, and the regulatory apparatus of AmeriCorps itself. I further argued that in this context, the learning organized within the program as civic engagement takes on a particular form, which is predicated on the abstraction of consciousness from matter. This appears as the consistent separation of experience from reflection and the emphasis on rational-technical explication of social problems, with attenuating obstruction of social relations of racism, sexism, and so on. AmeriCorps members experience this separation as an inability to talk about "real issues," and instead they only engage in a polemic about community service and good citizenship.

I temper this argument by further proposing that these forms of abstraction and disengagement within the program are not merely pedagogical problems. They emerge within the program *because* of the ideological forms that circulate through AmeriCorps on the subjects of democracy, citizenship, and social inequality. These forms of consciousness, which are put forward as foundational logics of the program, become interpretive frames that ask AmeriCorps members to contend with their explanations and complications. They are intimately connected to the social organization of the daily work done by AmeriCorps members, thus forming a praxis within the program. The learning environment of AmeriCorps, however, ensures that these frames are not encountered as possible explanations, but rather as objective truths. These truths can go by several names depending on how we understand their origins (discourses, ideologies, etc.), but I argue that they accomplish pedagogically the task Dorothy Smith describes as ideological practice.

> Ideological practices are an important form of inscription. They begin within the transcendent schemata of discourse or formal organization. An interpretive schema is used to assemble and order a set of particulars—descriptions or instances of actualities. These aim at and can be interpreted by the schema used to assemble them. The particulars become indices of an underlying pattern, corresponding to the schema, in terms of which they make sense. The ordering of events, objects, and so forth is thus pre-informed by the schema of discourse or formal organization. This is the ideological process at the boundaries of discourse or formal organization. It is of considerable significance in the exercise of power by the ruling apparatus.[19]

It is extremely important to understand what it is going on in the AmeriCorps program as not just the delivering of a particular interpretive frame or set of ideas. It is not the uncritical, mechanical imposition of an ideology produced by a ruling class. The ideology of a particular form of democracy, based in abstraction from material reality, is woven into the very operative practices of the program. In other words, AmeriCorps members live and work the ideology on a daily basis. However, the idea of this notion of ideology as a praxis is also different from other usages of the concept in critical education scholarship, notably the line of analysis developed by de Lissovoy in his study of the ideology of educational accountability. Following Žižek, de Lissovoy's analysis hinges on understanding ideology "not so much as within the subject as outside of it in its relationship to its surroundings. As a result, belief itself is not really a matter of an inner disposition so much as a compulsive repetition of the ideological ritual."[20] Ideological praxis, however, does not locate ideology as either inside or outside the subject.

Rather, ideologies are reproduced through the dialectics of thinking and being and through processes of objectified social consciousness. Objectified social consciousness can be seen in the socially organized and orchestrated forms of activity people engage in to co-construct their reality. In this way, ideological praxis relies on a notion of thinking/being and social reality, following Marx, as "sensuous human practice."[21]

The ultimate reality of the AmeriCorps program is a relation of bifurcation. Two competing processes of learning, the conceptual and the experiential, are set against each other after being violently abstracted from one another. The reality is that we are always thinking as we are acting; following Marx, there is only "conscious life."[22] This does not mean that our thinking and being exist harmoniously, but the expression of this conflict provoked with AmeriCorps is brought into relation through the organization of the program. The state, through the auspices of CNCS working within federal legislation, hands down a set of regulations, rules, and requirements that define the sites and practices of the AmeriCorps program. It also passes down the mandate for civic engagement curricula and AmeriCorps member training. It does not pass down an explicit definition of civic engagement. The state commission responds to the mandate for civic engagement by making it a deliverable outcome of the program, meaning that they will use it as an indicator to assess the program. The state commission also does not hand down an explicit definition of civic engagement, but does disseminate and monitor the evaluation criteria and accountability mechanisms. The programs receive the mandate to provide civic engagement, constantly working within an ensemble of institutional regulations and protocols. Program directors also have their own ideas vis-à-vis service, learning, and civic engagement. They combine these goals with the mandates from the state commission and the restrictions of the federal regulations in order to produce a civic engagement curriculum. This civic engagement curriculum becomes the interpretive frame of democracy and citizenship within the program.

This vacuous notion of democracy and citizenship brought forth through the conceptual apparatus of civic engagement exists in constant tension with individual AmeriCorps members' daily work experiences and practices. In one physical and mental location, their service site, they struggle daily to understand the violent realities of poverty, racism, sexism, inequality, cynicism, alienation, hopelessness, and indifference. They struggle to understand their service as part of the larger social and political landscape of the United States, to see the relationship between helping individuals and transforming social conditions, and to unearth the root causes of the social problems they face. They conduct this struggle on a largely individual basis and through informal conversation with other AmeriCorps members. These are the kinds of questions that are unsanctioned within AmeriCorps; they can only emerge through "brave" program directors that are willing to violate institutional regulations and risk the livelihood of their programs, their own material well-being, and the ongoing human needs their AmeriCorps members address in the community.

This bifurcation is resolved within the program through the implicit assertion that such violent social experiences can be understood as "community needs" and that the responsibility for meeting such needs should fall to citizens. A large part of this normative "should" is the notion that the only other option is to place such a responsibility in the hands of the state, which would surely create even greater inequality, inhumanity, and callousness. The question of the state, as such, is never a possibility for investigation. Juxtaposed to the state, the citizen must emerge as a particular form of democratic agent whose purpose is not confined merely to arrangements for collective self-governance. The purely democratic role of the citizen is augmented in AmeriCorps; the citizen has new tasks and responsibilities before them and through which the notions of citizen and civic responsibility transform. As President Obama argued in his remarks on the twentieth anniversary of the Points of Light Foundation,

> Once you've formed those connections, you'll find that it's a little harder to numb yourself to other people's suffering. It's a little harder to convince yourself that their struggles aren't your problem. It's a little harder to just stand by as a bystander. Once you've tutored young people in a struggling neighborhood, it's hard not to care about that ballot measure to fund their school. Once you've volunteered at a food bank, it's hard not to care about poverty and unemployment. Over time, the needs of the people you serve become your stake in the challenges of our time. In the end, service binds us to each other—and to our communities and our country—in a way that nothing else can. That's how we become more fully American. That's what it means to be American. It's always been the case in this country—that notion that we invest ourselves, our time, our energy, our vision, our purpose into the very fabric of this nation. That's the essence of our liberty—that we give back, freely.[23]

These relations of citizenship and democracy, with their implicit relations of power and inequality, have emerged, pedagogically, in a tidal form in not only AmeriCorps, but in universities, schools, the private sector, the nonprofit sector, and the public domain. These relations are no less than the "big citizenship" of the twenty-first century in which citizens assume responsibility for not only their own well-being, but for social welfare more broadly. They assume this responsibility, however, as individuals and without using any collective means of social redistribution.

In the following chapter, I want to discuss various explanations of how such relations of citizenship and democracy emerge and how that emergence aligns with the generation of ideological praxis. That is, I want to explore how the social relations of democracy make the ideology of civic engagement "real" and not "fake." This has everything to do with the reality of capitalist democracy and the temporal, spatial, social, material, and affective dislocation necessary to the reproduction of both. The implications of such relations in terms of how we learn what it means to live in a democracy are vast and disturbing, but can be significantly and strategically interrupted if we make epistemological and pedagogical moves to reconstruct that which was been fragmented through ideology. Historicizing and materializing these relations conceptually is the first challenge, which is necessarily coincident with the struggle to historicize and materialize these relations pedagogically.

Chapter Six

New Citizens for an Age of Uncertainty

> Service is a spark to rekindle the spirit of democracy in an age of uncertainty.
>
> —President Bill Clinton, "Remarks in a Swearing-In Ceremony for AmeriCorps Volunteers"

It is important to recognize the emergence of the CNCS and its programs, as well as the entry of the American government into the pedagogy of civic engagement, as not just the arrival of an idea whose time has come or the latest in a long line of American experiments in the revitalization of democracy. The establishment of this agency and these programs sits at the confluence of several political streams: the long-lobbied battle for civilian national service; the "failures" of the war on poverty; the rising costs of postsecondary education; and the intentional disinvestment and privatization of public welfare services. Its arrival is often interpreted, particularly by advocates of community service and civic engagement, as the successful outcome of a long-fought campaign for a good idea.[1] I think this is a naive and politically convenient interpretation; it leaves too much out to be taken seriously. The CNCS represents not just the establishment of a federal agency to facilitate community service, but also the emergence of an institution to normalize that which government "should not" do, in the words of Obama, and to reconstruct those activities as the appropriate terrain of community service and volunteer labor. This process involves the embodiment of, quite literally in the subjectivity of the volunteer and their labor, the ethics of capitalist efficiency: work harder and cost less.

As I come to the concluding moments of this research, I feel I have only begun to explore the complexity of the questions I posed for myself. What has become clear is that the ideology of civic engagement within AmeriCorps operates to produce a conceptualization and practice of citizenship grounded in service-labor. What I mean by this is that the dynamics of this ideology are that "good citizenship" can be articulated as unwaged labor organized at the local scale to address social problems through activities aimed ultimately at changing the individual or cultural modes of being within "communities of need." This fetishization of the local reflects the deeply held belief that the local scale is the only efficacious terrain for democratic action. Doing service in one's community, lobbying local officials, or being personally responsible for one's lifestyle are seen as the limit of democratic action, while the translocal scale, often thought of as the federal government, is seen as inefficient, unable to change, and largely a waste of energy. The reinforcement of this idea by both pedagogy and practice in AmeriCorps ultimately obscures the role that public policy, both local and translocal, plays in the reproduction and coordination of inequality, but also the ways in which political leadership liberate market forces to act "after their fashion," as Marx might say. This service-labor allows for no, or low, involvement of the state in addressing these problems, and can be constructed as a civic virtue, thus constituting a reiteration of other moral discourses of discipline and correction in capitalist colonialist societies, echoing the politics of charity and the white man's burden. This conceptualization obscures the roots, function, and morphology of social inequality, meaning that it becomes even more difficult, within this ideological frame, to see how racism, sexism, ableism, and other forms of oppression are dialectically related to forms of exploitation within capitalism and operate to produce "social problems" in need of community service interventions. This active side of citizenship, conceptualized as community service, is oriented toward cultivating personal and cultural responsibility among the poor. In this way, the work of citizens becomes managing the contradictions of inequality in daily life by focusing on the behaviors of the people who are left behind.

This ideology of civic engagement directs the citizens' gaze and activity in a particular manner, and it obscures two dialectical relationships that are important to an understanding of reproductive praxis, by which I mean modes of thinking/being that reproduce ideology, in democratic education: the local/global and the political/material. I am far from the only researcher to take up these questions in recent years, especially since they are tied to our efforts to understand the phenomenon termed *neoliberalism* and what it has to do with democracy. Ultimately, however, I have concluded from this research that the ideology of civic engagement cannot be reduced to new forms of governing or the reorganization of state-citizen relations, as is often argued in critiques of neoliberalism and democracy. These are important aspects of the ideology of civic engagement, but a further depth of analysis is necessary. To that end, in this chapter I want to expand on what a critique of neoliberalism brings to our understanding civic engagement, and then I want to push further and argue that neoliberalism, while generative, is not a sufficient explanation of what is happening with the project of AmeriCorps. To go further, we must explore more of the constitutive contradictions between democracy and capitalism.

Neoliberalism, Democracy, and Civic Engagement

The experience of AmeriCorps demonstrates that the American federal government is actively working to cultivate a particular notion of citizenship that is based on notions of responsibility and participation rather than rights and entitlements. This shift has been documented as a central component of the neoliberalization of citizenship. Neoliberalism is one of the most important, and debated, concepts in the last forty years of social theory. It is used pervasively by critics of policies that are market-oriented and by those who aim to resist the transformation of various public and social institutions along the lines of an economic, technical, and instrumental rationality. The historical emergence of neoliberalism has been charted as both a discursive logic of governance as well as a material response to crisis within capitalism. Some have even argued that it does not really exist and is simply a conceptual signifier articulated by its political opponents.[2] Nevertheless, the concept has been given tremendous explanatory power by its theorists. It is also, however, a concept that is used loosely and in reductionist terms. I often hear students and colleagues toss around the phrase, "That's neoliberalism for you," as if neoliberalism explains all, predicts all, and contains all. What is lost in the casual usage of the term is its specificity, particularly its historical specificity, which is key to understanding its emergence and operation as a political class-based project. I am wary of the use of concepts that obscure aspects of our social reality and limit our own agency. For this reason, it is important for me to take the time and space to say exactly what I mean by the concept of neoliberalism, its importance in understanding civic engagement as a political and pedagogical movement, and, additionally, how it might help us understand a changing politics of citizenship and democracy. It is equally important to take the time and space to do this in order to make the case that we should push our analysis of neoliberalism into closer relation to core contradictions within capitalism.

I understand neoliberalism as a political project brought forward by economic and political elites as a response to a particular historical moment of crisis in the accumulation of capital and resulting forms of political instability. In other words, I do not think of neoliberal initiatives or their effects as if these phenomena just happen outside the bounds of human agency, although the daily reality of neoliberal reform may feel as if the relations that produce these experiences are quite ephemeral and distant, much like the relations of capitalism writ large. In this regard, I understand neoliberalism as characterizing a particular political agenda for reshaping the relationships between state, market, civil society, and actual human beings, both individually and in social groups. As such, the phenomenon of neoliberalism is most visible in an ensemble of activities that stretches across multiple domains of policy. The characteristics of these policies express certain philosophical assumptions about what constitutes human freedom and how a society should be organized to create such freedom. As its most basic, this assumption can be described thus.

> Neoliberalism values market exchange as an 'ethic in itself, capable of acting as a guide to all human action, and substituting for all previously held ethical beliefs,' it emphasizes the significance of contractual relations in the marketplace. It holds that the social good will be maximized by maximizing the reach and frequency of market transactions, and it seeks to bring all human action into the domain of the market.[3]

In this way, neoliberal policy makers have not just reorganized the state's relationship to the market and civil society, but through instruments of policy that have allowed individual and corporate actors to utilize markets in such a way as to deeply alter the material reality of the majority of humanity. This material reality is characterized by the massive redistribution and concentration of wealth in the hands of the few, the severe deprivation of the many, the precarious insecurity of most, and the entrapment of everyday people in institutions that discipline their being to the normalization of this reality.[4] Further, the neoliberalization of varying aspects of society through instruments of public policy requires diverse and targeted discursive strategies in order to recast and legitimate previously understood aspects of the "public good" as being in need of reform.[5] Neoliberalism is no less than an effort to reorganize society. It is a strategy for social change.

A particularly glaring impact of this logic has been the argument for smaller or less government, which is facilitated through the downloading of public services onto smaller entities, such as regional and municipal governments or not-for-profit agencies, and through the devolution of public services to both the not-for-profit and for-profit sectors, effectively privatizing these services. Political efforts to reduce the size of government or to reduce tax expenditures have been popular rallying cries for an electorate long dissatisfied with the complexity, inaccessibility, and slowness of government services; this has been the strategy of political parties for decades at this point in time. The logic to reduce the size of the state in this way is largely made through the argument that services are either better managed at the local level or that the private sector is more efficient, creative, and responsive in the provision of services. The ethic of market behaviors, signified through supply and demand and embodied in discourses such as "choice" and "flexibility," mean that clients of public services will only pursue those options that maximize their own interests. Thus, it is argued that the market's self-regulating features will result in antiquated, poor, inefficient, or ineffective services simply disappearing from the marketplace. This has led to new discourses around the not-for-profit sector as well as a push by advocates of neoliberalism to see civil society as the preferred terrain of social action, resulting in a debate concerning the use of not-for-profits to deradicalize social movements.[6] This debate importantly extends into the NGO-ization of resistance movements in the Global South.[7]

An important aspect of neoliberalism—and one that is, at least superficially, most related to a discussion of civic engagement—involves complex social, material, and cultural processes for consolidating particular subjects or subjectivities, ways of being and thinking, within capitalist social relations. Within educational theory, the analysis of neoliberal subjectivity has heavily emphasized *homo oeconomicus*.[8] The emphasis on economic subjectivity makes perfect sense; educational policy and institutions have been a strategic target and linchpin of neoliberal advocates. Educational systems are key to the reproduction of both social and material relations and have long been the preferred institutions to enforce behavioral norms across the broadest section of the population. There is a strong argument to be made that the school and the prison are the two key disciplinary institutions of the capitalist state, and each has been remade under the terms of neoliberalism and, importantly, in relation to one another. In this respect, much of the critique of neoliberalism within education has focused on the instrumentalization of education toward the needs of the market, including processes of credentialization, requirements on individuals to upgrade skills, and the creation of a market out of education itself. This process involves transforming education from a social, public necessity into a privately accessed and held privilege that can be leveraged in moments of competition. The result is a certain sort of educational subject, or student, who I see in my classrooms on a daily basis; perpetually anxious, fraught with insecurity and uncertainty as to their future and value as a human being (embodied in both customer service and return on investment demands), and terrorized by either actual state violence or the threat of such violence, including the threat of downward class mobility. In other words, education has been repositioned not as something indispensable to a democratic society, but as an acquisition capable of separating individuals from a life of destitution. This acquisition of human capital is, of course, premised on the state abandoning human welfare to the market.

Neoliberal subjectivity, however, is not just about the extension of an economically determinant rationality to all domains of life. Rather, the economic recasting of self has necessitated and is constituted through its relation to a political and cultural reshaping as well. I will say, briefly, that a great deal has been written about the neoliberalization of citizenship. This shift has been documented as a central component of neoliberalism and has been analyzed by social scientists working in multiple theoretical traditions. Two popular approaches include the governmentality perspective, which understands neoliberalism as including the cultivation of new political subjectivities,[9] and scholars in the regulation school tradition, which uses the language of *citizenship regime* to describe changes in the overall apparatus of the state and its political relation to capital.[10] New articulations of active citizenship within education literature, as opposed to the passive enjoyment of status or rights, articulate similar shifts in thinking in which agency and activity become civic virtues. Newman argues that this focus has become the pedagogical aim of state policy.

> Citizenship is defined not as status, not an identity, nor even as a responsibility, but as set of practices ("votes," "participates," "works with") that together constitute the enactment or performance of effective citizenship . . . such practices require a set

of capacities (knowledge, skills, and a sense of empowerment) that can be elicited and encouraged.[11]

This active citizen is knowledgeable and empowered to participate in a variety of possible arenas of public life, including, but not necessarily, local governance and, in the case of AmeriCorps, "meeting community needs."

It is important to remember that neoliberalism is not just an economic, political, and epistemological project on the part of financial, political, and intellectual elites. It has also reconstituted material reality for the majority of the planet. The direness of the conditions of daily life is recounted in publication after publication as a dirge for the bulk of humanity. Not only are more and more of us living on less and less, but the relations we have used to organize our material lives, namely, relations of race and gender, seem to be shifting into fundamentalist and fanatical expressions of violence against women and people of color.[12] Given this articulation of neoliberalism, we should already be questioning the relationship between democracy and such a disastrous, antisocial formation as neoliberalism. What kind of democracy not only tolerates, but facilitates such a way of living? In many ways this is the central question of this book. Decades of neoliberal social policy have wrought an untenable way of life on this planet. The dismantling of the state, privatization, and the reorganization of society as a marketplace has created a daily reality that is destroying human life and the life of the planet itself; although it might be more accurate to say that neoliberalism does not create this reality so much as it exacerbates and concentrates it.

Neoliberalism, however, has not been an uncontested political project. Rather, what we see and experience of this social agenda is the outcome of what is made possible in the face of contestation. Rather than the neat, orderly dissemination of a set of ideals, neoliberalism has, much like capitalism itself, been shaped by local forms of enactment and resistance.[13] However, an equally important aspect of understanding the relation between enactment and resistance is the articulation of appropriate avenues for social and political change. In this regard, neoliberal actors have posited one arena of public life as the appropriate space through which contestation and amelioration may take place. The concept of civil society is thus intrinsic to the elaboration of neoliberalism as well as being particularly key to understanding the emergence of civic engagement as a political and pedagogical movement. The transformation of civil society involves complex process beyond the scope of my discussion; however, two interrelated aspects are paramount and in need of attention. I want to flag these processes here as this study of the AmeriCorps program provides an important way to conceptualize the relationships between these aspects of the neoliberalization of civil society. The first aspect is the downloading or devolution of public services onto both the not-for-profit sector and the privatization of these services within the private sector. The second aspect is the development of civil society as a space in opposition to the politicization of resistance movements. Effectually, this process concerns civil society as a space of depoliticization and deradicalization.

In the United States, the crafting of the volunteer citizen has been heavily influenced by the thinking of conservative communitarians, such as Amitai Etzioni.[14] Etzioni's work in this regard is significant for understanding the emergence of a state project such as AmeriCorps. Since the 1980s, Etzioni has made the argument that citizenship in the United States has been too focused on the provision of rights rather than the fulfillment of responsibilities. While his critique of entitlements does not take the same form as assaults against the welfare state, Etzioni sees his political and intellectual purpose as balancing the need for community with the protection of individual autonomy. Thus, he often argues that responsibilities to community are the antidote to the heartless individualism of American life, much like other communitarians such as Robert Bellah. This vision is well expressed in Etzioni's understanding of social justice, which has four components. The first component is individual responsibility, because "people have the moral responsibility to help themselves as best they can."[15] When individuals fall short of these responsibilities, "the second line of responsibility lies with those closest to the person, including kin, friends, neighbors, and other community members."[16] As opposed to ultra-conservatives like Charles Murray, Etzioni believes that, third, "as a rule every community ought to be expected to do the best it can to take care of its own."[17] When all else fails, "societies (which are nothing but communities of communities) must help those communities whose ability to help their members is severely limited."[18]

At first glance, we can see that the state, in any form, is absent from Etzioni's vision of communitarian "social justice." Further, social justice here has a pathological quality; it neither recognizes inequality nor the conditions that create it, thus it does not even approximate notions of social justice from the left, which see social difference and material inequality as fundamentally related.[19] It is purely individual in its implied definitions of inequality and locates social responsibility at the level of individuals and communities, not society or the state. When inequality is defined in these terms, it is perfectly acceptable to erase the state from the formulation. If inequality has nothing to do with the mediation of social, political, cultural, or economic power, then the power of the state is not necessary for addressing such conditions; these problems can be dealt with through networks of individuals working in communities. In order for a community to fulfill this responsibility, Etzioni argues that it must be "responsive," meaning that the community meets the "true needs" of its citizenry.[20] Communities, in Etzioni's vision, have three main characteristics: they are a "web of affect-laden relationships amongst individuals," and as such require a "shared culture" and are highly responsive.[21] Taken together, this implies a strong role for communities in the maintaining of individual and collective well-being and places a great deal of weight on the maintenance of shared culture, which Etzioni also refers to as the "centripetal force" that pulls toward "higher levels of community service, regulation, and mobilization."[22] The center of this vision is a balancing of rights and responsibilities, which differentiates the communitarian vision from the arguably more extreme antisocial rights position of neoliberalism, but at the same time colludes with a neoliberal perspective. Within this vision, citizens are responsible for the well-being of themselves and their communities; the state is absolved of both a responsibility to address inequality through policies of redistribution, *and* the state is obscured as an architect of inequality in the first place.

Etzioni's vision echoes some key tenets of neoliberal ethics and it also seems conspicuously similar to much of what happens within the AmeriCorps apparatus, deeply influencing the terms through which democracy can be conceptualized and practiced. These elements also reflect two key findings from this research: the fetishization of local spaces as the only terrain for democratic action and the orientation of service activities toward the work of cultivating personal and cultural responsibility for conditions of inequality. There is, however, nothing particularly innovative about Etzioni's diagnostic position; blaming poor people for their own poverty is the oldest trick in the book. In fact, his entire argument is a conservative retreading of old ideologies, including the idea that the work of addressing human welfare and managing the effects of material inequality in people's lives should be taken up by private citizens.

This is a process I call the management of inequality, by which I am referring to the social, cultural, and political processes of organizing and reproducing the inherent inequality of capitalist social relations at the same time that the sources of inequality are obscured through mechanisms such as choice, esteem, social pathology, and responsibility. I am taking the term from Paul Farmer, who refers, in passing, to international development specialists as Transnational Bureaucrats Managing Inequality (TBMIs).[23]

In Farmer's view, these actors specialize in managing poor people, moving them around, occupying them with projects, pinpointing their cultural and technological deficiencies, and then "developing" them in accordance with the demands of capitalist ethics. My articulation of this term is also strongly influenced by Teresa Funicello, who describes the poverty industry as not just capitalists profiteering from the direness of poor people, but also those who set out to help the poor through the mechanisms of not-for-profits or charities, the cornerstones of civil society, and who instead become focused on their own reproduction and subsistence.[24] Funicello's critique is echoed in Rodriguez's articulation of the not-for-profit industrial complex, which he describes as "the industrialized incorporation of pro-state liberal and progressive campaigns and movements into a spectrum of government proctored non-profit organizations."[25] These authors have directed attention to the very important problem of a vast network of organizations and practitioners whose purpose seems to be meeting the daily subsistence needs of poor people while offering escape to only the minor few who can or are willing to conform to the necessary vision of the entrepreneurial self. I propose that one of the political and material impacts of AmeriCorps and its ideology of civic engagement, one which is often unseen from the ideological positions of service, is the cultivation of a citizen identity that is both the subject and object of this project of "managing inequality." Those who are "being managed" are similarly constructed; as Kwoon argues,

> For citizen-subjects of a liberal democracy under neo-liberalism, citizenship and political activeness do not mean just acknowledging one's responsibility for economic growth and self-governance, but also the active and voluntary involvement in the management of one's potential for social risks (for example, poverty, unemployment, and disempowerment). In other words, this mode of governance or "bio-politics" of the population, in which marginalized people (such as the poor and "at-risk" youth) have become special objects of knowledge and targets of control, is amplified within a neoliberal regime that encourages self-responsibility and empowerment.[26]

Ultimately, the ideology of civic engagement constructs a citizen who must simultaneously learn not to rely on the state at the same time that it takes up the responsibility of ameliorating inequality through individual and collective acts of redress, which in turn offers a truncated political landscape that precludes, as Žižek stated and I will echo again, "any serious questioning of the way this liberal democratic order is complicit in the phenomena it officially condemns, and, of course any serious attempt to imagine a different sociopolitical order."[27]

Articulating a critique of civic engagement solely through an analysis of neoliberalism, however, leaves something not seen. It is crucial, in my opinion, to maintain an understanding of neoliberalism that sees it as a political, class-based response to a crisis within capitalism and capitalist political legitimacy. We have to be careful not to separate this political, social, cultural, and material phenomenon from the people who make it and their interests, particularly the interest to secure forms of capital accumulation in particular ways. Neoliberalism emerged out of, and has been deployed toward, the collapse of the welfare state. It is an explicitly moral project that aims to turn society away from itself and reconstruct any material or ethical bonds between people. The hyperindividualism of this social formation has an important duality to it; the self is the only entity capable of ensuring well-being at the same time that the self is the only source of suffering. This fundamentally obscures political and material relations in society, making it impossible to see what sorts of processes and relations allow for the exploitation of value and accumulation of wealth. It further renders invisible the ways in which racialization and gender constitute relations of exploitation and power.

This could lead us back to addressing why this type of obfuscation is so crucial not just to neoliberal interests, but to capitalist interests more broadly. The fundamental contradiction at the heart of the ideology of civic engagement is between political freedom, embodied in the concept of citizenship and democracy, and material and social unfreedom, generated through capitalist social relations. This contradiction requires us to ask why citizenship is such a productive space for obscuring this reality and how it can be so easily accomplished within the bounds of a democracy. To explore this, we will have to revisit the idea of democracy in a historical materialist manner.

Locating Civic Engagement in the Dislocation of the Political from the Material in Capitalist Social Relations

When I ask students to describe what the concept of citizenship means, they invariably resort to the language of freedom. To be a citizen, they tell me, is to have freedom, liberty, justice, and equality, all of which are embodied in the concept of rights. For many, citizenship equals rights. This conversation always gets more complicated as they then start to talk about obligations or duties, because they have been taught, through an admittedly paltry education in civics, that citizenship only exists in democracies and democracies are governments by the people for the people—and thus if they do not participate in their government in some way, then they will not have a democracy. Voting and paying taxes are usually the only agreed-on forms of participation and thus constitute the floor of democratic participation. The trajectory of this public brainstorming was echoed across my conversations with AmeriCorps members, and within it is the basic narrative of democracy that is taught in most liberal societies. I ask my students what they mean by freedom, and they tend to offer a framework. Freedom means *freedom from* particular things, such as tyranny of a nondemocratic government or the abuse of another person. Freedom also means *freedom to* do certain things, like assemble, speak, worship, and so forth. This is the basic conception of negative (freedom from) and positive (freedom to) rights. They are able to present, more or less, an outline of basic civil and political liberties.

The conversation gets more difficult when I ask them if they would describe being hungry and obtaining food with the language of freedom. In their society, which they describe as a democracy, I ask them, "Are you free to eat when you are hungry?" They go a few rounds about the morality of this question, and then they resolve that the answer is no. In fact, eating is a highly regulated activity, mediated through the market, and, under certain conditions, criminalized. If ones does not have money or land one may not eat, at least not with ease or safety. They puzzle over the reality that eating without money or land, for example through theft, is an illegal activity. Again they return to the morality of stealing to eat, but I often ask them to question how one can be free to say whatever one wants, but not eat whatever one wants. While we see restrictions on the freedom of the mind and expression as an affront to human dignity, starvation, apparently, is not.

There are many directions this conversation can go, one of which is toward the idea of social rights and entitlements as well as of social democracies, which do a better job than most in ensuring the right to eat. However, this is a leap to the question of how to address the contradiction the problem of eating poses rather than asking why this contradiction exists in the first place. One way to name this problem is to say that there is a contradiction between political freedom and material unfreedom within capitalist democracies. By this I mean that democracy allows a kind of formal, political equality at the same time that it also allows a substantive, material inequality. I have referenced this kind of contradiction several times throughout this research. It is another iteration of the problem of modernism, which is that the political project of liberalism, the establishment of the unfettered and free individual, has only succeeded in establishing relative and limited equality before the state and for only a small sector of the global society. Rather than creating an unfettered freedom, we seem to live in a situation of curtailed, alienated, vacant, and bereft freedoms. Within a society composed through social relations of race, gender, and class, people experience unfreedom in complex ways vis-à-vis the state, the economy, and through culture. In short, the way we live in raced, classed, and sexed lives, and the organization of social power through these relations, is in contradiction with the narrative of liberalism despite the emergence of some forms of political freedom for some people within this political formation.

It is crucial to recognize that for many people, there is no contradiction here. There is no problem with being a citizen with equal rights and equality before the law and also seeing people starving on the street. This is because these are seen as separate issues. The purpose of a democratic society, in this line of thought, is not to provide for the welfare of people, but to ensure that the rules of competition are fair, that everyone is treated equally and has the same recourse to justice if they are not. It is up to individuals to see to their well-being through their own hard work. In other words, democracy as a political system and capitalism as an economic system are in no way contradictory. For some, this is the perfect articulation of freedom because one is free to work as hard as one can for as long as one can in order to achieve one's own aspirations. Other people recognize that political freedom and material unfreedom pose limits on one another. When people struggle for their daily bread, they cannot participate or access the resources to press their interests in the same way as those who do not. Thus material inequality undermines political equality, and the contradiction should be resolved through public policy that ameliorates material inequality in some way, either through guaranteeing a standard of living or producing services that people can access to meet their needs. This can easily become a debate about the role of a democratic state in relation to capitalism. Should the state ensure that capitalists play fair with one another and no more, or should it attend to the problems of deprivation that capitalism creates through policies of redistribution? This struggle was present in the thinking of many of the AmeriCorps members.

What this struggle crucially represents is that our political lives and our material lives *appear* to us as separate spheres; thus, we are able to conceptualize them separately and not see any contradiction between them. This mode of analysis is based in an ahistorical understanding of the relationship between our political and material lives; it relies on conceptualizing the economic as separate from the political and then the imposition of this conceptualization on reality. This is the very definition of an ideological act, and the separation of the economic from the political is one of the most foundational ideologies of capitalism. I have argued that this is the contradiction in which the ideology of civic engagement is situated. However, to reduce it to the role or function of the state is also an ahistorical and abstracted framing of the problem between capitalism and democracy. The issue at hand here is whether we approach democracy as a concept and philosophy or whether we approach it as a historically specific set of human relations. To begin with human relations is to posit a historical materialist critique, which is exactly what I want to do here, attempting at the same time to return to dialectical conceptualization. I want to ground the ideology of civic engagement and its constitutive relations, namely, the conceptualization of citizenship as a means to address material inequality, within a larger discussion of how it operates ideologically within a capitalist democracy. This requires discussing what it even means to conceptualize democracy as *capitalist* democracy.

I have argued here that one of the primary functions of the ideology of civic engagement is to manage inequality in society through shifting the responsibility of social welfare off the state and on to citizens. But why does inequality need to be managed in the first place, and more specifically, why would this be taken up within a reconceptualization of citizenship? There are a wide variety of answers to this question, but I think three primary perspectives are helpful in the context of this research. One approach draws from the growing literature on the neoliberalization of citizenship and the study of citizenship regimes, which I discussed earlier in this chapter. A second comes from an older tradition within political sociology characterized by feminist, Marxist, and antiracist critiques of social welfare policy, which examine the regulatory policies of the welfare state.[28] A third comes from the political writing of Marx, who demonstrates that the material relations of capitalism are also political relations congealed in forms such as the state and citizenship and which have a necessary role in maintaining and expanding the logic of capitalism. While I have referred to the literature on neoliberalism and citizenship and I find that the literature on regulation addresses an important sociological dimension of this question, in this discussion I want to focus on Marx's writing because I believe his arguments are particularly important for educators and for the radical theorization of democratic learning, as they direct our attention toward a dialectical conceptualization of ideology, consciousness, and praxis.

The Contradiction of Freedom and Equality

Let me begin with a simple observation and statement of position. Many scholars of democracy trace a largely unbroken historical line from the democracies of ancient Greece and Rome to the "re-emergence" of democracy in Europe. Historians such as Ellen Meiksins Wood and Peter Linebaugh have, I believe, done the work necessary to demonstrate that this argument does not hold;[29] rather, they argue, to understand the emergence of modern democratic forms in Europe and their eventual elaboration in North America, one should begin with the social relations of feudalism. These social relations effectively merged the political and material lives of people, meaning that one's economic standing in society (as a serf or a lord or a yeoman) was also one's political standing. There was no separation between worker and "citizen" as in contemporary democracy; political relations were class relations. These relations cannot be described in the language of rights in the sense that we understand that term today. Serfs had certain duties and obligations to their lord, and vice versa. They also had certain privileges, particularly to the surplus produced through their labor, and certain entitlements to the land, the commons, on which they depended for their subsistence. Lords had duties to protect the community and to redistribute stored surpluses in times of dearth. These political material relations were based in important cultural meaning systems related to duty, fealty, and honor, but it is important to recognize them not as a monolithic belief system but as a mode of living generated through ongoing struggle between peasants and lords.[30] Acts of resistance including armed uprisings, work stoppages, and slowdowns, as well as different forms of protest and strike were the means through which peasants were able to assert their communal needs and make demands on feudal power. These struggles importantly resulted in local, village-based charters that increasingly established the parameters of the political lives of serfs, including limitations on taxes (a constant struggle) as well as on arbitrary arrest and abuse. Thus, present within feudal social relations were complex forms of political material relations that mediated the class relations of society. It would not be accurate to say that there was no self-government under feudalism, but it would also not be accurate to call these relations democracy as we understand it today.

The historical forces of privatization, enclosure, and accumulation that emerged within, and aided, the collapse of feudalism are too complex to recount here. However, for understanding the emergence of democracy as a political form, it is crucial to note that the transformation of a peasant serf into a waged laborer required separating these people from the land on which they depended for their subsistence. Through a long history of bloody struggle, the commons were enclosed, and peasants were no longer able to hunt, fish, or gather food and fuel on them. As these resources became privatized, they were increasingly only able to access the means of subsistence through waged labor. This material transformation in life also involved a social and political transformation. Wood argued,

> the individual and his property were detached from the community, as production increasingly fell outside communal regulation, whether by manorial courts or village community (the most obvious example of this process is the replacement of the English open-field system by enclosure); customary tenures became economic leaseholds subject to the impersonal competitive pressures of the market; smallholders lost their customary use-rights to common land; increasingly, they were dispossessed, whether by coercive eviction or the economic pressures of competition.[31]

That which had historically constituted the community was torn apart as families were cast off of lands and away from communities they had been tied to for generations. Charters and agreements between villages and lords were broken as villages were depopulated and violence was used to repress resistance. This process also produced and expanded the status of the wage worker. Ultimately, as Wood continues,

> as landholding became increasingly concentrated, the peasantry gave way to large landholders, on the one hand, and property-less wage laborers, on the other end. In the end, the "liberation" of the individual was complete, as capitalism, with its indifference to the "extra-economic" identities of the laboring multitude, dissipated prescriptive attributes and "extra-economic" differences in the solvent of the labor market, where individuals became

interchangeable units of labor abstracted from any specific personal or social identity.[32]

In other words, as the wage replaced forced labor, people gained the status of worker and the "freedom" to act as workers in a labor market, but they lost the political relations that tied them to community and land. They also lost the political power that allowed them to make demands for their own well-being. Instead of being a member of a village community, they were transformed into an isolated, private individual.

This abstracted individual is the citizen of modern democracy. Such citizens are formally equal before the state, which does not acknowledge any social identity, legally, as mediating their status as citizen, except the status of citizen itself. This, of course, is the outcome of long, violent, political struggle on the part of the multitudes that were denied access to the status of citizen for centuries, and has by no means been universally accomplished nor is it a status that is irrevocably held. Since September 11, we have seen the emergence of political factions using instruments of the state to restrict, deny, circumscribe, and strip away the legal status of citizen.[33]

Thus, in theory, citizens are "free" in very particular ways within modern democracy. I have argued that within capitalism, there is a contradiction between political freedom and material unfreedom. What do I mean by freedom and unfreedom? Freedom here has multiple definitions. On the one hand, it refers to the kind of freedoms we often associate with liberal democracy and that are embodied in the concept of rights, as I discussed earlier. These are formal freedoms, given and ensured by the state, and made real through juridical apparatuses. If these freedoms are violated, one may have recourse through judicial systems—or at least that is the promise made within a democratic society. These are political freedoms. Marx argued that other forms of freedom exist within human relations, particularly those organized as capitalism;[34] one is the freedom to labor, to work free from ties and commitments to land or person. This is the kind of freedom that was achieved by the "emancipation" of labor with the collapse of feudalism in Europe, when people were "freed" from servitude and able to set out from land they had been tied to through custom and tradition. In this kind of freedom, labor becomes a commodity, and it may move through the market as it sees fit. People become workers instead of serfs or slaves, and they are "free" to move between jobs, looking for better wages or better working conditions, maximizing their own potential and capacity.

This freedom, however, is necessarily related to a form of unfreedom. For labor to be free, it must also be dispossessed of the means of production and the ability to subsist. A political and material process of primitive accumulation and enclosure means that people have no other way to meet the needs of life, their material needs, than through the wage. Thus, they are "unfree" to live unless working for a wage. We can take my own life as an example. I own no property suitable for the cultivation of food. I cannot access materials to shelter or clothe myself without purchasing them as commodities. Health care is a commodity. Education is a commodity. Leisure, entertainment, and aesthetic pursuits are all commodities. My psychological well-being, or so corporations try to convince me, can be assured through the procurement of certain commodities. In short, my life is utterly dependent not on direct production, but rather on commodities produced by others in spaces and places that are largely far away from me. To imagine living outside this system is difficult; it requires either privatized resources (money and capital) to opt out of it or tremendous collective organization to arrange another way of meeting my material and social needs. Thus, I experience my material life within capitalism as a form of unfreedom, although the wage grants me the appearance of freedom through choice among and within markets.

This is the contradiction I began with; we can be "free" in a political way and "unfree" in a material way. The relative "freedoms," both political and material, that are enjoyed vary across time and space and are crisscrossed by geographically specific relations of race, gender, sexuality, and so on. This political freedom I enjoy is largely based on my identification with particular social categories, which are historical social constructions utilized to organize power in capitalist societies. As a white woman in North America, I experience few constraints on my political freedom, but there are some crucial ones. I do not feel overly threatened by the police and feel fairly confident they will not kill me for being a white woman, but if I take my political activities too far in particular directions, then the state will come after me—and I have experienced the realities of having my autonomy over my own body limited by the state. Citizenship is the embodiment of this political sort of freedom. However, the kinds of unfreedom that are necessary to capitalist social relations create inequality in everyday life. These unfreedoms are necessary because one of the realities that distinguishes capitalism from other material systems is not the use of money or markets, but the dependence on markets as well as the extraction of surplus value from labor and the transformation of that value into privatized resources utilized for the leveraging of further extraction. This is the relation of exploitation within capitalism, which is different from the sort of exploitation that existed within feudalism, but is exploitation nonetheless. Workers produce commodities, commodities are sold, and the difference between what is generated and what is paid out is privatized to the owner of the capital; workers must work because they cannot live otherwise, which is to say that they themselves must commodify their labor power. The transformation of feudal forms of exploitation into capitalist forms required not only the dispossession of the peasant class, but the transformation of gender relations into those in which reproductive labor was remade as valueless and women's bodies were commodified. It also required the construction of a system of racial classification used to justify hyper-exploitation and the appropriation of continents of land through colonization projects.[35] Thus, this difficult contradiction between political and material forms of freedom also involves contradictions between political freedom and material relations of gender, race, nation, and origin.

To situate democracy historically and within human relations means acknowledging that within capitalism, the way we go about meeting our material needs cannot be an equal process, because capitalism is organized to create inequality and to privatize that inequality. In fact, it cannot *begin* without inequality, in the form of private property, in the first place. The accumulation of private property was only accomplished through the transformation and concretization of existing class relations organized through relations of patriarchy and white supremacy. We do not begin, historically and in our social reality, from a position of equality. Thus, the category of equality has to emerge, at least in part, from its opposition to this already existing inequality. The equality of political freedom cannot negate the inequality of material life. Rather, the equality of political freedom is presupposed by inequality and ensures its continuity. Marx argued the following in *On the Jewish Question*:

> The state abolishes, after its fashion, the distinctions established by *birth, social rank, education, occupation*, when it decrees that birth, social rank, education, occupation are *non-political* distinctions; when it proclaims, without regard, to these distinctions, that every member of society is an *equal* partner in popular sovereignty, and treats all elements which compose the real life of the nation from the standpoint of the state. But the state, none-the-less, allows private property, education, occupation to

> *act* after *their* own fashion, namely as private property, education, occupation; and to manifest their *particular* nature. Far from abolishing these *effective* differences, it only exists so far as they are presupposed.[36]

His argument is twofold; the state does not create equality *and* it cannot create such conditions. In the processes of creating the formal equality known as equal rights, the relations of inequality in everyday, material life are reinscribed and cemented as components of social life. This extends not only to material relations of production, but to *social* relations as well, including processes of race and gender. Said differently, the only kind of equality the state can create, within capitalist social relations, is in the sphere of formal abstract relations. Marx referred to this form of equality as *political emancipation*, and while this freedom is an important reality of life, it should not be confused with *human emancipation* or the freedom from necessity. This differentiation is extremely important; when combined with Marx's analysis of the capitalist mode of production, we can see further how political emancipation is the limit of freedom under capitalism. Equality and freedom, the central tenets of citizenship and democracy, can only exist in a specific form: politically, legally, formally, and abstractly, but not objectively, materially, or concretely. This is rooted in the fundamental contradiction between capital and labor that produces surplus value in capitalist societies—we cannot avoid this reality; capitalism is the appropriation of value and the privatized accumulation of value.

Specific and General Forms of the Ideology of Citizenship

Locating the ideology of civic engagement within this contradiction between freedom/unfreedom and equality/inequality helps us to understand why this contradiction must be managed within capitalism. Obviously, it would not be good for profit or accumulation for masses of people to recognize that the condition of material suffering is not due to individual deficits or cultural failings, but is rather necessary to capitalism as a mode of life. When this has happened, historically, those who choose to resist have met a massive force of violence from the state. Recognizing this contradiction, however, does not explain why it exists. That can only be done by conceptualizing political and material relations as dialectically related. Further, such recognition does not help us understand why the ideology of civic engagement—which is actually just a specific form of the more general ideology of citizenship—feels real, nor does it help us to understand why citizenship and democracy are such effective ideological relations for obscuring this contradiction.

What was significant about the liberal revolutions of the eighteenth and nineteenth centuries—that is, the revolution against monarchies, absolute and otherwise, and the establishment of republican or parliamentary states utilizing constitutions, elected representation, and legislative systems—was the emergence of parliamentary and representative democratic states. These democratic states, such as the United States, have claimed historical continuity with these early democratic experiments ever since. Sometimes it seems there is not a single political debate in the United States that does not contain reference to the "founding fathers," for example. This suggests the extent of the belief that these democracies are fixed, absolute, and transhistorical. According to Sayer, and following on the discussion of Wood, above, Marx's early political writings begin from the assumption that the democratic state emerged out of the political formations of feudalism.[37] In this vein, in order to understand the novel forms of the new democratic society, in particular the appearance of separate economic and political spheres of life, Marx developed his understanding of the state from the historical processes of the division of labor and the development of private property.[38] The development of private property is a part of the process by which direct producers are violently separated from the means of production and ownership, access, and use of natural resources and forms of technology are concentrated in the hands of the few. This process is necessarily a process of class formation. Privatization also dismantles previous feudal relations of dependence; the shattering of any notion of communal bond separates the political and economic. The appropriator and the producer now confront one another through terms of exchange. The social relations governing human interaction and cooperation are no longer based on communal ties, privileges, or deference, but on legal relations. These coincident social processes, the creation of private property and the reforming of social relations, create the need for the state to become a "separate entity, beside and outside civil society."[39]

The division of labor is a second and simultaneous development that plays an intricate role in the development of the state as such. The division of labor should be understood as a process of class formation, whereby societies produce and distribute resources in a differentiated and hierarchical fashion. Traditionally, this division of labor is recognized as being segmented into mental and manual labor. However, feminist critique also recognizes the historical processes that divided labor categories of productive and reproductive; reproductive labor being understood as having less value, or no value, when compared to productive labor. It has been feminist scholars who have advanced work on the concept of division of labor by demonstrating the ways in which this division has the overall effect of decreasing the value of all labor. Further, the historical, and ongoing, processes generating divisions of labor are colonial and imperial processes. This segmentation is both a precondition and result of capitalist social formation. However, organizing our societies in this way also creates a contradiction between the private interests of the individual and the general interest of the public.[40] We fix private interests by connecting one's subsistence to a segregated role in society and production. In this way, we experience our lives exactly as the Enlightenment philosophers postulated we did: as egotistical individuals advancing our private interests. The mistake of these theorists, according to Marx and Engels, is to suppose those lives constitute a *natural* condition as opposed to the real, lived outcomes of a socially organized division of labor historically produced through violent force. This natural individual, egoist man, is the philosophical presupposition of the state, the justification of the need for legal relations and for the establishment of a general interest outside the private interests of individuals. In short, the presumption of the self-interested, private individual is the basis for the argument that the state is a representation of the public interest, which acts to limit the gross egoism of the individual.

The contradiction between freedom and unfreedom, how to subsist and thrive within social relations premised on the exploitation and appropriation of one's labor, is for Marx the central relation that gives rise to the state. This is essentially a class contradiction, but it is also a paradox. As Sayer pointed out, one of the peculiar functions of divided relations of labor in which we live is to make us feel and act as though we are alone at the same time that we become increasingly interdependent with others to meet our needs.[41] For example, returning to the right to eat, our food is obtained through the simple act of exchange. In reality, our food, our subsistence, is premised on the combined and cooperative labor of many thousands of people. However, one of the outcomes of the division of labor, or capitalist social relations in general, is to make this interdependence invisible. The state then exists as an expression of the only communal relations we understand ourselves to have and which we experience in daily life, relations mediated through laws, rights, duties, and obligations. These acts, rights, laws, and so on circumscribe our spheres of action and are experienced as a limit. They matter. It is for this reason that Marx and Engels argued that out of this very contradiction between the interests of the individual and that of the community, the latter takes an independent form as the *state*, divorced from the real interests of individual and community, and at the same time as an illusory communal life, always based, however, on the real ties existing in every family . . . and especially . . . on the classes, already determined by the division of labor, which in every such mass of men separate out, and of which, one dominates the others.[42]

The notion that the state is an "illusory community," particularly as argued by Ollman, must be understood as articulating the particularities of the capitalist democratic state.[43] It must also not be abstracted from Marx's analysis and simply thought of as "an illusion." While this notion may explain the paradox of individualism and interdependence that exists in capitalist social life, it does not explain the specific class relation embodied in the state, which is implied through its formation in private property and the division of labor and which is manifested in the project of "managing inequality." For this reason, Sayer advised that it is best to understand the state itself as an "ideal" expression of capitalist material relations.[44]

To say that the state is an ideological form of appearance is not to say that it is a falsification or a floating entity that exist only in people's heads. The state is a real entity with institutions and practices. Similarly, citizenship as an ideology is not a fake or false illusion. Having this status, one enshrined in a piece of paper, is crucial to one's safety in today's world. To say that the state is ideal in this way is to say that it is, above all, an expression of the social relations of actual living working people. To this end, Marx and Engels argued that

> The social structure and the State are continually evolving out of the life-process of definite individuals, not as they may appear in their own or other people's imagination, but as they really are; i.e. as they operate, produce materially, and hence as they work under definite material limits, presuppositions and conditions independent of their will.[45]

The state exists as an objectified form of social consciousness. However, and I cannot stress this point enough, the state is not a transhistorical category that expresses all political relationships through time. The state is most importantly a historical category; "in other words the concept is not a synonym for any and all forms of government (or ways in which ruling classes rule), but describes a definite and historically delimited social form: the social form, specifically, of bourgeois class rule."[46] In this way, the state is an ideal form of the class relations of capitalism. The citizen is a mediation of class relations.

For Marx, the state not only expressed all of the paradoxical and alienated social relations found within civil society, but it was also the form in which the bourgeoisie ruled *as a class*. The notion that the state predicates the arrangements of capitalism through legal relations or wields its monopoly on violence in the interests of the bourgeoisie seems obvious enough. Even the most alienated American voter can argue that the rich get richer and the poor get poorer and the government is the reason for this; but the question is why capitalist social relations require the state as such to secure their position. Sayer answered the question thusly.

> The clue to the necessity of bourgeois rule taking the form of an ideally independent state enforcing the rule of law lies, for Marx, in the atomized, fissiparous character—precisely the individualized nature—of the bourgeois class itself. . . . The individuals of the bourgeoisie, Marx considers, "form a class only in so far as they have to carry on a common battle against another class; otherwise they are on hostile terms with each other as competitors." Their common class interest can be secured only by maintaining conditions—above all the defense of individual property rights—in which they can continue to act freely as individuals, each pursuing his own private interests, in apparent isolation from one another. This entails both the safeguarding of bourgeois rights against the political and moral economies of other classes . . . and the maintenance of equal rights among bourgeois individuals themselves. The "rule of law" is the paradigm form of such regulation.[47]

In other words, the state expresses the interests of the bourgeoisie by protecting the capitalist forms through which their class position is formed in the first place, namely, via private property, *and* by creating a public sphere in which equality is only predicated on political grounds. Politically, but not materially, equal individuals remain the private, competitive, "free" individuals of civil society formed through the division of labor, alienated from their labor and their community, and secured in their status, both materially and politically, through the abstract notion of "the State." In this way, as an expression of a bourgeois relation, the state finds its articulation through the core categories of legal rights and citizenship. Citizenship can thus be seen as an expression of the contradiction between the political and the material within capitalism.

In his critique of citizenship as an abstract notion, Marx identified several sides of this relation between the political and the material. The first relation develops by premising citizenship and the relations of the state on abstract equality, the state obscures all of the social relations that make up civil society. According to Arthur,

> we see that a political, merely political, emancipation leaves intact the world of private interests, of domination and subordination, exploitation and competition, because the State establishes its universality, and the citizens their communality, only by abstracting away from the real differences and interests that separate the members of civil society and set them against one another.[48]

In this way, the state declares that it will not recognize differences between "free" competitors so that they may remain "free" in their exchanges. And in this way, Marx was demonstrating that class antagonisms remain despite the appearance of equality before the state. It is also what he meant when he argued that the limit of political emancipation is that the state can be free while people are not. The state posits itself as "free" from the complexities and complications of material and social life in civil society. This is perhaps the most popular lesson that scholars have taken from *On the Jewish Question*, and it is well used in analyzing, in particular, the ways in which democracy and racism coexist in discursive forms and is the very experience that set me on the path of this research many years ago. However, Marx also argued a second side of this relation, which is that the establishment of the state through the political emancipation of civil society is actually a presupposition of the unequal relations in civil society in the first place. In many ways this is a reiteration of the analysis of the foundation of the state as a capitalist relation and is what Marx meant when he argued that "the consummation of the idealism of the state was at the same time the consummation of the materialism of civil society."[49] In civil society, individuals coproduce under relations of inequality created through private property, the division of labor, and the accumulation of capital. The state is unable to abolish these inequalities through the mechanism of citizenship precisely because the state exists in the first place to secure these relations; the state arises out of the contradictions of civil society, not, as Hegel had argued, the other way around.[50] Thus, it can only abolish inequality theoretically or abstractly, formally. It cannot undo how inequality is built into the ways we have organized our productive and social lives. If it were to try and do so, if the state were to be "aware of itself" as such, Marx argued that it would be in a state of permanent revolution by trying to abolish the social relations that give birth to it. For this reason, a third relation arises from the contradiction of abstracted citizenship, which is that political emancipation develops as the limit of freedom within capitalist society.

A fourth relation of citizenship as the contradiction between the political and the material is best developed through Marx's discussion of rights. In *On the Jewish Question* Marx takes the time to ask what exactly these "rights" are that define citizenship. His answer is that the so-called immutable and natural "rights of man" are in actuality the right to exist as an egotistical individual in civil society.[51] These rights, which we classically associate with liberalism as negative rights, the "freedom from" rights, and positive rights, the "freedom to" rights: the rights of person, equality, liberty, security and property. They protect the citizen from incursions by his fellow citizens and the state. For Marx, these are legal expressions of the social relations of the capitalist mode of production, such as the right to be separated from others in ones' community (the division of labor), the right to acquire and appropriate (private property), and the right to be self-interested. Or as Žižek provocatively argues on the subject of the international expression of legal political relations, human rights, we can see that

> the experience of our post-political liberal-permissive society amply demonstrates, human rights are ultimately, at their core, simply rights to violate the Ten Commandments. "The right to privacy"—the right to adultery, in secret, where no one sees me or has the right to probe my life. "The right to pursue happiness and to possess private property"—the right to steal (to exploit others). "Freedom of the press and the expression of opinion"—the right to lie. "The right of free citizens to possess weapons"—the right to kill. And, ultimately, "freedom of religious belief"—the right to worship false gods.[52]

At the same time that these rights appear to ameliorate the inequality of civil society, it is Marx's argument that they actually affirm the inequality and class antagonisms of civil society. Further, as they exist in a completely paradoxical relation to their expression as *common* rights of political community; they are completely predicated on the separation of individuals within community. Marx argued that in the frame of liberal rights,

> Man is far from being considered as a species-being; on the contrary, species-life itself—society—appears as a system which is external to the individual as a limitation of his original independence. The only bond between men is natural necessity, need, and private interest.[53]

In this way, the bourgeois notions of citizenship and rights reduce human community to a notion of political community whose purpose is solely to reproduce, or at best mediate, the social relations of capitalism. But again, these notions of citizenship and rights are predicated on the actual existing relations of civil society. These natural rights of the citizen are actually "the recognition of the frenzied movement of the cultural and material elements of which form the content of life."[54] It is for this reason that Marx proposed that political emancipation is the limit of emancipation within capitalism, and that in order to transform these relations the emphasis must be on human emancipation. Human emancipation requires the negation of the state as a capitalist relation as well as the negation of the artificial division between the private and the public, the material and the political, and social and political power.

Reproducing and Revolutionizing the Ideology of Civic Engagement

Thus, within the political relations of capitalism, the right to equality becomes the right to inequality.[55] The existence of such inequality, however, is fundamentally in contradiction with the moral claims of capitalism, particularly the claims that through such relations equality, freedom, and liberty can be achieved. Inequality within capitalism, therefore, must be managed; it must be organized and coordinated in such a way that our consciousness about the existence of inequality does not oppose its existence. It must be naturalized, desocialized, abstracted, and obscured. This is a vast ideological project of democratic capitalism, constructed through the category of citizenship and visible over time in projects such as the undeserving poor, the foreign national, or "welfare queens" through which women, people of color, and immigrants become subject to violent social processes legitimating their social and political exclusion and the hyperexploitation of their labor.[56] A good deal of citizenship discourse and theory has been devoted to maintaining such divisions between those who are "decent" and "indecent" or "deserving" or "undeserving" in the eyes of the nation. For example, the National Commission on Civic Renewal put this platform forward in their final report on the state of civic engagement in the United States.

> Our moral and civic ills are most often discussed in the context of our troubled urban areas. There is no doubt that the civic condition of communities is affected by their economic condition. The breakdown of families, public safety, and neighborhoods is compounded by economic misery and diminished opportunities. The decline in civic and political disengagement is especially pronounced among individuals who are sliding down the economic ladder, or those who have never taken the first step up that ladder.[57]

Put differently, creating "bad citizens" out of those who must be "managed" is a major component of capitalist social relations. For the idea of democratic participation of citizens to be reorganized an essential part of this process speaks to an evolution in the historical development of ideologies that pathologize the poor. It also points to a historical development in the relation between civil society and the state.

Creating citizens who "manage inequality," who feel responsible for the well-being of others and understand care as part of their democratic duty, is a pedagogical project for both the state and capital. As such, it has become a major aim of public policy and appears in multiple forms such as projects for citizenship education, character education, and moral education; it is often visible in the trifecta I referred to in the introduction to this text: the knowledge, skills, and attitudes of "good citizens." Newman aptly summarizes this project.

> Welfare beyond the welfare state also depends on citizens taking greater responsibility for the health and wellbeing of themselves, their families, and neighbours and their "communities." This is turn requires skills, capacities, and orientations that need to be inculcated, whether it is on how to eat healthy, to be better parents, to make responsible lifestyle choices, to engage in the

"co-production" of services or to participate in democratic spaces of decision making.[58]

I argue that this project appears explicitly in forms such as AmeriCorps, but it also appears in the work of those who uncritically accept and naturalize the political economy of democratic relations. It happens through the well-intentioned actions of those who simply want to help those in need and understand themselves as having a moral obligation to address social problems. The impulse to help is not the problem; rather, it is the contextualization of this ethical position within the reproduction of capitalist social relations. In order to move beyond the limits of this ideology, we must revolutionize learning for democracy.

Chapter Seven

Beyond a Better Democracy

Rehistoricizing and Rematerializing Critical Education

> Justice is not a natural part of the lifecycle of the United States, nor is it a product of evolution; it is always the outcome of struggle.
>
> —Keeanga-Yamahtta Taylor,
> *From #BlackLivesMatter to Black Liberation*

Democracy feels like a different sort of beast today than it did when I first began this research. The American presidential administration has changed and, for maybe the first time in decades, educators are having serious conversations about how best to respond to fascism and white nationalism as realities in our classrooms. These, however, are not the only conversations that are challenging us. New social movements against settler colonialism, anti-Black racism, state violence, and sexual violence have once again captured national conversations. These forms of violence are being named in public discourse, although perhaps their constitutive relations of capitalism, patriarchy, and white supremacy are not. My good friend and comrade Amir Hassanpour once told me that he believed fundamentalisms are most violent when they are most threatened by historical change. The change, however, is not pregiven; we do not yet know what kind of society will emerge from the struggles we are waging today. The future depends entirely on the actions of the present, and thus the kind of historical change that will occur is the question for educators, activists, community workers, cultural workers, and everyday people (some of whom are "citizens") to take up and act on in this moment. The manner through which this kind of change might occur, however, is something we should make clear among ourselves. I still believe bell hooks was right when she argued that "since we live historically (as individuals who change and are changed by events and circumstances), we have the power to transform reality, if we choose to act. Simply naming and identifying a problem does not solve it; naming is only one stage in the process of transformation."[1]

I have attempted, through my research, to name the problem around civic engagement as ideology and to name some of the terms on which we should understand this phenomenon. Civic engagement, at its broadest, is the enclosure of political imagination; it is the capture of possibility within the confines of the orchestrated denigration of humanity. The issue is not simply that there is an ideology of civic engagement circulating among educators, policy makers, not-for-profit workers, and young people that is predicated on the depoliticization of democratic life. If so, the answer would be robust social movements for policy reform. The problem is also not simply that the form of citizenship embodied in this concept of civic engagement is itself a component of a larger political project to reconfigure the citizen in relation to state and capital, a project that I have labeled neoliberalism. If this was the case, we could continue our argument over the role of the state in mediating the excess violence of capitalism. What is evidenced in the AmeriCorps program, and in the civic engagement argument more broadly, is the fetishization of democracy. Fetishism, within Marx's conceptual economy, refers to a very specific mode of thinking and being. It is a type of reification, which is a way of thinking that objectifies social processes and relations and turns them into things. As a form of reification, fetishism is special because of the consequences of this way of thinking. Again, as Allman describes, through fetishistic thought "the attributes and powers, the essence, of the person or social relation appear as natural, intrinsic, attributes or power of the 'thing' . . . social relations between people are misconstrued as relations between things."[2] Fetishism not only turns processes and relations into things, it obscures the human agency and activity at the core of our social relations.

I have attempted to demonstrate the ways in which teaching and learning about democracy through the concept of civic engagement embodies profound and violent abstractions from the historical, social, and material reality we live within. I have also attempted to move us beyond an argument of bad versus good ways to talk about democracy, or that it is sufficient to struggle against neoliberalism apart from the broader historical struggle against capitalism. I have argued against the reification of democracy as a set of ideals, practices, or modes of governance that can be discussed abstractly or philosophically apart from the actual world and its historical constitution. I have done this because I believe we are at a crucial moment in which we cannot continue to recycle the same platitudes about a political system that does not work for the majority of people, and that was never designed to do so. I believe that getting beyond a "better democracy" argument means thinking outside the borders that the concept of democracy imposes on our thinking and our ways of living; it means examining the social relations that constitute democracy in our world and seriously considering if this is how we want to live and, of course, whether we are capable of more.

The problem I have attempted to illuminate is also that the ways we teach about democracy, and pedagogically how we approach the notion, play a tremendous role in normalizing and naturalizing the underlying and essential relations of capitalist democracy, thus forcing us into modes of analysis that are cut off from deeper, more revolutionary forms of praxis. In that way, we become locked in cycles of reformist, albeit often progressive, modes of analysis and social change; we leave undisturbed the bedrock relations of injustice and violence in our society; we cut ourselves off from the forms of knowledge and struggle necessary to address them. The ideology of civic engagement renders invisible, both in thought and action, the constitutive relations of capitalism that create the very needs of communities in the first place. The ultimate cost of this ideology, I believe, is the reification of the social relations of capitalism, which has the effect of fragmenting reality and undermining the emergence of solidarities that we desperately need. These solidarities will not be created without a painful, even violent, struggle to bring them into being and not without our utter commitment to their necessity. Because I have written this text for educators, I am going to focus on the problems before them, which are pedagogical in character. These problems have to do with the production of knowledge and the facilitation of learning as well as the relation between the two.

I believe that all purposeful social change, any kind of critical praxis, is fundamentally a pedagogical project. If we cannot learn to think about ourselves, our planet, and the other people and species on this planet differently, then we have nothing ahead of us except the barbarism and ecocide we seemed headed toward in this particular moment. At the same time, I also believe that there is only so much our consciousness can change without engaging in historical struggle with others. It is in and through struggle that we begin to think about how we might live differently and how we might reorganize our social relations. It is through these relations that we come to recognize the limitations of our own thinking and ways of being. This leaves us with a conundrum. Learning is necessarily relational, but the experiences necessary for this kind of learning are not accessible to educators unless they go out and forge relationships. To participate in the creation of these spaces, we must think differently and work relationally, which is extremely difficult. The work of critical education is, as described by Paula Allman, the ongoing work of self-social transformation.[3] This is the possibility and limitation of praxis.

I also believe that the work of critical education needs to change in some key ways in order for us to be able to contend with the reformist and reactionary tendencies we see present in the ideology of civic engagement and to begin to talk about the ways in which "learning for democracy" traps our thinking and our political imagination. For too long, the assumptions guiding critical education work have been premised on a reductive critique of capitalism, a fragmentation of the political and the material, a marginalization and often a dismissal of feminist antiracist anticolonialist scholarship, a fear of radical and collectivized social change, and a preoccupation with fixing consciousness. Most critical educators I have encountered operate within a perverse inversion of the banking model, Freire's now classical critique of the commodification of knowledge and its pedagogical realization in didactic, nondialogical teaching methods.[4] The problem, as many educators have articulated it, is that their students, be they children or young adults or the "oppressed" or the "community," do not have the "correct" analysis. They do not have the "right" consciousness; they are not critical or "awake," and they may even be suffering from false consciousness. None of this, in my opinion, is helpful. The attempt to replace the wrong consciousness with the right one does not actually facilitate the emergence of historical actors who are ready to take up social struggle. Further, if we as educators follow this logic we risk developing our teaching into another iteration of teaching through domination, another banking model run amok.[5] This mode of conceptualizing consciousness cannot negate the contradiction between teaching and learning established within capitalist social relations, specifically knowledge relationships premised on power, accumulation, and privatization. It is therefore not able to address the epistemological and ontological fragmentation of capitalist social relations. It also cannot imagine learning as anything other than the accumulation of the "right" pieces of knowledge, and it absolutely cannot recognize the complexity of knowledge that will be necessary to not only understand the histories and realities of capitalism, but also actualize its transformation.

What is required to begin this work, I argue, is the ability to think about how you think. This is not some empty call for critical thinking; it is a robust call for a particular kind of critical thinking, one that does not shy away from historical materialist critique and aims to expand that critique into the fulsomeness of the social relations of capitalism and its constitution through colonialism, imperialism, and patriarchy. Rehistoricizing and rematerializing critical education praxis ultimately means shifting our focus from the function and content of ideology to the social relations that produce ideologies in the first place. I believe this can only be done through a return to a dialectical epistemology and ontology that is based on understanding material reality as cooperative social relations and relations with the earth. This means: (1) pushing our understanding of our material reality into its constitutive relations; and (2) locating problems of ideology in the dislocations (both spatial and temporal) of these material relations, not in idealist constructions or fetishized activities.

At the end of every course I teach, I always tell my students that the end of any learning experience, be it a class or a text, is both a point of arrival and a point of departure. As a researcher and writer, this text for me has posed a tremendous challenge for my own learning; for readers, I imagine it has challenged some and (hopefully) offered something to be learned. In this way, we have together, both writer and reader, come to understand new ideas about learning and democracy. What we have come to understand should serve to spin us into something else; we will jump off from here, whether you as a reader agree with what has been written or not. In this way, we have arrived and we must depart. In that same way, I want to conclude this text by situating the implications of this analysis of the ideology of civic engagement within the broader conceptualization of how we should respond as educators and scholars of education to our historical moment. In what follows, I will elaborate on the two points I raised in the previous paragraph: what it means to push our thinking toward the constitutive relations of our material reality and to locate the problems of ideology within that reality.

Returning to Social Relations:
History, Materiality, and Ideology in Praxis

There are many ways I could approach the two points I've made above. The way I want to do this, however, is by respectfully referencing a teaching from Faith Spotted Eagle, a Yankton Sioux Nation elder and a leader of the resistance at Standing Rock against the continued dispossession of Indigenous people. In January of 2017 she gave an interview that was distributed by Longhouse Media. In it, she discussed the problem of non-Indigenous people coming to the encampment at Standing Rock. She summed up the challenge of the presence of non-Indigenous people very succinctly; our challenge, she said, is "not to reify colonialism,"[6] that is, not to turn colonialism into a historical event, something over and done, rather than recognize it as the social relations we continue to live within. To reify something, again, is to turn a process and a relation into an object; in this case to turn colonialism into an historical artifact. Because the non-Indigenous allies at the camp do not fully recognize the realities of colonialism as the foundational social relations of the United States, she describes settlers joining the resistance at Standing Rock as allies and very quickly attempting to "settle" the encampment by marking off territory in the camp and privatizing space. They have, she says succinctly, "that settler mind."[7] In my study I have taken up a similar challenge, of not reifying democracy, although I have not taken it far enough. I want to examine now how Faith Spotted Eagle's challenge pushes back against my own account of the ideology of civic engagement and through this to demonstrate what I mean by the need to rehistoricize and rematerialize any kind of critical education for democracy.

By way of review, I began this text with a particular problem, which was to understand how civic engagement is constituted as a thing that can be learned. This was a different kind of question than research to understand what young people learn about civic engagement through their participation in AmeriCorps. I engaged in a dialectical analysis of the program, which meant, from the outset, not to begin the research from the concept of civic engagement, but from a human activity that people call civic engagement. To do this, I selected a practice, community service, and an institutionalized form in which this practice takes place. I did this because I wanted to understand how this practice can be understood as civic engagement within the confines of a state-sponsored program that was explicitly aiming to craft political participation among young adults. I asked questions concerning under what conditions civic engagement can be learned through the experience of community service in this federally sponsored program. Thinking dialectically also meant historicizing the practice of community service as civic engagement within a broader set of social relations. I argued that it was through these relations of state and civil society that the equation of national civilian service with community service came into being and that it was within a particular historical moment that this articulation of service became a form of citizen participation. I also tried to ground the pedagogical argument that community service is a way to "learn democracy" within its historical emergence, both its initial iteration in the progressive reform movement of the early twentieth century and its reenvisioning during the emergence of a civil society discourse in the late twentieth century. I then grounded the study of AmeriCorps within an analysis of its particular institutional context, which allowed me to understand what institutional relationships shape the way civic engagement can be conceptualized and practiced by actors within the program. Based on this ethnographic research, I argued that in addition to the explicit institutional regulations that govern permissible and sanctioned democracy within the program, there are also implicit regulations within it that exert a great deal of force on the activity of people. These regulations are crucially involved in the circulation of knowledge within the program. I located particular forms of abstraction in experience and knowledge as the terrain on which the idea of democracy can be engaged within the program and then demonstrated how this notion of democracy becomes the basis of an articulation of civic engagement. I attempted to show how the concept and practice of democracy are also abstractions from the material relations of the capitalist mode of production. I concluded this analysis with the argument that the ideology of civic engagement is the fetishization of democracy and the reification of democracy in a particular way, a process that ultimately renders invisible the social relations that constitute society itself.

Why did I do this? I could have easily developed a survey of the knowledge, skills, and attitudes of civic engagement (many such tools already exist) and administered this survey to AmeriCorps participants or some other group that regularly participates in community service. As I have discussed, there are many such studies already in existence, and there are also many studies that detail how difficult it is for young people to learn the hard lessons of democracy. Democracy, in that body of research, is understood to be a hard thing to do. It involves negotiating and navigating complex interests and positions. It requires a great deal of intellectual, emotional, and physical labor and an outstanding moral, secular commitment to the ideal of a democratic society. I rejected this approach because I did not want to reify democracy; that is, I did not want to impose it on young people as something outside of them that they must internalize and then do properly. I also did not want to treat democracy as if it was a rose among thorns, perfect except for that which tries to corrupt it. I have learned enough from the historical study of democracy to know that this is not the case. But above all, I was attempting to learn to do research following Marx's critique of ideological processes and utilizing Dorothy Smith's interpretation of this critique. To summarize, she argues that

> This critique is not simply of an idealist theory that represents society and history as determined by consciousness but of methods of reasoning that treat concepts, even of those of political economy, as determinants. His view of how consciousness is determined historically by our social being does not envisage some kind of mechanical transfer from 'economic structure' or 'material situation' to consciousness. Rather, he works with an epistemology that takes the concepts foundational to political economy as expressions or reflections of the social relations of a mode of production. The difference between ideology and science is the difference between treating concepts as the primitives of theory and treating them as sites for exploring the social relations that are expressed in them.[8]

I committed myself to begin not from the concept of democracy or its expression in the concept of civic engagement, but rather in the practice of human beings, organized and coordinated as social relations. The challenge here was to constantly and consistently locate inquiry in social relations and to not revert to the reification of any aspect of the research—including the reification of my critique itself—as the "ideology of civic engagement." Again, the challenge to think against reification is the challenge to think of our world as constituted through processes and relations and not as the accumulation of things, whether those things are events, people, or even time.

This struggle, which is really the only word that can describe this process, has also been a struggle for understanding this mode of critique and its political application. When Faith Spotted Eagle says that the challenge at Standing Rock is to not reify colonialism, she is reminding us that colonialism is not a thing in the past; it is the relations we live within on this land and in relation to the land. It is not just the exercising of white privilege by allies at the encampment, and it is not just the actions they take that contradict their stated beliefs. It is the praxis they engage within that reproduces, concretizes, and normalizes the social relations of colonialism and capitalism. This reification can happen anywhere and anytime, including within this research despite my struggle. Arriving at this point of departure in my own scholarship is part of that same struggle.

It is with this in mind that I argue that those with the heart and soul for critical education work must take up these challenges posed by reification and engage in efforts to rehistoricize and rematerialize critical education praxis. I say this because critical educators have not easily integrated forms of knowledge based in feminist, antiracist, and anticolonial praxis. It has led to an inability to reckon with the relationship between capitalist modes of domination and those based in gender, sexuality, and race. It has led to us now being unable to grasp some of the clear limits on our own thinking. We have a long history in critical education of a limited articulation of the relationship between our material reality and our social relations, including, crucially, our modes of consciousness. Glenn Rikowski, I believe, has done the necessary work for understanding how, specifically within educational theory, we have labored to our own detriment under nondialectical conceptualizations of social relations.[9] To think nondialectically about social relations is to pull them apart from one another, either assuming they have an independent existence or that they relate in an external way. Twenty years ago, Rikowski laid these problems out clearly. He argued that Marxist educational theorizing suffered from five key "debilitating theoretical problematic": the base-superstructure metaphor, the influence of structural functionalism, the concept of relative autonomy, resistance theory, and the "tension between education autonomy and socialism."[10] I'm not going to repeat his analysis here, but the major problem that Rikowski identifies is a mode of interpretation based in objectification, reification, fragmentation, and, ultimately, ossified theory. This happens when we do things like think about "the economy" as a thing outside of ourselves made by people who do high-end drugs and wear expensive suits. Or we think of it as natural like the weather and as containing its own logic that goes on and on independent of human beings taking action in society. Or we think of it without history, as this is just always how it has been, can be, will be. There's even an acronym for this: TINA (which stands for there is no alternative). Or we think that "the economy" determines all. This problem of thinking nondialectically is also what constitutes the whole of the analysis in *The German Ideology*. To separate the relation of our material lives from our cultural lives, that is, to think that the ways in which we produce and reproduce life itself are not also historically specific, in actuality further reifies both aspects of this relation. Our material ways of subsistence and our relation to the planet become fixed and transhistorical; our cultural ways of being, thinking, and doing become natural to either our biology or to particular groups. We can then argue about which aspect of this fragmented whole determines the other. Neither of these approaches allows us to be conscious, living, acting human beings who live in—and through our living make—intricate webs of social relations.

What would it mean to think about social relations in a dialectical way? This is the entirety of Marx's intellectual project, and since we cannot reproduce here those many thousands of pages, we can begin with just a little sentence: "The chief defect of all hitherto existing materialism . . . is that the thing, reality, sensuousness, is conceived only in the form of the *object or of contemplation*, but not as *sensuous human activity, practice*, not subjectively."[11] This opening sentence of the first thesis on Feuerbach is very famous, and for a very good reason. It points to an important distinction in the ways in which we can think about our social reality. We can think of social reality as a thing that exists outside of us, that is as fixed and natural as a mineral deposit, or we can think of it as something that human beings create for themselves through their conscious activity, meaning their ways of thinking, being, seeing, and doing. Immediately, however, my mineral deposit analogy breaks down. Solid stone, as the saying goes, is just sand and water and a million years gone by. When I visited Death Valley, I was captivated by the beauty of the mineral deposits in the landscape. They have been there for a very long time, a longer history than my mind can grasp, but in order for them to be there many other things had to happen in very specific ways. The mineral in the rock has its own history; it is not pregiven, but made from many different forces interacting with one another, their action of course being influenced by those forces acting on them: sand, water, time. To think about human relations dialectically means exactly this; conscious people, living with each other, within historical conditions.

It is very difficult to learn to think dialectically. It might not actually be something you learn, that is, have mastery over, but a way of seeing the world that you are constantly coaxing from yourself despite all the challenges of fragmentation and abstraction in daily life. There is a danger here, and it is something I have done in the past. While one can *materialize* their thinking about social reality, it is equally required to *socialize* one's thinking about material reality. Both of these require historical analysis to accomplish. What I mean by this is that the danger can be found in reifying capitalism or, said differently, not taking the dialectics of capitalism far enough. For example, I believe this is what Fanon meant when he argued that Marxist analysis must be "slightly stretched every time we have to do with the colonial problem."[12] "Slightly stretched" is perhaps too kind. I would argue that Marxist analysis must incorporate Fanon's insights into its center. The colonial problem is not dislocated from capitalism temporally or spatially. It is a problem in the colonies, it is a problem in the land of the colonizers, it is a problem in the settlement, it is a problem for the whole world—and one that involves the whole world. Colonialism in all its dirty workings, including settlement, appropriation, dispossession, enslavement, genocide, erasure, and exploitation, was the strategy that allowed for the development of the capitalism we now live. As Leanne Simpson has argued, settler colonialism remains a principle form of extraction of value from land and people.[13] The stretching has to include not just the social relations of race wrought by the colonial project, but the relations of gender transformed through this history, as patriarchy was a precondition for the transformation of exploitation into capitalist exploitation in Europe.[14] What I and many Marxists have done in the past is to follow the first thesis on Feuerbach to its conclusion as it relates to the constitution and transformation of labor in the abstract. There is always a relation, however, between abstract and concrete labor. Labor is also concrete and embodied because it is done by a person, with their body and mind, under definite historical conditions and within specific social relations. It cannot be taken out of history and it cannot be removed from social relations. This means that understanding how "sensuous human activity" actually happens, how certain ways of being, doing, and thinking have emerged out of other historical forms, how embodied labor becomes abstract labor with the relations of the capitalist mode of production, and how power is organized within these relations is necessary to shift our thinking toward a more coherent understanding of our world, one that is premised on people actively making their social reality.

The other manner in which this stretching and pushing—perhaps pulling—of dialectics is necessary is in having to look to not only the constitution and transformation of labor, but of land as well. Peter Linebaugh, in discussing the criminalization of customary rights, Marcus Rediker, in a history of the slave trade, and together in their analysis of the relations across the Atlantic, have made a key observation about land: not only is land a crucial mechanism for the accumulation of capital, it must also be transformed or readied so as to be a site of accumulation.[15] Within a capitalist mode of production, the activity of people, including the technologies they develop, and land are the only ways in which value, and thus wealth, can be created. For this reason, so much of our history of conflict and war is centrally tied to controlling people and land. Taken a step further, these conflicts are often about dictating the terms on which people access their material subsistence and ensuring that this access does not occur through a direct relationship with land. We live a profoundly alienated existence from our environment, and the consequences of that alienation have captured our attention thanks to movements against ecocide. However, by focusing on consequences, we make it difficult to understand what the roots of these problems are and how those roots can change and emerge as new forms of exploitation and violence. Enclosures and colonization are processes of transforming land and people and peoples' relationships with land into a privatized, objectified relation. Without a historical understanding of this material and social process, we cannot understand it or what we must do today to address it. When we do this work, as educators, we can begin to understand how the way we live is constituted through gendered and racialized relations as well as how gendered and racialized relations are used to constitute land as an object for capitalist accumulation. Here also, people are part of the land; they too must be transformed. Historical analysis helps us to know and understand these processes as part of our reality; historicizing critical education helps us to internalize these relations and understand their constitution in the modes of ideology we presently live within.

There are two interrelated implications of this argument for critical education praxis. The first is, perhaps obviously, that pedagogically the focus should shift toward understanding the historical preconditions of our contemporary moment, including the forms of consciousness and ideology that are, and have been, part of this history. This is the only way to avoid the reification of the past, present, and future; it requires a turn away from a sole emphasis on the deconstructive critique of ideology as systems of thought or the teaching of the categories and concepts of critical analysis of political economy. There is a place for these approaches, but I am suggesting that we should turn to teaching Marx's method of historical study. This leads to the second implication, which is that the study of ideology must be grounded in the study of the social relations that produce particular forms of experiential and epistemological abstraction. This is where an understanding of Marx's argument around ideology is key. When we equate the notion of ideology with discourse, we abstract ideas from the material and social relations in which they are generated. When we are captured by a reified ideology, we participate in the ideas of the ruling class and as such abstract those ideas from social relations, but we also turn a process of knowledge creation into a thing. We then focus our critique on the ideas rather than the social relations that produce the ideas.

The theorization of ideology—and pedagogically what to do—within critical education theory has been plagued by the same problems in dialectical conceptualization that have undermined our attempts at understanding the constitutive relations of our social reality. I have written about the problem of ideology extensively with my collaborator Shahrzad Mojab, but I will say briefly that the major problem in this articulation is the separation and reification of thinking from being.[16] Because of this reification, we have a wide variety of ways of understanding what ideology means. I discussed this issue in chapter 2 of this book, but to briefly revisit this argument, ideology often stands in for the concept of "ideas," sometimes understood as systems of ideas. In this instance, ideologies have particular characteristics and can be grouped; for example, the ideology of multiculturalism. Depending on one's mode of analysis, ideologies can be relative or not; as a system of ideas, everyone can have ideology regardless of whether or not that ideology has any social power. We can have liberal media elite ideology and a conservative ideology. You can even have no ideology and claim neutrality, objectivity, for example, as when Obama asserted that "being pragmatic" is not contaminated by ideology.[17] For others, ideology is only meaningful when we are talking about, as Marx and Engels famously said, "the ideas of the ruling class."[18] To my way of thinking, this reduction is equally problematic. The consequences of such a way of thinking can be profound. Notice here that the emphasis is on the *content* of thought.

For others, ideology is only ever illusion. Ideology represents systems of ideas that cover up what is really happening in society, creating fictions and fantasies that distract us from understanding what is going on around us. To this way of thinking, ideology is like some kind of beautiful toxic mist, obscuring our thought and clouding our vision. I think that this conceptualization of ideology confuses its form with its function. Ideology does act to obscure and to make certain aspects of reality not visible to us. And, yes, there are people in the world who are propagating particular ideas so that we don't see what they are doing and why. Many of these people are political strategists, creating discourses and code words and ways of talking about the world that cloud our thinking and judgment as they work very hard to convince us of the reality of those words. But this understanding of ideology leaves unresolved the question of why these modes of thinking, why these ideologies, emerge in the first place and operate so powerfully. It also leaves us in the political position of looking for the Wizard of Oz.

But ideology, in Marx's conceptual universe, is fundamentally about processes of abstraction. It is about knowledge created through dislocation from processes of material production and within social relations that organize that dislocation. It is about the production of ideas being separated from, both experientially and philosophically, what is happening within people's lives under specific historical conditions. Earlier in this book, I used the example of walking home from my office and thinking about the road on which I am walking. I talked about the numerous forms of abstraction that are required in order for me to not think about the land beneath my feet in its historical context. Through those abstractions, I am able to obscure the relationship between the road and the settler colonial history of where I live and my own history within this relationship. I also talked about how I am experiencing the road as a road, not as these social relations although these social relations are present. This is the temporal and spatial dislocation of these capitalist social relations. There are particular systems of thought that obscure this reality or normalize this abstraction, but the process of creating knowledge from within these dislocations makes ideology feel real. Thus, there is nothing really illusory or fantastical about it. When we understand ideology as a form of praxis, then we direct our attention to the inner relation between abstracted forms of knowledge and practice that normalizes those abstractions. To be caught in the midst of it is a kind of uncritical reproductive praxis.[19]

By way of example, let me speak to three issues that have contextualized the debate around democracy in America's current historical moment. The first is fascist and white supremacist campaign against immigration. The second is the debate around gun control. The third is the struggle around police and state violence, particularly in relation to the African American community. The terms of these debates are premised on the reification of colonialism, both settler colonialism in North America and the colonization of Africa resulting in the slave trade and also the ongoing imperialist conquest of Asia, Latin America, Africa, and the Middle East. All of the relations of racism and patriarchy are present in this reification as well. For example, concerning immigration, we ignore the historical continuity of settler colonialism when we argue positions for or against the "Americanness" of open borders. When we debate gun violence, we forget who was given the right to bear arms against whom. When we defend police violence, we forget how our police forces came into existence and who they were designed to police. It is actually not accurate to say that this has been forgotten; we don't teach these histories and tell these stories and so they are actively obscured, not passively lost to time.

A very common response from self-identified critical educators is to insist that these problems are antithetical to democracy. This response could be characterized as what Keeanga-Yamahtta Taylor (and many others) refers to as "American exceptionalism." She argues that "American exceptionalism operates as a mythology of convenience that does a tremendous amount of work to simplify the contradiction between the apparent creed of US society and its much more complicated reality."[20] American exceptionalism, for the political left, is the idea that democracy, in some ideal form, is our weapon against fascism and capitalism. American exceptionalism is premised on Indigenous erasure. Alternatively, we could also critique these debates as representative of particular ideologies and thus begin a process of unpacking the ideological composition of these problems. I suggest a different way; rather than beginning from the standpoint of critiquing ideology alone, we begin from the commitment to examine social relations through historical study. We can then ask what kinds of abstractions have been made, what kinds of relations have been reified, and what kinds of separations are necessary to produce the common sense ways in which we talk about these problems. It is a redirection away from studying the "mythology" and back toward "the complicated reality" in order to understand the very emergence of the mythology.

Final Thought: The Way Out Is Back Through

I do not remember exactly when I learned this phrase "the way out is back through." I do remember it was in a community discussion of the language we use to describe terrible events: Nakba, Maafa, Holocaust. I was young when it was taught to me, perhaps only eighteen or nineteen years old. It has always echoed in my mind, a reminder of the value of the past and its relationship to the present and future. To me this has always been the purpose of learning, especially a kind of learning that wants to change the world. If we are able to do what I have suggested in this chapter, I think we will be better able to engage with the complexities of social relations as well as with modes of critique that isolate or fragment the social totality. This means being able to address settler colonialism, imperialism, white supremacy, heteropatriarchy, and ableism as social forces and constitutive relations of capitalist accumulation. I believe this is the future direction of Marxian analysis in education.

The kind of learning and teaching that I am advocating is based in struggle, and because struggle is upheaval it leads to some kind of suffering for someone.[21] When I was a young(er) adult, one of my mentors in community work explained the animosity I was experiencing within a workplace as a "propensity to speak truth to power." It got me in trouble, quite often, and manifested the alienation I felt at a level that could not be ignored. Not only could I feel it, but the people around me could see it. It resulted not so much in the burning of bridges as the closing quietly of doors behind oneself as you leave. I went through a long period of silencing myself as I thought through the consequences of this kind of act. This process was painful and shameful because there are of course multiple sets of consequences; those that emerge if you do speak and those that emerge when you do not. There are also many forms of struggle, but the ones, in my experience, that lead to deep-rooted transformation hurt like hell.

For those who find or have found themselves deeply wedded to American democracy, I expect this text has been very difficult to read. I sympathize because I have been through the experience of breaking apart the belief that we can carry on as we have with just a little bit more fairness, justice, and equality. I have also tried to see my way around the idea that the only way out is back through. But my study and my attempt at building relations in this world has led me to an inevitable conclusion that has been pointed out in far more powerful ways by many before me—the American dream is a nightmare. In my opinion this is the only moral conclusion one can come to in the study of history. The difficult paradox is that this nightmare has produced some of the most important tools we have in dismantling it, but let's stop lying to ourselves about this reality. The American dream is a constant dissonance. It is not a dream in the sense of fantasy; this has all been very real. This is not a fatalism or nihilism. I am proposing that any kind of learning for democracy must be first and foremost a kind of reckoning, but one that is based in a deep love for the possibility of humanity. I do believe we can have a different society. It will be much harder than we thought. That is a terrible reality to contend with, but it is necessary if we are to move through and beyond where we are now.

The very last thing I will say about the need to rehistoricize and thus rematerialize critical education is this: We are within history all the time, like waves in the ocean. We have to understand ourselves as part of this continuity between the generations before and the generations after. We cannot understand ourselves as part of a process of change if we do not understand ourselves as part of the process of what *has* changed and *how* it has changed.

Notes

Chapter 1

1. David McNally, *The Global Slump: The Economics and Politics of Crisis and Resistance* (Oakland, CA: PM Press, 2011), 24.

2. Stuart Hall, "Race, Articulation and Societies Structured in Dominance," in *Sociological Theories: Race and Colonialism*, edited by Bernan Associates (Hamburg, Germany: UNESCO, 1980), 341.

3. Julia Berndt and Cara James, *The Effects of the Economic Recession on Communities of Color, Issue Brief No. 7953* (Menlo Park, CA: Henry J. Kaiser Family Foundation, 2009), 2. www.kff.org/minorityhealth/upload/7953.pdf.

4. Barack Obama. "Presidential address announcing United We Serve program," Speech, Washington, DC, June 17, 2009. https://obamawhitehouse.archives.gov/blog/2009/06/17/united-we-serve.

5. Jean Bricmont, *Humanitarian Imperialism: Using Human Rights to Sell War* (New York: Monthly Review Press, 2006), 105.

6. Ellen Meiksins Wood, "Democracy as Ideology of Empire," in *The New Imperialist: Ideologies of Empire*, edited by Colin Mooers (Oxford, UK: Oneworld, 2006), 11.

7. Slavoj Žižek, "Afterword: Lenin's Choice," in *Revolution at the Gates: A Selection of Writings from February to October 1917*, edited by Slavoj Žižek (London: Verso, 2002), 167.

8. Keeanga-Yamahtta Taylor, *From #BlackLivesMatter to Black Liberation* (Chicago, IL: Haymarket Press, 2016), 131.

9. Teresa Ebert, *Ludic Feminism and After: Postmodernism, Desire, and Labor in Late Capitalism* (Ann Arbor: University of Michigan Press, 1996), 150.

10. Saskia Sassen, *Expulsions: Brutality and Complexity in the Global Economy* (Cambridge, MA: Belkamp, 2014), 215.

11. Samir Amin, *The Liberal Virus: Permanent War and the Americanization of the World* (New York: Monthly Review Press, 2004), 24.

12. This is an obvious reference to Heidi Hartmann's famous essay on the unhappy marriage of Marxism and feminism. See Heidi Hartmann. "The Unhappy Marriage of Marxism and Feminism: Towards a More Progressive Union," *Capital & Class 3*, no. 2 (1979): 1–33. For a substantial treatment of this argument see Himani Bannerji, *Thinking Through: Essays on Feminism, Marxism, and Anti-Racism* (Toronto, ON: Canada Womens' Press, 1995) and Shahrzad Mojab, "Introduction: Marxism and Feminism" in *Marxism and Feminism*, edited by Shahrzad Mojab (London: Zed Books, 2015).

13. For Bertell Ollman's expansive work on the philosophy of dialectics, see Bertell Ollman, *Dialectical Investigations* (New York: Routledge, 1993) and Bertell Ollman, *Dance of the Dialectic. Steps in Marx's Method* (Champaign-Urbana: University of Illinois Press, 2003).

14. Paula Allman, *Revolutionary Social Transformation: Democratic Hopes, Political Possibilities, and Critical Education* (Westport, CT: Bergin & Garvey, 1999), 63.

15. Ollman, *Dialectical Investigations*, 10.

16. Karl Marx, "Theses on Feuerbach," in *The German Ideology* (Moscow: Progress, 1968), 662.

17. This argument is elaborated throughout the entirety of *The German Ideology*, but particularly in part I.

18. Karl Marx and Friedrich Engels, *The German Ideology* (Moscow: Progress, 1968), 31.

19. Paula Allman, and John Wallis, "Praxis: Implications for 'Really' Radical Education," *Studies in the Education of Adults* 22, no. 1 (1990): 15.

20. Peter David Thomas, *The Gramscian Moment: Philosophy, Hegemony, and Marxism* (Chicago, IL: Haymarket Books, 2011), 3.

21. Marx, "Theses on Feuerbach," 659. Emphasis in original.

22. It is imperative to note, especially for the extension of Marx and Engel's argument into the actual social relations in which we live, that we understand "the material," the objective reality as being culturally constituted. To be clear, by "material" I do not mean economic in some abstract, mechanical way. I mean the socially organized, conscious, and sensuous ways that human beings go about producing and reproducing a mode of life, both in its social and material forms. This implies that culture is not separate from or determined by materiality, but is itself material in that materiality is produced through human relations that are cultural. Forms, appearances, and systems of meaning that may popularly be understood as "cultural" are thus material in character, and our material reality is constituted through these forms and meanings. This has real consequences in the conceptualization of social difference, identity, and forms of power, as I will discuss in later chapters. For further elaboration of the culture–materiality dialect, see Himani Bannerji, *Thinking Through*; Himani Bannerji, "Building from Marx: Reflections on Class and Race," *Social Justice* 32, no. 4 (2005): 144–60; Himani Bannerji, *Demography and Democracy: Essays on Nationalism, Gender, and Ideology* (Toronto, ON: Canadian Scholars' Press, 2011).

23. Sara Carpenter and Shahrzad Mojab, eds., *Educating from Marx: Race, Gender, and Learning* (New York: Palgrave, 2011); Sara Carpenter, "Centering Marxist Feminism in Adult Learning," *Adult Education Quarterly* 62, no. 1 (2012): 19–35; Sara Carpenter and Shahrzad Mojab, *Revolutionary Learning: Marxism, Feminism and Knowledge* (London: Pluto, 2017).

24. Allman, *On Marx*, 37.

25. Carpenter and Mojab, *Revolutionary*, 50.

26. Alan Sears and James Cairns, *A Good Book, In Theory*, 2nd ed. (Toronto, ON: University of Toronto Press, 2015), 85.

27. Allman, *On Marx*, 32.

28. Allman, *On Marx*, 33.

29. I am thinking here of the first few chapters of *Capital Volume 1*, but also of a thread of analysis that moves through the *Grundrisse*. For a discussion of this see David Harvey, *A Companion of Marx's Capital: Vol. 1* (London: Verso, 2010).

30. A good overview of the "third way" articulation and some of its detractors can be found in Anthony Giddens, *The Third Way and Its Critics* (London: Polity, 2000).

31. This argument is developed throughout John Ehrenberg, *Civil Society: A Critical History of an Idea* (New York: New York University Press, 1999).

32. Derek Sayer, "The Critique of Politics and Political Economy: Capitalism, Communism, and the State in Marx's Writing of the Mid-1840s," *Sociological Review* 33, no. 2 (1985): 225.

33. Michael Edwards, *Civil Society*, 2nd ed. (Cambridge, UK: Polity, 2009), 9.

34. Alex Callinicos, *Social Theory: A Historical Introduction* (New York: New York University Press, 1999), 36.

35. Christopher J. Arthur, ed. "Editor's Introduction" in *The German Ideology: Part One* (New York: International Publishers, 1991), 5.

36. Sayer, "Critique of Politics," 236.

37. Throughout this research I drew heavily from Ellen Meiksins Wood's extensive scholarship on the historical transition from feudalism to capitalism. The point I am referencing is made in several texts, but for the most explicit discussion see Ellen Meiksins Wood, *Democracy Against Capitalism: Renewing Historical Materialism* (Cambridge, UK: Cambridge University Press, 1995).

38. Karl Marx, *Capital, Volume 1* (New York: International Publishers, 1967), 713.

39. Bannerji, "Building from Marx," 147.

40. To see this argument expanded across Marxist feminist scholarship see: Leopoldina Fortunati, *The Arcane of Reproduction* (Brooklyn: Autonomedia, 1995); Maria Mies. *Patriarchy and Accumulation on a World Scale*, 2nd ed. (London: Zed Books, 1998); Silvia Federici, *Caliban and the Witch: Women, the Body, and Primitive Accumulation* (Brooklyn, NY: Autonomedia, 2004).

41. Federici, *Caliban*, 104.

42. Bannerji, "Building from Marx," 147.
43. Dorothy Smith, "Ideology, Science, and Social Relations: A Reinterpretation of Marx's Epistemology," *European Journal of Social Theory* 7, no. 4 (2004): 445.
44. Dorothy Smith, *The Conceptual Practices of Power: A Feminist Sociology of Knowledge* (Boston, MA: Northeastern University Press, 1990), 33.
45. Dorothy Smith, *Writing the Social: Critique, Theory, and Investigations* (Toronto, ON: University of Toronto Press, 1999), 98.
46. Allman, *Revolutionary*, 37.
47. Dorothy Smith, *Institutional Ethnography: A Sociology for People* (Lanham, MD: AltaMira Press, 2005), 35.
48. Karl Marx, "The Eighteenth Brumaire of Louis Bonaparte," in *The Marx-Engels Reader*, edited by Robert Tucker (London: Norton, 1978), 595.
49. Smith, *Institutional Ethnography*, 56.
50. Smith, *Institutional Ethnography*, 13.
51. Smith, *Writing*, 73.
52. Smith, *Institutional Ethnography*, 13.
53. Allman, *Revolutionary*, 37.
54. Smith, *Writing*, 77.
55. Smith, *Writing*, 134.
56. Bryan Palmer, *Descent into Discourse: The Reification of Language and the Writing of Social History* (Philadelphia: Temple University Press, 1990), 25.
57. Smith, *Institutional Ethnography*, 17.
58. Smith, *Writing*, 80.
59. Smith, *Writing*, 80.
60. Smith, *Institutional Ethnography*, 111.
61. Marie Campbell and Francis Gregor, *Mapping Social Relations: A Primer in Doing Institutional Ethnography* (Aurora, ON: Garamond Press, 2002), 46.
62. Dorothy Smith and Catherine Schryer, "On Documentary Society," in *Handbook on Research on Writing: History, Society, School, Individual, Text*, edited by Charles Bazerman (New York: Routledge, 2008), 142.
63. Smith, *Writing*, 79.
64. Smith and Schryer, "On Documentary," 139.
65. Allman, *On Marx*, 37.
66. Ellen Pence's work with the Duluth Domestic Abuse Project is discussed extensively by Smith, *Institutional Ethnography*, 170.
67. Smith, *Institutional Ethnography*, 113.

Chapter 2

1. Peter Jarvis, *Learning in Later Life: An Introduction for Educators and Carers* (New York: Routledge, 2001), 46.

2. It is not entirely within, nor outside, the scope of this study to discuss the relationship between the state's project of domestic democracy promotion in the same historical moment that the American government began imperialist wars, primarily in the Middle East, under the rhetoric of "democracy promotion." Needless to say, this is a crucial historical linkage. For a good discussion of this relationship, see Adam Hanieh, *Lineages of Revolt: Issues of Contemporary Capitalism in the Middle East* (Chicago: Haymarket Books, 2013).

3. Robert Putnam. "Bowling Alone? America's Declining Social Capital," *Journal of Democracy* 6 (1995), 65–78.

4. Michel Crozier, Samuel P. Huntington, and Joji Watanuki, *The Crisis of Democracy: Report on the Governability of Democracies to the Trilateral Commission* (New York: New York University Press, 1975). The Trilateral Commission is a nongovernmental research and policy organization founded by David Rockefeller in 1973. It was founded with the purpose of aligning international policy between the major capitalist industrialist centers of North America, Europe, and Asia. http://trilateral.org/.

5. Crozier, Huntington, and Watanuki, *Crisis*, 162.

6. This argument is developed across the text. See Robert Bellah, Richard Madsen, William Sullivan, Ann Swidler, and Steven Tipton, *Habits of the Heart: Individualism and Commitment in American Life* (Berkeley: University of California Press, 1985).

7. William Kymlicka and Wayne Norman, "Return of the Citizen: A Survey of Recent Work in Citizenship Theory," *Ethics* 104, no. 2 (1994): 360.

8. National Commission on Civic Renewal, *A Nation of Spectators: How Civic Disengagement Weakens America and What We Can Do about It* (College Park, MD: University of Maryland, 1998).

9. For a discussion of the expansion of mandated civics curricula in the United States, see Alistair Ross, *A European Education: Citizenship, Identities and Young People* (Stoke-on-Trent: Trentham, 2008); Karen Kedrowski, "Civic Education by Mandate: A State-by-State Analysis," *PS: Political Science & Politics* 36, no. 2 (2003): 225–27; for international mandates see Ross, 2008.

10. Of particular interest in this regard is the development of positivist survey assessment of youth civic engagement, headquartered through the work CIRCLE (The Center for Information & Research on Civic Learning and Engagement). https://civicyouth.org/. For examples of this type of typology development see Judith Torney-Purta, John Schwille, and Jo-Ann Amadeo, *Civic Education across Countries: Twenty-Four National Case Studies from the IEA Civic Education Project* (Amsterdam: International Association for the Evaluation of Educational Achievement, 1999).

11. Joel Westheimer and Joseph Kahne, "What Kind of Citizen? The Politics of Educating for Democracy," *American Educational Research Journal* 41, no. 2 (2004): 240.

12. Sara Carpenter, "Examining the Social Relations of Learning Citizenship: Citizenship and Ideology in Adult Education," in *Educating from Marx:*

Race, Gender, and Learning, eds. Sara Carpenter and Shahrzad Mojab (New York: Palgrave, 2011), 65.

13. For foundational documents of the civic engagement and higher education argument see: Harry Boyte and Elizabeth Hollander, "Wingspread Declaration on Renewing the Civic Mission of the American Research University," *The Wingspread Conference*. Presented at the Wingspread Conference (Racine, WI: Wingspread Conference, 1999); Campus Compact, "President's Declaration on the Civic Responsibility of Higher Education," Campus Compact (Providence: Campus Compact, 2000), www.compact.org/resources/declaration.

14. For examples of the proliferation of civic engagement and higher education research, see: Anne Colby, Elizabeth Beaumont, Thomas Ehrlich, and Jason Stephens, *Educating Citizens: Preparing America's Undergraduates for Lives of Moral and Civic Responsibility* (New York: John Wiley & Sons, 2003); Thomas Ehrlich, ed., *Civic Responsibility and Higher Education* (Phoenix: American Council on Education & Oryx Press, 2000); Abby Kiesa, Alexander Orlowski, Peter Levine, Deborah Both, Emily Hogan Kirby, Mark Hugo Lopez, and Karlo Barrios Marcelo, *Millennials Talk Politics: A Study of College Student Political Engagement* (College Park: The Center for Information & Research on Civic Learning and Engagement, 2007).

15. For examples on the emphasis on civic engagement of youth beyond higher education, see: Eldin Fahmy, *Young Citizens: Young People's Involvement in Politics and Decision Making* (Farnham, UK: Ashgate, 2006); Peter Levine, *The Future of Democracy: Developing the Next Generation of American Citizens* (Boston, MA: Tufts University Press, 2007); Murray Print and Henry Milner, eds., *Civic Education and Youth Political Participation* (Rotterdam, the Netherlands: Sense Publishers, 2009); Craig Rimmerman, *The New Citizenship: Unconventional Politics, Activism, and Service* (Boulder, CO: Westview Press, 2011); James Youniss and Peter Levine, eds., *Engaging Young People in Civic Life* (Nashville, TN: Vanderbilt University Press, 2009); Cliff Zukin, Scott Keeter, Molly Andolina, Krista Jenkins, and Michael Delli Carpini, *A New Engagement? Political Participation, Civic Life, and the Changing American Citizen* (Oxford, UK: Oxford University Press, 2006).

16. Jennifer Simpson's work stands out in this regard for its critical engagement with the concept of civic engagement, although still struggling to make sense of this amorphous and a historical concept. See Jennifer Simpson, *Longing for Justice: Higher Education and Democracy's Agenda* (Toronto, ON: University of Toronto Press, 2014).

17. Joel Westheimer and Joseph Kahne, "What Kind of Citizen," 240.

18. Himani Bannerji, "The Tradition of Sociology and the Sociology of Tradition." *Qualitative Studies in Education* 16, no. 2 (2003): 159–60.

19. Stephen Goldsmith and David Eisner. *Corporation for National and Community Service Strategic Plan: 2006–2010* (Washington, DC: Corporation for National and Community Service, 2006): 3. https://www.nationalservice.gov/about/strategic-plan/2006-2010-strategic-plan.

20. Stephen Waldeman, *The Bill: How Legislation Really Becomes Law: A Case Study of the National Service Bill* (New York: Penguin, 1995), 5.

21. Corporation for National and Community Service. "What Is AmeriCorps?" last modified December 15, 2017. https://www.nationalservice.gov/programs/americorps/join-americorps/what-americorps.

22. For excellent historical accounts of these processes in North America see: Desmond King, *Making Americans: Immigration, Race, and the Origins of the Diverse Democracy* (Cambridge, MA: Harvard University Press, 2000); Lisa Lowe, *Immigrant Acts: On Asian American Cultural Politics* (Durham, NC: Duke University Press, 1996); Sunera Thobani, *Exalted Subjects: Studies in the Making of Race and Nation in Canada* (Toronto, ON: University of Toronto Press, 2007).

23. Robert A. Carlson, *The Quest for Conformity: Americanization through Education* (San Francisco, CA: Wiley, 1975), 108.

24. William James, "The Moral Equivalent of War," *Peace and Conflict: Journal of Peace Psychology* 1, no. 1 (1995): 25.

25. Donald Eberly and Michael Sherraden, "United States: Several Noteworthy Programs," in *The Moral Equivalent of War? A Study of Non-Military Service in Nine Nations*, edited by Donald Eberly and Michael Sherraden (New York: Greenwood, 1990), 116.

26. Michael Gillette, *Launching the War on Poverty: An Oral History* (New York: Oxford University Press, 1996), 2.

27. Robert F. Clark, *The War on Poverty: History, Selected Programs, and Ongoing Impact* (New York: University Press of America, 2002), 125.

28. Gillette, *Launching*, 238.

29. Melissa Bass, *The Politics and Civics of National Service: Lessons from the Civilian Conservation Corps, VISTA, and AmeriCorps* (Washington, DC: Brookings Institute Press, 2013), 90.

30. Clark, *War on Poverty*, 132.

31. Gillette, *Launching*, 294.

32. William Crook and Ross Thomas, *Warriors for the Poor: The Story of VISTA, Volunteers in Service to America* (New York: William Morrow, 1969), 61.

33. Melissa Bass, "National Service in America: Policy (Dis)Connections Over Time." CIRCLE Working Paper No. 11 (College Park: University of Maryland, 2003), 8. https://civicyouth.org/PopUps/WorkingPapers/WP11Bass.pdf.

34. Susan Chambre, "Kindling Points of Light: Volunteering as Public Policy," *Non-Profit and Voluntary Sector Quarterly* 18, no. 3 (1989): 256.

35. See Morris Janowitz, *The Reconstruction of Patriotism: Education for Civic Consciousness* (Chicago, IL: University of Chicago Press, 1983); Charles Moskos, *A Call to Civic Service: National Service for Country and Community* (New York: Free Press, 1988).

36. Janowitz, *Reconstruction of Patriotism*, 8.

37. Bass, "National Service," 9.
38. Moskos, *A Call*, 6.
39. 103rd Congress of the United States of America, *National and Community Service Trust Act of 1993*, PL 103-82 [H.R. 2010]: Subtitle C, Part 4.
40. David Osborne and Ted Gaebler, *Reinventing Government: How the Entrepreneurial Spirit Is Transforming the Public Sector* (New York: Plume, 1992), 16.
41. Bass, "National Service," 12.
42. George H. Bush, "State of the Union Address," Speech, Washington, DC, January 29, 2002. Accessed on December 10, 2010. https://georgewbush-whitehouse.archives.gov/news/releases/2002/01/20020129-11.html.
43. Barack Obama, "Obama Issues Call for Public Service," *The Caucus: The Politics and Government Blog of the Times*. New York Times, December 5, 2007. https://thecaucus.blogs.nytimes.com/2007/12/05/obama-issues-call-for-public-service/.
44. Barack Obama, "Obama, in Texas, Hails Bush I and Volunteerism: Remarks by President Obama at the 20th Anniversary of Points of Light." *Top of the Ticket, Los Angeles Times*, October 16, 2009. https://latimesblogs.latimes.com/washington/2009/10/barack-obama-george-h-w-bush-texas-speech-text.html.
45. Obama, "Call for Public Service," para. 1.
46. Michel Foucault, *The Birth of Biopolitics: Lectures at the College de France, 1978–79*, trans. Graham Burchell (New York: Picador, 2008), 19.
47. Foucault, *Birth of Biopolitics*, 18.
48. Mitchell Dean, *Governmentality: Power and Rule in Modern Society* (London: Sage, 1999), 19.
49. Dean, *Governmentality*, 18.
50. Barbara Cruikshank, *The Will to Empower: Democratic Citizens and Other Subjects* (Ithaca, NY: Cornell University Press, 1999), 4.
51. Soo Ah Kwon, *Uncivil youth: Race, Activism, and Affirmative Governmentality* (Durham, NC: Duke University Press, 2013), 9.
52. Kwon, *Uncivil Youth*, 119.
53. James, "Moral Equivalent," 25.
54. This type of evaluation and assessment research includes examples such as: Abt Associates, Inc., *Serving Country and Community: A Longitudinal Study of Service in AmeriCorps* (Washington, DC: Corporation for National and Community Service, 2004); Abt Associates, Inc., *Still Serving: Measuring the 8-Year Impact of AmeriCorps on Alumni* (Washington, DC: Corporation for National and Community Service, 2008); Christopher Simon and Changhua Wang, *Impact of AmeriCorps on Members' Political and Social Efficacy, Social Trust, Institutional Confidence and Values in Idaho, Montana, Oregon, and Washington* (Portland, OR: Northwest Education Research Laboratory, 1999); Christopher Simon and Changhua Wang, *First Follow-up Study: Impact of AmeriCorps on Members' Political and Social Efficacy, Social Trust, Institutional Confidence and Values in Idaho, Montana, Oregon, and Washington* (Portland.

OR: Northwest Education Research Laboratory, 2000); Christopher Simon and Changhua Wang, "The Impact of AmeriCorps Service on Volunteer Participants: Results from a 2-Year Study in Four Western States," *Administration & Society*, 34, no. 5 (2002): 522–40; Christina Standerfer, "Engaging Theory, Engaging Citizens: An Exploration of the Relationships Among Civic Participation, National Service, and Rhetoric" (Ph.D. diss., University of Colorado, 2003).

55. Peter Frumkin, Joann Jastrzab, Margaret Vaaler, Adam Greeney, Robert T. Grimm, Kevin Cramer, and Nathan Dietz, "Inside National Service: AmeriCorps' Impact on Participants," *Journal of Policy Analysis and Management* 28, no. 3 (2009): 396.

56. See: Aaron Einfeld and Denise Collins, "The Relationships Between Service-Learning, Social Justice, Multicultural Competence, and Civic Engagement," *Journal of College Student Development* 49 no. 2 (2008): 95–109; Maria Hernandez Ferrier, "Ordinary Citizens in an Extraordinary Era of Big Citizenship," *Community Education Journal* 25, no. 1–2 (1998): 52–54; Christopher Simon, "Testing for Bias in the Impact of AmeriCorps Service on Volunteer Participants: Evidence of Success in Achieving a Neutrality Program Objective," *Public Administration Review* 6 (2002): 670–78.

57. See Deborah Cassidy, Susan Hicks, Alice Henderson Hall, Dale Farran, and Jackie Gray. "The North Carolina Child Care Corps: The Role of National Service in Child Care," *Early Childhood Research Quarterly* 13, no. 4 (1998): 589–602; Barry Checkoway, "Institutional Impacts of AmeriCorps on the University of Michigan," *Journal of Public Service and Outreach* 2, no. 1 (1997): 70–79; Nancy Naples, "From Maximum Feasible Participation to Disenfranchisement," *Social Justice* 25, Spring (1998): 47–66; Ann Marie Thomson and James Perry, "Can AmeriCorps Build Communities?" *Non-Profit and Voluntary Sector Quarterly* 27, no. 4 (1998): 399–420.

58. Nina Eliasoph, *The Politics of Volunteering* (London: Polity, 2013), 12.

59. Federici, *Caliban*, 94.

60. Walter Trattner, *From Poor Law to Welfare State: A History of Social Welfare in America*, 4th ed. (New York: The Free Press, 1989), 84.

61. Keith Morton and John Saltmarsh, "Addams, Day, and Dewey: The Emergence of Community Service in American Culture," *Michigan Journal of Community Service Learning* 4, no. 1 (1997): 137.

62. Trattner, *From Poor Law*, 87.

63. Important texts in this regard are: Jane Addams, *Democracy and Social Ethics* (New York: Macmillan, 1902); Jane Addams, "Charity and Social Justice," *North American Review* 192, no. 656 (1910): 68–81; Jane Addams, *Twenty Years at Hull House* (New York: Macmillan, 1912).

64. Gary Daynes and Nick Longo, "Jane Addams and the Origins of Service-Learning Practice in the United States," *Michigan Journal of Community Service-Learning* 11 (Fall 2004): 7.

65. Similarly to Addams, Dewey made this argument in multiple places. Key texts are, I believe, John Dewey, *The Public and Its Problems* (Athens, OH: Swallow Press, 2016); John Dewey, *Democracy and Education* (New York: The Free Press, 1966).

66. Shirley Sagawa, *The American Way to Change: How National Service and Volunteers Are Transforming America* (San Francisco, CA: John Wiley & Sons, 2010), 43.

67. Janowitz, *Reconstruction of Patriotism*, 192.

68. Ivan Illich. "To Hell with Good Intentions" in *Combining Service and Learning: A Resource Book for Community and Public Service*, edited by Jane Kendall (Raleigh: National Society for Experiential Education, 1990), 316.

69. Bruce Speck and Sherry Hoppe, eds., *Service-Learning: History, Theory, and Issues* (Westport, CT: Praeger, 2004), 87.

70. Dan Butin, *Service Learning in Theory and Practice: The Future of Community Engagement in Higher Education* (New York: Palgrave, 2010), 14.

71. Dwight Giles and Janet Eyler, "The Theoretical Roots of Service-Learning in John Dewey: Toward a Theory of Service-Learning," *Michigan Journal of Community Service Learning* 1, no. 1 (1994): 77–85.

72. John Saltmarsh, "Education for Critical Citizenship: John Dewey's Contribution to the Pedagogy of Service-Learning," *Michigan Journal for Community Service Learning* 3, no. 1 (1996): 13–21.

73. John Dewey, *The School and Society* and *the Child and the Curriculum* (Chicago, IL: University of Chicago Press, 1990), 14.

74. Dewey, *The School*, 14.

75. Saltmarsh, "Education," 15.

76. John Dewey, *Experience and Education* (New York: The Free Press, 1997), 25.

77. John Dewey, "The Need for a Philosophy of Education," in *John Dewey: On Education, Selected Writings*, edited by Reginald Archambault (Chicago: University of Chicago Press, 1964), 4.

78. Dewey, *Experience*, 37.

79. John Dewey, *How We Think* (Amherst, NY: Prometheus Books, 1991), 3.

80. David Kolb, *Experiential Learning: Experience as the Source of Learning and Development* (Englewood Cliffs, NJ: Prentice-Hall, 1984), 41.

81. Saltmarsh, "Education," 16.

82. John Dewey, "Creative Democracy: The Task Before Us," in *John Dewey: The Political Writings*, edited by Debra Morris and Ian Shapiro (Indianapolis, IN: Hackett Publishing, 1993), 244.

83. Dewey, "Creative Democracy," 244.

84. For the breadth of these critiques, see: Dan Butin, *Service-Learning in Higher Education: Critical Issues and Directions*. New York: Palgrave Macmillan, 2005; Dan Butin, *Service Learning in Theory and Practice*; Calderón, José Z., ed., *Race, Poverty, and Social Justice: Multidisciplinary Perspectives through Service Learning*

(Sterling: Stylus, 2007); Susan Benigni Cipolle, *Service-Learning and Social Justice: Engaging Students in Social Change* (New York: Rowan & Littlefield, 2010).

85. Derek Sayer, *The Violence of Abstraction: The Analytic Foundations of Historical Materialism* (New York: Basil Blackwell, 1987).

Chapter 3

1. Himani Bannerji, *Inventing Subjects: Studies in Hegemony, Patriarchy, and Colonialism* (New Delhi, India: Tulika, 2001), 3.

2. Code of Federal Regulations, *The Corporation for National and Community Service*, No. CFR 45, chapter XXV, Subtitle B (Washington, DC: United States Congress, 2008), 644.

3. 101st Congress of the United States of America, *National and Community Service Act of 1990*. PL 106–70 (42 U.S.C.A. 12501), 1990; 111th Congress of the United States of America, *Edward Kennedy Serve America Act*. PL 111–13 (H. R. 1388), 2009.

4. Corporation for National and Community Service, *Instructions for Applications: Notice of Federal Funds Offered: AmeriCorps*. OMB Control #: 3045-0047 (Washington, DC: Corporation for National and Community Service, 2006), 7.

5. 111th Congress, *Edward Kennedy Serve America Act*, 1575.

6. 99th Congress of the United States of America, *United States Internal Revenue Code: Title 26, Subtitle A, Chapter 1, Subchapter F, 501* (Washington DC: Congress of the United States of America, 1986), 1456.

7. Internal Revenue Service, "The Restriction of Political Campaign Intervention by Section 501(c)(3) Tax-Exempt Organizations" (Washington, DC: Department of Treasury, 2016a). Accessed January 15, 2017. https://www.irs.gov/charities-non-profits/charitable-organizations/the-restriction-of-political-campaign-intervention-by-section-501c3-tax-exempt-organizations.

8. Internal Revenue Service, "Restriction of Political Campaign," para. 3.

9. Internal Revenue Service, "Lobbying" (Washington, DC: Department of Treasury, 2016b). Accessed January 15, 2017. https://www.irs.gov/charities-non-profits/lobbying.

10. Internal Revenue Service, "Lobbying," para. 1.

11. John Francis Reilly, Carter C. Hull, and Barbara A. Braig Allen, *IRC 501c(4) organizations: Technical Instructions Program for FY 2003* (Washington, DC: Department of Treasury, 2003), I-2. www.irs.gov/pub/irs-tege/eotopici03.pdf.

12. Internal Revenue Service, "Social Welfare Organizations" (Washington, DC: Department of Treasury, 2016c). Accessed January 15, 2017. https://www.irs.gov/charities-non-profits/other-non-profits/social-welfare-organizations.

13. Federal Register, "Corporation for National and Community Service," *Federal Register* 70, no. 130 (2005): 39562.

14. Federal Register, "Corporation," 39562.
15. Federal Register, "Corporation," 39564.
16. David Eisner and Rosie Mauk, *AmeriCorps Rule: Message from CEO and Director* (Internal Communication) (Washington, DC: Corporation for National and Community Service, 2005), 2.
17. Eisner and Mauk, "AmeriCorps Rule," 2.
18. Dylan Rodriguez, "The Political Logic of the Non-Profit Industrial Complex," in *The Revolution Will Not Be Funded: Beyond the Non-Profit Industrial Complex*, edited by INCITE! (Cambridge, MA: South End Press, 2007), 21.
19. William Foster and Jeffrey Bradach, "Should Non-Profits Seek Profits?" *Harvard Business Review* 83, no. 2 (2005): 99.
20. Corporation for National and Community Service, *2009 AmeriCorps State: Application Instructions for Programs*. OMB # 3045-0047 (Washington, DC: CNCS, 2008), 10.
21. Alan Khazei, *Big Citizenship: How Pragmatic Idealism Can Bring Out the Best in America* (Philadelphia. PA: PublicAffairs, 2010), 3.
22. Smith, *Institutional Ethnography*, 152.
23. Smith, *Institutional Ethnography*, 151.
24. Code of Federal Regulations, *Corporation*, 642.
25. Code of Federal Regulations, *Corporation*, 642.
26. Code of Federal Regulations, *Corporation*, 644–45.
27. 111th Congress of the United States, 42 USC 12584a.
28. Code of Federal Regulations, *Corporation*, 642.
29. Code of Federal Regulations, *Corporation*, 644–45.
30. Bricmont, *Humanitarian Imperialism*, 35.
31. For a more expansive critique of logic models, see Sara Carpenter, "'Modeling' Youth Work: Logic Models, Neoliberalism, and Community Praxis," *International Studies in Sociology of Education* 26, no. 2 (2017): 105–20.
32. Sue Kaplan and Katherine Garrett, "The Use of Logic Models by Community-Based Initiatives," *Evaluation and Program Planning* 28 (2005): 167.
33. John Dwyer and Susan Makin, "Using a Program Logic Model that Focuses on Performance Measurement to Develop a Program," *Canadian Journal of Public Health* 88, no. 6 (1997): 421.
34. Ralph Renger, "Consequences to Federal Programs when the Logic Modeling Process Is Not Followed with Fidelity," *American Journal of Evaluation* 27, no. 4 (2006): 452.
35. Renger, "Consequences," 453.
36. Nancy Porteous, Barbara Sheldrick, and Paula Stewart, "Introducing Program Teams to Logic Models: Facilitating the Learning Process," *Canadian Journal of Program Evaluation* 17, no. 3 (2002): 116–17.
37. Leonard Bickman, *Using Program Theory in Evaluation: New Directions in Program Evaluation* (San Francisco, CA: Jossey-Bass, 1987), 14.

38. Renger, "Consequences," 455.
39. Kaplan and Garrett, "Use of Logic Models," 170.
40. Renger, "Consequences," 462.
41. Bickman, Using Program Theory, 14.
42. Kaplan & Garrett, "The Use of Logic Models," 171.
43. Code of Federal Regulations, *Corporation*, 641.
44. For further research on the importance of paperwork and administrative processes, see: Naomi Nichols, "Gimme Shelter! Investigating the Social Service Interface from the Standpoint of Youth," *Journal of Youth Studies* 11, no. 6 (2008): 685–99; Naomi Nichols and Allison Griffith, "Talk, Texts, and Educational Action: An Institutional Ethnography of Policy in Practice," *Cambridge Journal of Education* 39, no. 2 (2009): 241–55; Frank Ridzi, *Processing Private Lives in Public: An Institutional Ethnography of Front-Line Welfare Intake Staff Post Welfare Reform* (Syracuse, NY: Syracuse University, 2003); Frank Ridzi, "Making TANF Work: Organizational Restructuring, Staff Buy-In, and Performance Monitoring in Local Implementation," *Journal of Sociology and Social Welfare* 31, no. 2 (2004): 27–48.
45. Taylor, *From #BlackLivesMatter*, 40.
46. Daniel Patrick Moynihan, *The Negro Family: The Case for National Action* (Washington, DC: Department of Labor, 1965), 29.
47. Allison Griffith and Dorothy Smith, "Introduction," in *Under New Public Management: Institutional Ethnographies of Changing Frontline Work*, edited by Allison Griffith and Dorothy Smith (Toronto, ON: University of Toronto Press, 2014), 5.

Chapter 4

1. 101st Congress of the United States, *National and Community Service Act*, 1.
2. Waldeman, *The Bill*, 7.
3. Elizabeth Diller, *Citizens in Service: The Challenge of Delivering Civic Engagement Training to National Service Programs* (Washington, DC: Corporation for National and Community Service, 2001), 1.
4. George W. Bush, "State of the Union Address," Speech, Washington, DC, January 29, 2002, para. 52. https://georgewbush-whitehouse.archives.gov/news/releases/2002/01/20020129-11.html.
5. Bush, "State of the Union," para. 56.
6. Congressional Record, "Citizen Service Act," *Congressional Record* 148, no. 69 (May 24, 2002), E933.
7. Corporation for National and Community Service, *2003 AmeriCorps Guidelines*, 3.
8. Corporation for National and Community Service, *2003 AmeriCorps Guidelines*, 4.

9. Corporation for National and Community Service, *2003 AmeriCorps Guidelines*, 49.
10. Corporation for National and Community Service, *2003 AmeriCorps Guidelines*, 17.
11. Corporation for National and Community Service, *2003 AmeriCorps Guidelines*, 16.
12. Michael Peters, "Education, Enterprise Culture, and the Entrepreneurial Self: A Foucauldian Perspective," *Journal of Educational Enquiry* 2, no. 2 (2001): 66.
13. Dewey, *Experience*, 37.
14. Diller, *Citizens in Service*, 5.

Chapter 5

1. Noah de Lissovoy, *Education and Emancipation in the Neoliberal Era: Being, Teaching, and Power* (New York: Palgrave, 2015), 36.
2. Paula Allman, *Critical Education against Global Capitalism: Karl Marx and Revolutionary Critical Education*, 2nd ed. (Rotterdam, the Netherlands: Sense, 2010), 167.
3. Corporation for National and Community Service. About this website, para. 2. https://www.nationalservice.gov/vcla/about-website.
4. George Smith, "Political Activist as Ethnographer," *Social Problems* 37, no. 4 (1990): 633.
5. Dorothy Smith, *Texts, Facts, and Femininity: Exploring the Relations of Ruling* (New York: Routledge, 1993), 139.
6. Smith, "Ideology," 449.
7. Westheimer and Kahne, "What Kind of Citizen?," 240.
8. John Tevlin, "Bachman's Wayward Son Up and Joins AmeriCorps." *Star Tribune*. Minneapolis, MN (August 12, 2009). http://www.startribune.com/local/53002167.html?elr=KArksL.
9. Obama, "Obama, in Texas," para. 42.
10. Corporation for National and Community Service, *2011–2015 Strategic Plan* (Washington, DC: Corporation for National and Community Service, 2011), 5.
11. Mark Purcell, "Urban Democracy and the Local Trap," *Urban Studies* 43, no. 11 (2006): 1924.
12. For a complex discussion of the ways in which the concept of community can be used to reinscribe racialized and gendered modes of differentiation and collusion with capitalist social relations, see Miranda Joseph, *Against the Romance of Community* (Minneapolis: University of Minnesota Press, 2002).
13. Neil Brenner and Nik Theodore, "Preface: From the "New Localism" to the Spaces of Neo Liberalism," *Antipode* 34, no. 3 (2002): 341.

14. Sara Carpenter, "The 'Local' Fetish as Reproductive Praxis in Democratic Learning," *Discourse: Studies in the Cultural Politics of Education* 36, no. 1 (2015): 133–43.

15. Allman, *On Marx*, 37.

16. Corporation for National and Community Service, *2011–2015 Strategic Plan*, 12–13.

17. For discussion of these debates see Frances Cleaver, "Paradoxes of Participation: Questioning Participatory Approaches to Development," *Journal of International Development* 11, no. 4 (1999): 597–612; Samuel Hickey and Giles Mohan, *Participation: From Tyranny to Transformation? Exploring New Approaches to Participation in Development* (London: ZED Books, 2004); Carolyn Long, *Participation of the Poor in Development Initiatives: Taking Their Rightful Places* (London: Earthscan, 2001).

18. Feminist social reproduction theory and feminist political theory has extensively taken up this question. See: Johanna Brenner, *Women and the Politics of Class* (New York: Monthly Review Press, 2000); Nancy Fraser, "Women, Welfare and the Politics of Need Interpretation," *Hypatia* 2, no. 1 (1987): 103–21; Nancy Fraser. *Justice Interruptus: Critical Reflections on the "Postsocialist" Condition* (New York: Routledge, 1997); Ruth Lister, *Citizenship: Feminist Perspectives*, 2nd ed. (New York: New York University Press, 2000).

19. Smith, *Texts*, 217.

20. de Lissovoy, *Education and Emancipation*, 36.

21. Marx, "Theses on Feuerbach," 659.

22. Marx and Engels, *German Ideology*, 37.

23. Obama, "Obama, in Texas," paras. 39–41.

Chapter 6

1. This refrain is echoed across several celebratory works on civilian national service. See: Bass, *Politics and Civics*; Khazei, *Big Citizenship*; Sagawa, *American Way*.

2. Wendy Brown, *Undoing the Demos: Neoliberalism's Stealth Revolution* (New York: Zone Books, 2015), 20.

3. David Harvey, *A Brief History of Neoliberalism* (Oxford: Oxford University Press, 2005), 3.

4. Sassen, *Expulsions*, 68.

5. Aihwa Ong, *Neoliberalism as Exception: Mutations in Citizenship and Sovereignty* (Durham, NC: Duke University Press, 2006), 4.

6. Victoria Bernal and Inderpal Grewal, "The NGO Form: Feminist Struggles, States, and Neoliberalim," in *Theorizing NGOs: States, Feminism, and Neoliberalism*, Victoria Bernal and Inderpal Grewal, eds. (Durham, NC: Duke University Press, 2014), 11.

7. Dip Kapoor, "Social Action and NGOization in Contexts of Development Dispossession in Rural India: Explorations into the Un-civility of Civil Society," in *NGOization: Complicity, Contradictions, and Prospects*, Aziz Choudry and Dip Kapoor, eds. (London: ZED, 2013), 13.

8. Foucault, *Birth of Biopolitics*, 147.

9. See chapter 2 for a more detailed discussion of governmentality.

10. For examples of the regulation tradition, see: Jane Jenson and Susan Phillips, "Regime Shift: New Citizenship Practice in Canada," *International Journal of Canadian Studies* 14 (1996): 111–36; Jane Jenson and Susan Phillips, "Redesigning the Canadian citizenship regime: Remaking the institutions of representation," in *Citizenship, Markets, and the State*, edited by Colin Crouch, Klau Eder, and Damian Tambini (Oxford, UK: Oxford University Press, 2001), 69–89.

11. Janet Newman, "Towards a Pedagogical State? Summoning the 'Empowered' Citizen," *Citizenship Studies* 14, no. 6 (2010): 715.

12. Himani Bannerji, "Politics and Ideology," *Socialist Studies* 11, no. 1 (2016): 10.

13. Neil Smith, *Uneven Development: Nature, Capital, and the Production of Space* (Athens: University of Georgia Press, 2008), 132.

14. Etzioni's arguments concerning citizenship and civil society are developed across multiple texts. See: Amitai Etzioni, *The Spirit of Community: Rights, Responsibilities, and the Communitarian Agenda* (New York: Crown Publishers, 1994); Amitai Etzioni, "The Responsive Community: A Communitarian Perspective," *American Sociological Review* 61, no. 1 (1996): 1–11; Amitai Etzioni, *The New Golden Rule: Community and Morality in a Democratic Society* (New York: Basic Books, 1998); Amitai Etzioni, *The Common Good* (San Francisco: Wiley-Blackwell, 2004).

15. Etzioni, *Spirit of Community*, 144.

16. Etzioni, *Spirit of Community*, 144.

17. Etzioni, *Spirit of Community*, 146.

18. Etzioni, *Spirit of Community*, 146.

19. Fraser, *Justus Interruptus*, 13.

20. Etzioni, "The Responsive Community," 5.

21. Etzioni, "The Responsive Community," 5.

22. Etzioni, "The Responsive Community," 6.

23. Tracey Kidder, *Mountains Beyond Mountains: The Quest of Dr. Paul Farmer, A Man Who Would Cure the World* (New York: Random House, 2004), 216.

24. Teresa Funicello, *Tyranny of Kindness: Dismantling the Welfare System to End Poverty in America* (New York: Atlantic Monthly Press, 1993), 252.

25. Rodriguez, "Political Logic," 21.

26. Kwoon, *Uncivil Youth*, 10.

27. Žižek, *Lenin's Choice*, 167.

28. There is a great deal of literature developed in this line. See: Martin Gilens, *Why Americans Hate Welfare: Race, Media, and the Politics of Anti-Poverty Policy*

(Chicago, IL: University of Chicago Press, 1999); King and Waldron, "Citizenship"; Wendy Limbert and Heather Bullock, "'Playing the Fool': US Welfare Policy from a Critical Race Perspective," *Feminism & Psychology* 15, no. 3 (2005), 253–74; Francis Fox Piven and Richard Cloward, *Regulating the Poor: The Functions of Public Welfare* (New York: Taylor & Francis, 1972); Premilla Nadasen, *Welfare Warriors: The Welfare Rights Movement in the United States* (New York: Routledge, 2005).

29. See: Peter Linebaugh, *The London Hanged: Crime and Civil Society in the Eighteenth Century* (London: Verso, 2007); Peter Linebaugh, *The Magna Carta Manifesto: Liberties and Commons for All* (Berkeley: University of California Press, 2008); Wood, *Democracy against Capitalism*; Ellen Meiksins Wood, *The Origin of Capitalism: A Longer View* (London: Verso, 2002); Ellen Meiksins Wood, *Citizens to Lords: A Social History of Western Political Thought from Antiquity to Middle Ages* (London: Verso, 2008); Ellen Meiksins Wood, *Liberty and Property: A Social History of Western Political Thought from Renaissance to Enlightenment* (London: Verso, 2012).

30. Federici, *Caliban*, 28.

31. Wood, *Democracy Against Capitalism*, 210.

32. Wood, *Democracy Against Capitalism*, 210–11.

33. Luin Goldring and Patricia Landolt, "The Conditionality of Legal Status and Rights: Conceptualizing Precarious Non-Citizenship in Canada" in *Producing and Negotiating Non-Citizenship: Precarious Legal Status in Canada*, edited by Luin Goldring and Patricia Landolt (Toronto: University of Toronto Press, 2015), 6.

34. Marx, *Capital*, 714.

35. Federici, *Caliban*, 220.

36. Karl Marx, "On the Jewish Question," in *The Marx-Engels Reader*, edited by Robert Tucker (New York: Norton, 1978), 33, emphasis in original.

37. Sayer, "Critique of Politics," 233.

38. Wood, *Democracy against Capitalism*, 30.

39. Marx and Engels, *The German Ideology*, 78.

40. Federici, *Caliban*, 75.

41. Sayer, "Critique of Politics," 236.

42. Marx and Engels, *The German Ideology*, 45.

43. Bertell Ollman, "Imperialism, Then and Now," interview by Azfar Hussain, *Meghbarta: A Journal for Activism*, 2004. Available at https://www.nyu.edu/projects/ollman/docs/interview03.php.

44. Sayer, "Critique of Politics," 233.

45. Marx and Engels, *German Ideology*, 37.

46. Sayer, "Critique of Politics," 231.

47. Sayer, *Violence*, 107.

48. Arthur, "Editor's Introduction," 8.

49. Marx, "On the Jewish Question," 40.

50. Callinicos, *Social Theory*, 83.

51. Marx, "On the Jewish Question," 42.

52. Slavoj Žižek, *The Fragile Absolute: Or, Why Is the Christian Legacy Worth Fighting For?* (London: Verso, 2001), 100.
53. Marx, "On the Jewish Question," 40.
54. Marx, "On the Jewish Question," 45.
55. Karl Marx, "Critique of the Gotha Programme" in *The Marx-Engels Reader*, edited by Robert Tucker (New York: W. W. Norton & Company, 1978), 530.
56. For examples of this argument see: Vivyan Adair, *From Good Ma to Welfare Queen: A Genealogy of the Poor Woman in American Literature, Photography and Culture* (New York: Routledge, 2000); Ange-Marie Hancock, *The Politics of Disgust: The Public Identity of the Welfare Queen* (New York: NYU Press, 2004); Joel Handler and Yehenskel Hasenfeld, *The Moral Construction of Poverty: Welfare Reform in America* (New York: Sage, 1991); Michael Katz, *The Undeserving Poor: From the War on Poverty to the War on Welfare* (New York: Pantheon Books, 1990).
57. National Commission on Civic Renewal, *Spectators*, 5.
58. Newman, "Pedagogical State," 714.

Chapter 7

1. bell hooks, *Talking Back: Thinking Feminist, Thinking Black* (Boston, MA: Sound End Press, 1989), 70.
2. Allman, *On Marx*, 37.
3. Allman, *On Marx*, 58.
4. Paulo Freire, *The Pedagogy of the Oppressed* (New York: Continuum, 1973).
5. hooks, *Talking Back*, 101.
6. Faith Spotted Eagle, "Faith Spotted Eagle on the Settler Colonial Mind Set," interview by Tracey Rector, *Indian Country Today*, January 17, 2017. https://newsmaven.io/indiancountrytoday/archive/faith-spotted-eagle-on-the-settler-colonial-mind-set-GRbqpCUEv0WG-Ev0UhyXYQ/.
7. Faith Spotted Eagle, Interview, 01:06.
8. Smith, "Ideology," 446.
9. Glenn Rikowski, "Scorched Earth: Prelude to Rebuilding Marxist Educational Theory," *British Journal of Sociology of Education* 18, no. 4 (1997): 553.
10. Rikowski, "Scorched Earth," 553.
11. Marx, "Theses on Feuerbach," 659, emphasis in original.
12. Franz Fanon, *The Wretched of the Earth*, translated by Constance Farrington (New York: Grove Press, 1963), 40.
13. Leanne Betasamosake Simpson, "Dancing the World into Being: A Conversation with Idle No More's Leanne Simpson," interview by Naomi Klein. *Yes! Magazine*, March 5, 2013. http://www.yesmagazine.org/peace-justice/dancing-the-world-into-being-a-conversation-with-idle-no-more-leanne-simpson.
14. Federici, *Caliban*, 92.

15. See Linebaugh, *The London Hanged* (London: Verso, 1991); Marcus Rediker, *The Slave Ship: A Human History* (London: Penguin, 2007); Peter Linebaugh and Marcus Rediker, *The Many-Headed Hydra: Sailors, Slaves, Commoners, and the Hidden History of the Revolutionary Atlantic* (Boston, MA: Beacon Press, 2000).

16. Carpenter and Mojab, *Revolutionary*, 5.

17. Chris Hayes, "The Pragmatist," *The Nation*, December 10, 2008. https://www.thenation.com/article/pragmatist/.

18. Marx and Engels, *German Ideology*, 61.

19. Allman, *On Marx*, 59.

20. Taylor, *From #BlackLivesMatter*, 29.

21. Fanon, *Wretched*, 34.

Bibliography

Abt Associates, *Serving Country and Community: A Longitudinal Study of Service in AmeriCorps*. Washington, DC: Corporation for National and Community Service, 2004. https://www.nationalservice.gov/pdf/06_1223_longstudy_report.pdf.

———. *Still Serving: Measuring the 8-Year Impact of AmeriCorps on Alumni*. Washington, DC: Corporation for National and Community Service, 2008. https://www.nationalservice.gov/pdf/08_0513_longstudy_executive.pdf.

Addams, Jane. *Democracy and Social Ethics*. New York: Macmillan, 1902.

———. "Charity and Social Justice." *North American Review* 192, no. 656 (1910): 68–81.

———. *Twenty Years at Hull House*. New York: Macmillan, 1912.

Adair, Vivyan. *From Good Ma to Welfare Queen: A Genealogy of the Poor Woman in American Literature, Photography and Culture*. New York: Routledge, 2000.

Allman, Paula. *Revolutionary Social Transformation: Democratic Hoes, Political Possibilities, and Critical Education*. Westport, CT: Bergin & Garvey, 1999.

———. *On Marx: An Introduction to the Revolutionary Intellect of Karl Marx*. Rotterdam, the Netherlands: Sense, 2007.

———. *Critical Education against Global Capitalism: Karl Marx and Revolutionary Critical Education*. 2nd ed. Rotterdam, the Netherlands: Sense, 2010.

Allman, Paula, and John Wallis. "Praxis: Implications for 'Really' Radical Education." *Studies in the Education of Adults* 22, no. 1 (1990): 14–30.

Amin, Samir. *The Liberal Virus: Permanent War and the Americanization of the World*. New York: Monthly Review Press, 2004.

Arthur, Christopher J. "Editor's introduction." In *The German Ideology, Part One*, edited by Christopher J. Arthur, 4–34. New York: International Publishers, 1991.

Bannerji, Himani. *Thinking Through: Essays on Feminism, Marxism, and Anti-Racism*. Toronto, ON: Women's Press, 1995.

———. *Inventing Subjects: Studies in Hegemony, Patriarchy, and Colonialism*. New Delhi, India: Tulika, 2001.

———. "The Tradition of Sociology and the Sociology of Tradition." *Qualitative Studies in Education* 16, no. 2 (2003): 157–73.

———. "Building from Marx: Reflections on Class and Race." *Social Justice* 32, no. 4 (2005): 144–60.

———. *Demography and Democracy: Essays on Nationalism, Gender, and Ideology.* Toronto: Canadian Scholars' Press, 2011.

———. "Politics and Ideology," *Socialist Studies* 11, no. 1 (2016): 3–23.

Bass, Melissa. "National Service in America: Policy (Dis)Connections over Time." CIRCLE Working Paper No. 11. College Park: University of Maryland, 2003. https://civicyouth.org/PopUps/WorkingPapers/WP11Bass.pdf.

———. *The Politics and Civics of National Service: Lessons from the Civilian Conservation Corps, VISTA, and AmeriCorps.* Washington, DC: Brookings Institute Press, 2013.

Bellah, Robert, Richard Madsen, William Sullivan, Ann Swidler, and Steven Tipton. *Habits of the Heart: Individualism and Commitment in American Life.* Berkeley: University of California Press, 1985.

Bernal, Victoria, and Inderpal Grewal. "The NGO Form: Feminist Struggles, States, and Neoliberalim." In *Theorizing NGOs: States, Feminism, and Neoliberalism*, edited by Victoria Bernal and Inderpal Grewal, 1–18. Durham, NC: Duke University Press, 2014.

Berndt, Julia, and Cara James. *The Effects of the Economic Recession on Communities of Color, Issue Brief No. 7953.* Menlo Park, CA: The Henry J. Kaiser Family Foundation, 2009. www.kff.org/minorityhealth/upload/7953.pdf.

Bickman, Leonard. "The Functions of Program Theory." *New Directions in Program Evaluation* 33 (Spring 1987): 5–18.

Boyte, Harry, ed. *By the People.* Washington, DC: Corporation for National and Community Service, 2001.

Boyte, Harry, and Elizabeth Hollander. "Wingspread Declaration on Renewing the Civic Mission of the American Research University." *The Wingspread Conference.* Presented at the Wingspread Conference, Racine, WI, 1999. https://compact.org/wingspread-declaration-on-the-civic-responsibilities-of-research-universities/.

Brenner, Johanna. *Women and the Politics of Class.* New York: Monthly Review Press, 2000.

Brenner, Neil, and Nik Theodore, "Preface: From the "New Localism" to the Spaces of Neo Liberalism," *Antipode* 34, no. 3 (2002): 341–47.

Bricmont, Jean. *Humanitarian Imperialism: Using Human Rights to Sell War.* New York: Monthly Review Press, 2006.

Brown, Wendy. *Undoing the Demos: Neoliberalism's Stealth Revolution.* New York: Zone Books, 2015.

Bush, George H. W. "State of the Union Address." Speech, Washington, DC, January 29, 2002. https://georgewbush-whitehouse.archives.gov/news/releases/2002/01/20020129-11.html.

Butin, Dan. *Service-Learning in Higher Education: Critical Issues and Directions.* New York: Palgrave Macmillan, 2005.

———. *Service Learning in Theory and Practice: The Future of Community Engagement in Higher Education*. New York: Palgrave, 2010.
Callinicos, Alex. *Social Theory: A Historical Introduction*. New York: New York University Press, 1999.
Calderón, José Z., ed. *Race, Poverty, and Social Justice: Multidisciplinary Perspectives through Service Learning*. Sterling, VA: Stylus, 2007.
Campbell, Marie Louise and Frances Mary Gregor, *Mapping Social Relations: A Primer in Doing Institutional Ethnography*. Aurora, ON: Garamond Press, 2002.
Campus Compact (blog). *President's Declaration on the Civic Responsibility of Higher Education*. Providence: Campus Compact, 2000. www.compact.org/resources/declaration.
Carlson, Robert A. *The Quest for Conformity: Americanization through Education*. San Francisco, CA: Wiley, 1975.
Carpenter, Sara. "Examining the Social Relations of Learning Citizenship: Citizenship and Ideology in Adult Education." In *Educating from Marx: Race, Gender, and Learning*, edited by Sara Carpenter and Shahrzad Mojab, 63–86. New York: Palgrave, 2011.
———. "Centering Marxist Feminism in Adult Learning." *Adult Education Quarterly* 62, no. 1 (2012): 19–35.
———. "The 'Local' Fetish as Reproductive Praxis in Democratic Learning," *Discourse: Studies in the Cultural Politics of Education* 36, no. 1 (2015): 133–43.
———. "'Modeling' Youth Work: Logic Models, Neoliberalism, and Community Praxis." *International Studies in Sociology of Education* 26, no. 2 (2017): 105–20. DOI:10.1080/09620214.2016.1191963.
Carpenter, Sara, and Shahrzad Mojab, ed. *Educating from Marx: Race, Gender, and Learning*. New York: Palgrave, 2011.
———. *Revolutionary Learning: Marxism, Feminism and Knowledge*. London, UK: Pluto, 2017.
Cassidy, Deborah, Susan Hicks, Alice Henderson Hall, Dale Farran, and Jackie Gray. "The North Carolina Child Care Corps: The Role of National Service in Child Care." *Early Childhood Research Quarterly* 13, no. 4 (1998): 589–602. DOI:10.1016/S0885-2006(99)80062-3.
Chambre, Susan. "Kindling Points of Light: Volunteering as Public Policy." *Non-Profit and Voluntary Sector Quarterly* 18, no. 3 (1989): 249–68.
Checkoway, Barry. "Institutional Impacts of AmeriCorps on the University of Michigan." *Journal of Public Service and Outreach* 2, no. 1 (1997): 70–79.
Choudry, Aziz, and Dip Kapoor, eds. *NGOization: Complicity, Contradictions and Prospects*. London, UK: ZED Books, 2013.
Cipolle, Susan Benigni. *Service-Learning and Social Justice: Engaging Students in Social Change*. New York: Rowman & Littlefield, 2010.
Clark, Robert F. *The War on Poverty: History, Selected Programs, and Ongoing Impact*. New York: University Press of America, 2002.

Cleaver, Frances. "Paradoxes of Participation: Questioning Participatory Approaches to Development." *Journal of International Development* 11, no. 4 (1999): 597–612.

Clinton, William J. "Remarks in a Swearing-In Ceremony for AmeriCorps Volunteers," Speech, Washington, DC, September 12, 1994, para. 6. http://www.presidency.ucsb.edu/ws/index.php?pid=49067.

Code of Federal Regulations. *The Corporation for National and Community Service* (No. CFR 45, Chapter XXV, Subtitle B). Washington, DC: United States Congress, 2008.

Colby, Anne, Elizabeth Beaumont, Thomas Ehrlich, and Jason Stephens. *Educating Citizens: Preparing America's Undergraduates for Lives of Moral and Civic Responsibility*. New York: John Wiley & Sons, 2003.

Congressional Record. "Citizen Service Act." May 24, 2002. Hon. Peter Hoekstra. Congressional Record 148, no. 69 (2002): E932–33.

Constitutional Rights Foundation. *Effective Citizenship through AmeriCorps*. Washington, DC: Corporation for National and Community Service, 2001. https://www.nationalservice.gov/sites/default/files/resource/w1952-a-guide-to-effective-citizenship-through-ac.pdf.

Corporation for National and Community Service. *2003 AmeriCorps Guidelines* (Internal Memo). Washington, DC: Corporation for National and Community Service, 2003.

———. Instructions for Applications: Notice of Federal Funds Offered: AmeriCorps. OMB Control #: 3045-0047. Washington, DC: Corporation for National and Community Service, 2006.

———. 2008 AmeriCorps State: Application instructions for programs. OMB # 3045-0047. Washington, DC: Corporation for National and Community Service, 2007.

———. 2009 AmeriCorps State: Application instructions for programs. OMB # 3045-0047. Washington, DC: Corporation for National and Community Service, 2008.

———. *2011–2015 Strategic Plan*. Washington, DC: Corporation for National and Community Service, 2011. https://www.nationalservice.gov/sites/default/files/documents/11_0203_cncs_strategic_plan.pdf.

———. "About This Website." https://www.nationalservice.gov/vcla/about-website.

Crook, William, and Ross Thomas. *Warriors for the Poor: The Story of VISTA, Volunteers in Service to America*. New York: William Morrow, 1969.

Crozier, Michel, Samuel P. Huntington, and Joji Watanuki. *The Crisis of Democracy: Report on the Governability of Democracies to the Trilateral Commission*. New York: New York University Press, 1975.

Cruikshank, Barbara. *The Will to Empower: Democratic Citizens and Other Subjects*. Ithaca, NY: Cornell University Press, 1999.

Daynes, Gary, and Nick Longo. "Jane Addams and the Origins of Service-Learning Practice in the United States." *Michigan Journal of Community Service-Learning* 11 (Fall 2004): 5–13.

de Lissovoy, Noah. *Education and Emancipation in the Neoliberal Era: Being, Teaching, and Power.* New York: Palgrave, 2015.

Dean, Mitchell. *Governmentality: Power and Rule in Modern Society.* London, UK: Sage, 1999.

Dewey, John. "The Need for a Philosophy of Education," in *John Dewey: On Education, Selected Writings,* edited by Reginald Archambault, 3–14. Chicago, IL: University of Chicago Press, 1964.

———. *Democracy and Education.* New York: The Free Press, 1966.

———. *The School and Society* and *The Child and the Curriculum.* Chicago: University of Chicago Press, 1990.

———. *How We Think.* Amherst, NY: Prometheus Books, 1991.

———. "Creative Democracy: The Task Before Us," in *John Dewey: The Political Writings,* edited by Debra Morris and Ian Shapiro, 240–45. Indianapolis, IN: Hackett Publishing, 1993.

———. *Experience and Education.* New York: The Free Press, 1997.

———. *The Public and Its Problems.* Athens, GA: Swallow Press, 2016.

Diller, Elizabeth. *Citizens in Service: The Challenge of Delivering Civic Engagement Training to National Service Programs.* Report of the National Service Fellow. Washington, DC: Corporation for National and Community Service, 2001. www.ibrarian.net/navon/.../Citizens_in_Service?The_Challenge_of_Delivering_.pdf.

Dwyer, John, and Susan Makin. "Using a Program Logic Model that Focuses on Performance Measurement to Develop a Program." *Canadian Journal of Public Health* 88, no. 6 (1997): 421–25.

Eberly, Donald, and Michael Sherraden. "United States: Several Noteworthy Programs." In *The Moral Equivalent of War? A Study of Non-Military Service in Nine Nations,* edited by Donald Eberly and Michael Sherraden, 115–26. New York: Greenwood, 1990.

Ebert, Teresa. *Ludic Feminism and After: Postmodernism, Desire, and Labor in Late Capitalism.* Ann Arbor: University of Michigan Press, 1996.

Edwards, Michael. *Civil Society,* 2nd ed. Cambridge, UK: Polity, 2009.

Ehrenberg, John. *Civil Society: A Critical History of an Idea.* New York: New York University Press, 1999.

Ehrlich, Thomas, ed. *Civic Responsibility and Higher Education.* Phoenix: American Council on Education & Oryx Press, 2000.

Einfeld, Aaron, and Denise Collins. "The Relationships Between Service-Learning, Social Justice, Multicultural Competence, and Civic Engagement." *Journal of College Student Development* 49, no. 2 (2008): 95–109.

Eisner, David, and Rosie Mauk. *AmeriCorps Rule: Message from CEO and Director* (Internal Communication). Washington, DC: Corporation for National and Community Service, 2005.

Eliasoph, Nina. *The Politics of Volunteering.* London: Polity, 2013.

Etzioni, Amitai. *The Spirit of Community: Rights, Responsibilities, and the Communitarian Agenda.* New York: Crown Publishers, 1994.

———. "The Responsive Community: A Communitarian Perspective." *American Sociological Review* 61, no. 1 (1996): 1–11.
———. *The New Golden Rule: Community and Morality in a Democratic Society.* New York: Basic Books, 1998.
———. *The Common Good.* San Francisco, CA: Wiley-Blackwell, 2004.
Fahmy, Eldin. *Young Citizens: Young People's Involvement in Politics and Decision Making.* Farnham, VA: Ashgate, 2006.
Fanon, Frantz. *The Wretched of the Earth.* Translated by Constance Farrington. New York: Grove Press, 1963.
Federal Register. Corporation for National and Community Service. *Federal Register* 70 (130), 39562–7. July 8, 2005.
Federici, Silvia. *Caliban and the Witch: Women, the Body, and Primitive Accumulation.* Brooklyn, NY: Autonomedia, 2004.
Ferrier, Maria Hernandez. "Ordinary Citizens in an Extraordinary Era of Big Citizenship." *Community Education Journal* 25, no. 1–2 (1998): 52–54.
Fortunati, Leopoldina. *The Arcane of Reproduction.* Brooklyn, NY: Autonomedia, 1995.
Foster, William, and Jeffrey Bradach. "Should Non-Profits Seek Profits?" *Harvard Business Review* 83, no. 2 (2005): 92–100.
Foucault, Michel. *The Birth of Biopolitics: Lectures at the College de France, 1978–79.* Translated by Graham Burchell. New York: Picador, 2008.
Fraser, Nancy. "Women, Welfare and the Politics of Need Interpretation," *Hypatia* 2, no. 1 (1987): 103–21.
———. *Justice Interruptus: Critical Reflections on the "Postsocialist" Condition.* New York: Routledge, 1997.
Freire, Paulo. *The Pedagogy of the Oppressed.* New York: Continuum, 1973.
Frumkin, Peter, Joann Jastrzab, Margaret Vaaler, Adam Greeney, Robert T. Grimm, Kevin Cramer, and Nathan Dietz. "Inside National Service: AmeriCorps' Impact on Participants," *Journal of Policy Analysis and Management* 28, no. 3 (2009): 394–416.
Funicello, Theresa. *Tyranny of Kindness: Dismantling the Welfare System to End Poverty in America.* New York: Atlantic Monthly Press, 1993.
Giddens, Anthony. *The Third Way and Its Critics.* London: Polity, 2000.
Gilens, Martin. *Why Americans Hate Welfare: Race, Media, and the Politics of Anti-Poverty Policy.* Chicago: University of Chicago Press, 1999.
Giles, Dwight, and Janet Eyler. "The Theoretical Roots of Service-Learning in John Dewey: Toward a Theory of Service-Learning." *Michigan Journal of Community Service Learning* 1, no. 1 (1994): 77–85.
Gillette, Michael. *Launching the War on Poverty: An Oral History.* New York: Oxford University Press, 1996.
Goldring, Luin, and Patricia Landolt. "The Conditionality of Legal Status and Rights: Conceptualizing Precarious Non-Citizenship in Canada." In *Producing and Negotiating Non-Citizenship: Precarious Legal Status in Canada*, edited

by Luin Goldring and Patricia Landolt, 3–30. Toronto, ON: University of Toronto Press, 2015.

Goldsmith, Stephen, and David Eisner. *Corporation for National and Community Service Strategic Plan: 2006–2010*. Washington, DC: Corporation for National and Community Service, 2006. https://www.nationalservice.gov/about/strategic-plan/2006-2010-strategic-plan.

Goldsmith, Stephen, Gigi Georges, and Tim Glynn Burke. *The Power of Social Innovation: How Civic Entrepreneurs Ignite Community Networks for Good*. New York: John Wiley and Sons, 2010.

Griffith, Allison, and Dorothy Smith. "Introduction." In *Under New Public Management: Institutional Ethnographies of Changing Frontline Work*, edited by Allison Griffith and Dorothy Smith, 3–24. Toronto, ON: University of Toronto Press, 2014.

Hall, Stuart. "Race, Articulation and Societies Structured in Dominance," in *Sociological Theories: Race and Colonialism*, edited by Bernan Associates, 305–45. Hamburg, Germany: UNESCO, 1980.

Hancock, Ange-Marie. *The Politics of Disgust: The Public Identity of the Welfare Queen*. New York: NYU Press, 2004.

Handler, Joel, and Yehenskel Hasenfeld. *The Moral Construction of Poverty: Welfare Reform in America*. New York: Sage, 1991.

Hanieh, Adam. *Lineages of Revolt: Issues of Contemporary Capitalism in the Middle East* Chicago, IL: Haymarket Books, 2013.

Hartmann, Heidi. "The Unhappy Marriage of Marxism and Feminism: Towards a More Progressive Union." *Capital & Class 3*, no. 2 (1979): 1–33.

Harvey, David. *A Brief History of Neoliberalism*. Oxford: Oxford University Press, 2005.

———. *A Companion of Marx's Capital: Volume 1*. London: Verso, 2010.

Hayes, Chris. "The Pragmatist." *The Nation* (blog). December 10, 2008. https://www.thenation.com/article/pragmatist/.

Hickey, Samuel, and Giles Mohan. *Participation: From Tyranny to Transformation? Exploring New Approaches to Participation in Development*. London: ZED Books, 2004.

hooks, bell. *Talking Back: Thinking Feminist, Thinking Black*. Boston, MA: South End Press, 1989.

Illich, Ivan. "To Hell with Good Intentions." In *Combining Service and Learning: A Resource Book for Community and Public Service*, edited by Jane Kendall, 314–320. Raleigh: National Society for Experiential Education, 1990.

Internal Revenue Service. "The Restriction of Political Campaign Intervention by Section 501(c)(3) Tax-Exempt organizations." Washington, DC: Department of Treasury, 2016a. https://www.irs.gov/charities-non-profits/charitable-organizations/the-restriction-of-political-campaign-intervention-by-section-501c3-tax-exempt-organizations.

———. "Lobbying." Washington, DC: Department of Treasury, 2016b. https://www.irs.gov/charities-non-profits/lobbying.

———. "Social welfare organizations." Washington, DC: Department of Treasury, 2016c. https://www.irs.gov/charities-non-profits/other-non-profits/social-welfare-organizations.

James, William. "The Moral Equivalent of War." *Peace and Conflict: Journal of Peace Psychology* 1, no. 1 (1995): 17–26.

Janowitz, Morris. *The Reconstruction of Patriotism: Education for Civic Consciousness.* Chicago, IL: University of Chicago Press, 1983.

Jarvis, Peter. *Learning in Later Life: An Introduction for Educators and Carers.* New York: Routledge, 2001.

Jenson, Jane, and Susan Phillips. "Regime Shift: New Citizenship Practice in Canada." *International Journal of Canadian Studies* 14 (1996): 111–36.

———. "Redesigning the Canadian Citizenship Regime: Remaking the Institutions of Representation." In *Citizenship, Markets, and the State*, edited by Colin Crouch, Klau Eder, and Damian Tambini, 69–89. Oxford, UK: Oxford University Press, 2001.

Jessop, Bob. *The Capitalist State: Marxist Theories and Methods.* New York: NYU Press, 1982.

Joseph, Miranda. *Against the Romance of Community.* Minneapolis, MN: University of Minnesota Press, 2002.

Kaplan, Sue, and Katherine Garrett. "The Use of Logic Models by Community-Based Initiatives." *Evaluation and Program Planning* 28 (2005): 167–72.

Kapoor, Dip. "Social Action and NGOization in Contexts of Development Dispossession in Rural India: Explorations into the Un-Civility of Civil Society." In *NGOization: Complicity, Contradictions, and Prospects*, edited by Aziz Choudry and Dip Kapoor, 45–74. London, Canada: ZED, 2013.

Katz, Michael. *The Undeserving Poor: From the War on Poverty to the War on Welfare.* New York: Pantheon Books, 1990.

Kedrowski, Karen. "Civic Education by Mandate: A State-by-State Analysis." *PS: Political Science & Politics* 36, no. 2 (2003): 225–27.

Khazei, Alan. *Big Citizenship: How Pragmatic Idealism Can Bring Out the Best in America.* Philadelphia, PA: PublicAffairs, 2010.

Kidder, Tracey. *Mountains beyond Mountains: The Quest of Dr. Paul Farmer, a Man Who Would Cure the World.* New York: Random House, 2004.

Kiesa, Abby, Alexander Orlowski, Peter Levine, Deborah Both, Emily Hogan Kirby, Mark Hugo Lopez, and Karlo Barrios Marcelo. *Millennials Talk Politics: A Study of College Student Political Engagement.* College Park: The Center for Information & Research on Civic Learning and Engagement, 2007. http://www.civicyouth.org/PopUps/CSTP.pdf.

King, Desmond. *Making Americans: Immigration, Race, and the Origins of the Diverse Democracy.* Cambridge, MA: Harvard University Press, 2000.

King, Desmond, and Jeremy Waldron. "Citizenship, Social Citizenship, and the Defense of Welfare Provision." *British Journal of Political Science* 18, no. 4 (1988), 415–43.

Kolb, David. *Experiential Learning: Experience as the Source of Learning and Development.* Englewood Cliffs, NJ: Prentice-Hall, 1984.

Kwon, Soo Ah. *Uncivil Youth: Race, Activism, and Affirmative Governmentality.* Durham, NC: Duke University Press, 2013.

Kymlicka, Will, and Wayne Norman. "Return of the Citizen: A Survey of Recent Work in Citizenship Theory." *Ethics* 104, no. 2 (1994), 352–81.

Levine, Peter. *The Future of Democracy: Developing the Next Generation of American Citizens.* Boston, MA: Tufts University Press, 2007.

Limbert, Wendy, and Heather Bullock. "'Playing the Fool': US Welfare Policy from a Critical Race Perspective." *Feminism & Psychology* 15, no. 3 (2005), 253–74.

———. *The London Hanged: Crime and Civil Society in the Eighteenth Century.* London: Verso, 2007.

———. *The Magna Carta Manifesto: Liberties and Commons for All.* Berkeley: University of California Press, 2008.

Linebaugh, Peter, and Marcus Rediker. *The Many-Headed Hydra: The Hidden History of the Revolutionary Atlantic.* London: Verso, 2000.

Lister, Ruth. *Citizenship: Feminist Perspectives.* 2nd ed. New York: New York University Press, 2000.

Long, Carolyn. *Participation of the Poor in Development Initiatives: Taking Their Rightful Places.* London: Earthscan, 2001.

Lowe, Lisa. *Immigrant Acts: On Asian American Cultural Politics.* Durham, NC: Duke University Press, 1996.

Mark, Karl. *Capital, Volume I: The Process of Capitalist Production.* New York International Publishers, 1967.

Marx, Karl. "On the Jewish Question." In *The Marx-Engels Reader*, edited by Robert Tucker, 26–52. New York: W. W. Norton, 1978.

Marx, Karl. "Theses on Feuerbach," in *The German Ideology.* Moscow: Progress, 1968: 659–62.

———. "The Eighteenth Brumaire of Louis Bonaparte." In *The Marx-Engels Reader*, edited by Robert Tucker. London: Norton, 1978: 594–617.

———. "Critique of the Gotha Programme." In *The Marx-Engels Reader*, edited by Robert Tucker, 525–41. New York: W. W. Norton, 1978.

Marx, Karl, and Frederick Engels. *The German Ideology.* Moscow: Progress, 1968.

McNally, David. *Global Slump: The Economics and Politics of Crisis and Resistance.* Oakland, CA: PM Press, 2011.

Mies, Maria. *Patriarchy and Accumulation on a World Scale.* London: ZED Books, 1998.

Mojab, Shahrzad. "Introduction: Marxism and Feminism." In *Marxism and Feminism*, edited by Shahrzad Mojab, 1–29. London: ZED Books, 2015.

Morton, Keith, and John Saltmarsh. "Addams, Day, and Dewey: The Emergence of Community Service in American Culture." *Michigan Journal of Community Service Learning* 4, no. 1 (1997): 137–49.
Moskos, Charles. *A Call to Civic Service: National Service for Country and Community*. New York: Free Press, 1988.
Moynihan, Daniel Patrick. *The Negro Family: The Case for National Action*. Washington, DC: US Department of Labor, 1965. https://www.dol.gov/oasam/programs/history/webid-meynihan.htm.
Nadasen, Premilla. *Welfare Warriors: The Welfare Rights Movement in the United States*. New York: Routledge, 2005.
Naples, Nancy. "From Maximum Feasible Participation to Disenfranchisement." *Social Justice* 25, Spring (1998): 47–66.
National Commission on Civic Renewal. *A Nation of Spectators: How Civic Disengagement Weakens America and What We Can Do about It*. College Park: University of Maryland, College Park, 1998. https://archive.org/stream/ERIC_ED424174/ERIC_ED424174_djvu.txt.
Newman, Janet. "Towards a Pedagogical State? Summoning the 'Empowered' Citizen," *Citizenship Studies* 14, no. 6 (2010): 711–23.
Nichols, Naomi. "Gimme Shelter! Investigating the Social Service Interface from the Standpoint of Youth," *Journal of Youth Studies* 11, no. 6 (2008): 685–99. doi:10.1080/13676260802392957.
Nichols, Naomi, and Allison Griffith. "Talk, Texts, and Educational Action: An Institutional Ethnography of Policy in Practice," *Cambridge Journal of Education* 39, no. 2 (2009): 241–55. doi:10.1080/03057640902902286.
Obama, Barack. "Presidential Address Announcing United We Serve Program." Speech, Washington, DC, June 17, 2009. https://obamawhitehouse.archives.gov/blog/2009/06/17/united-we-serve.
———. "Obama Issues Call for Public Service." *The Caucus: The Politics and Government Blog of The Times. New York Times*, December 5, 2007. https://thecaucus.blogs.nytimes.com/2007/12/05/obama-issues-call-for-public-service/.
———. "Obama, in Texas, Hails Bush I and Volunteerism: Remarks by President Obama at the 20th Anniversary of Points of Light." *Top of the Ticket, Los Angeles Times*, October 16, 2009. https://latimesblogs.latimes.com/washington/2009/10/barack-obama-george-h-w-bush-texas-speech-text.html.
———. *Dialectical Investigations*. New York: Routledge, 1993.
Ollman, Bertell. *Dance of the Dialectic: Steps in Marx's Method*. Champaign-Urbana: University of Illinois Press, 2003.
———. "Imperialism, Then and Now." Interview by Azfar Hussain, Meghbarta: A Journal for Activism, 2004. https://www.nyu.edu/projects/ollman/docs/interview03.php.
Ong, Aihwa. *Neoliberalism as Exception: Mutations in Citizenship and Sovereignty*. Durham, NC: Duke University Press, 2006.

Osborne, David, and Ted Gaebler. *Reinventing Government: How the Entrepreneurial Spirit Is Transforming the Public Sector*. New York: Plume, 1992.
Palmer, Bryan. *Descent into Discourse: The Reification of Language and the Writing of Social History*. Philadelphia, PA: Temple University Press, 1990.
Peters, Michael. "Education, Enterprise Culture, and the Entrepreneurial Self: A Foucauldian Perspective." *Journal of Educational Enquiry* 2, no. 2 (2001): 58–71.
Piven, Francis Fox, and Richard Cloward. *Regulating the Poor: The Functions of Public Welfare*. New York: Taylor & Francis, 1972.
Print, Murray, and Henry Milner, eds. *Civic Education and Youth Political Participation*. Rotterdam: Sense, 2009.
Putnam, Robert. "Bowling Alone? America's Declining Social Capital," *Journal of Democracy*, 6 (1995): 65–78.
Porteous, Nancy, Barbara Sheldrick, and Paula Stewart. "Introducing Program Teams to Logic Models: Facilitating the Learning Process." *Canadian Journal of Program Evaluation* 17, no. 3 (2002): 113–41.
Purcell, Mark. "Urban Democracy and the Local Trap." *Urban Studies* 43, no. 11 (2006): 1921–1941.
Rediker, Marcus. *The Slave Ship: A Human History*. New York: Penguin, 2007.
Reilly, John Francis, Carter C. Hull, and Barbara A. Braig Allen. *IRC 501c(4) Organizations: Technical Instructions Program for FY 2003*. Washington, DC: Internal Revenue Service, 2003. www.irs.gov/pub/irs-tege/eotopici03.pdf.
Renger, Ralph. "Consequences to Federal Programs when the Logic Modeling Process Is Not Followed with Fidelity." *American Journal of Evaluation* 27, no. 4 (2006): 452–63.
Ridzi, Frank. *Processing Private Lives in Public: An Institutional Ethnography of Front-Line Welfare Intake Staff Post Welfare Reform*. Syracuse, NY: Syracuse University, 2003.
———. "Making TANF Work: Organizational Restructuring, Staff Buy-In, and Performance Monitoring in Local Implementation." *Journal of Sociology and Social Welfare* 31, no. 2 (2004): 27–48.
Rikowski, Glenn. "Scorched Earth: Prelude to Rebuilding Marxist Educational Theory." *British Journal of Sociology of Education* 18, no. 4 (1997): 551–74.
Rimmerman, Craig. *The New Citizenship: Unconventional Politics, Activism, and Service*. Boulder, CO: Westview Press, 2011.
Rodriguez, Dylan. "The Political Logic of the Non-Profit Industrial Complex." In *The Revolution Will Not Be Funded: Beyond the Non-Profit Industrial Complex*, edited by Incite!, 21–40. Cambridge, MA: South End Press, 2007.
Ross, Alistair. *A European Education: Citizenship, Identities and Young People*. Stoke-on-Trent, UK: Trentham, 2008.
Sagawa, Shirley. *The American Way to Change: How National Service and Volunteers Are Transforming America*. San Francisco: John Wiley & Sons, 2010.

Saltmarsh, John. "Education for Critical Citizenship: John Dewey's Contribution to the Pedagogy of Service-Learning." *Michigan Journal for Community Service Learning* 3, no. 1 (1996): 13–21.

Sassen, Saskia. *Expulsions: Brutality and Complexity in the Global Economy*. Cambridge, MA: Belknap, 2014.

Sayer, Derek. "The Critique of Politics and Political Economy: Capitalism, Communism, and the State in Marx's Writing of the Mid-1840s." *Sociological Review* 33, no. 2 (1985), 221–53.

———. *The Violence of Abstraction: The Analytic Foundations of Historical Materialism*. New York: Basil Blackwell, 1987.

Sears, Alan, and James Cairns. *A Good Book, In Theory*. 2nd ed. Toronto, ON: University of Toronto Press, 2015.

Simon, Christopher. "Testing for Bias in the Impact of AmeriCorps Service on Volunteer Participants: Evidence of Success in Achieving a Neutrality Program Objective." *Public Administration Review* 6 (2002): 670–78.

Simon, Christopher, and Changhua Wang. *Impact of AmeriCorps on Members' Political and Social Efficacy, Social Trust, Institutional Confidence and Values in Idaho, Montana, Oregon, and Washington*. Portland, OR: Northwest Education Research Laboratory, 1999.

———. *First Follow-up Study: Impact of AmeriCorps on Members' Political and Social Efficacy, Social Trust, Institutional Confidence and Values in Idaho, Montana, Oregon, and Washington*. Portland, OR: Northwest Education Research Laboratory, 2000.

———. "The Impact of AmeriCorps Service on Volunteer Participants: Results From a 2-Year Study in Four Western States." *Administration & Society*, 34, no. 5 (2002): 522–40.

Simpson, Leanne Betasamosake. "Dancing the World into Being: A Conversation with Idle No More's Leanne Simpson." Interview by Naomi Klein. *Yes! Magazine*, March 5, 2013. http://www.yesmagazine.org/peace-justice/dancing-the-world-into-being-a-conversation-with-idle-no-more-leanne-simpson.

Simpson, Leanne Betasamosake. "Land as Pedagogy: Nishnaabeg Intelligence and Rebellious Transformation." *Decolonization: Indigeneity, Education, & Society* 3, no. 3 (2014): 1–25.

Simpson, Jennifer. *Longing for Justice: Higher Education and Democracy's Agenda*. Toronto, ON: University of Toronto Press, 2014.

Smith, Dorothy. *The Conceptual Practices of Power: A Feminist Sociology of Knowledge*. Boston, MA: Northeastern University Press, 1990.

———. *Texts, Facts, and Femininity: Exploring the Relations of Ruling*. New York: Routledge, 1993.

———. *Writing the Social: Critique, Theory, and Investigations*. Toronto, ON: University of Toronto Press, 1999.

———. "Ideology, Science, and Social Relations: A Reinterpretation of Marx's Epistemology," *European Journal of Social Theory* 7, no. 4 (2004): 445–62.

———. *Institutional Ethnography: A Sociology for People*. Lanham, MD: AltaMira Press, 2005.

Smith, Dorothy, and Catherine Schryer. "On Documentary Society." In *Handbook on Research on Writing: History, Society, School, Individual, Text*, edited by Charles Bazerman, 138–54. New York: Routledge, 2008.

Smith, George. "Political Activist as Ethnographer." *Social Problems* 37, no. 4 (1990): 629–48.

Smith, Neil. *Uneven Development: Nature, Capital, and the Production of Space*. Athens, GA: University of Georgia Press, 2008.

Speck, Bruce, and Sherry Hoppe, eds. *Service-Learning: History, Theory, and Issues*. Westport, CT: Praeger, 2004.

Spotted Eagle, Faith. "Faith Spotted Eagle on the Settler Colonial Mind Set." Interview by Tracey Rector. *Indian Country Today*, January 17, 2017. Audio: 00:08. https://indiancountrymedianetwork.com/news/native-news/faith-spotted-eagle-settler-colonial-mind-set/.

Standerfer, Christina. "Engaging Theory, Engaging Citizens: An Exploration of the Relationships among Civic Participation, National Service, and Rhetoric." PhD diss., University of Colorado, 2003.

Taylor, Keeanga-Yamahtta. *From #BlackLivesMatter to Black Liberation*. Chicago, IL: Haymarket Books, 2016.

Tevlin, Jon. Bachman's Wayward Son up and Joins AmeriCorps. *Star Tribune*. Minneapolis, MN, August 12, 2009. http://www.startribune.com/local/53002167.html?elr=KArksL.

Thobani, Sunera. *Exalted Subjects: Studies in the Making of Race and Nation in Canada*. Toronto. ON: University of Toronto Press, 2007.

Thomas, Peter David. *The Gramscian Moment: Philosophy, Hegemony, and Marxism*. Chicago, IL: Haymarket Books, 2011.

Thomson, Ann Marie, and James Perry. "Can AmeriCorps Build Communities?" *Non-Profit and Voluntary Sector Quarterly* 27, no. 4 (1998): 399–420.

Torney-Purta, Judith, John Schwille, and Jo-Ann Amadeo. *Civic Education across Countries: Twenty-Four National Case Studies from the IEA Civic Education Project*. Amsterdam, the Netherlands: International Association for the Evaluation of Educational Achievement, 1999.

Trattner, Walter. *From Poor Law to Welfare State: A History of Social Welfare in America*. 4th ed. New York: The Free Press, 1989.

US Congress. United States Internal Revenue Code of 1986. Title 26, Subtitle A, Chapter 1, Subchapter F, 501. 99th Congress of the United States of America.

———. House. National and Community Service Act of 1990. PL 106–70 [42 U.S.C.A. 12501]. 101st Congress of the United States of America.

———. House. National and Community Service Trust Act of 1993. PL 103–82 [H.R. 2010]. 103rd Congress of the United States of America.

———. House. Edward Kennedy Serve America Act of 2009. PL 111–13 [H. R. 1388]. 111th Congress of the United States of America.

Waldeman, Stephen. *The Bill: How Legislation Really Becomes Law, A Case Study of the National Service Bill.* New York: Penguin, 1995.

Westheimer, Joel, and Joseph Kahne. "What Kind of Citizen? The Politics of Educating for Democracy." *American Educational Research Journal* 41, no. 2 (2004): 237–69. doi:10.3102/00028312041002237.

Wood, Ellen Meiksins. *Democracy against Capitalism: Renewing Historical Materialism.* Cambridge, MA: Cambridge University Press, 1995.

———. *The Origin of Capitalism: A Longer View.* London: Verso, 2002.

———. "Democracy as Ideology of Empire." In *The New Imperialist: Ideologies of Empire*, edited by Colin Mooers, 9–23. Oxford, UK: Oneworld, 2006.

———. *Citizens to Lords: A Social History of Western Political Thought from Antiquity to Middle Ages.* London: Verso, 2008.

———. *Liberty and Property: A Social History of Western Political Thought from Renaissance to Enlightenment.* London: Verso, 2012.

Youniss, James, and Peter Levine, eds. *Engaging Young People in Civic Life.* Nashville, TN: Vanderbilt University Press, 2009.

Žižek, Slavoj. *The Fragile Absolute: Or, Why Is The Christian Legacy Worth Fighting For?* London: Verso, 2001.

———. "Afterword: Lenin's Choice." In *Revolution at the Gates: Žižek on Lenin, The 1917 Writings*, edited by Slavoj Žižek, 167–336. London: Verso, 2002.

Zukin, Cliff, Scott Keeter, Molly Andolina, Krista Jenkins, and Michael Delli Carpini. *A New Engagement? Political Participation, Civic Life, and the Changing American Citizen.* Oxford, UK: Oxford University Press, 2006.

Index

abstraction
  within AmeriCorps, 33, 116, 124, 135, 145, 165–166, 207
  within capitalism, 18, 207, 213–214
  civic engagement, 6, 42, 135, 202
  consciousness, 16–18, 165
  critical education, 212
  critique of, 10–11, 17, 24–25
  Dewey, John, 66
  experience, 16–18, 124
  fetishism, 161
  ideology, 18, 213–214
  logic models, 98
ACTION Agency, 48
American exceptionalism, 215
American Recovery and Reinvestment Act of 2009, 2, 51
AmeriCorps
  2005 Rule, 77–78, 82
  bifurcation within, 94–95, 104, 167–168
  civic engagement action plan, 114, 116–117, 121–123, 139
  civic engagement curricula, 108–112, 114–116, 120–122, 145, 157, 167
  civic mandate, 55, 105, 108, 113, 144, 167
  civic engagement performance measure, 33, 78, 96, 99–101, 105, 108, 112–116, 118 120–121, 124, 130–131
  civic engagement service projects, 113–114, 130–133
  civic engagement training, 5, 109–111, 114–115, 117–119, 121, 123–124, 129, 140, 144
  community needs, 84, 94, 96, 99, 101, 103, 113, 154, 168, 177
  consciousness, 107, 128, 139, 144–149, 158–160, 165–166
  democracy, 93, 104–105, 109, 116, 136–137, 139, 141–142, 145, 147–148, 156, 160–162, 165
  direct service activities, 48, 88, 94, 96, 104, 145
  eligibility, 32, 71–73
  epistemological relations, 6, 40, 67, 117, 124, 129, 135, 146–147, 169, 177
  experiential learning, 67, 70, 104, 129
  fetishism within, 160–161, 171, 179, 202, 205, 207
  financial sustainability, 71, 77–78, 81–82, 84–85, 99, 100, 104
  funding match, 78, 81–84
  history, 44, 48–51, 108
  member training, 48, 50, 67, 70, 83, 87, 94, 97, 104, 109–111, 114, 167

251

AmeriCorps *(continued)*
  not-for-profit organizations, 72–74,
    77–78, 80–84, 87–88, 91, 95,
    130, 135, 137–138
  organization, 44
  pedagogical relations, 124, 129, 135,
    146
  permissible service activities, 32, 72,
    76, 87–88, 94–95, 99, 105, 115,
    137, 151, 207
  praxis, 104, 139, 145–146, 148,
    166–167, 169, 172
  prohibited activities, 72, 74–75, 80,
    87–91, 93–95, 121, 127, 135–
    135, 138–139, 151
  racism, 124–125
  reflection, 117, 128–129, 131–133,
    141, 163, 165
  regulation of, 32, 67, 71–74, 76–78,
    82, 87–95, 100, 112, 115, 117,
    124, 135, 137–139 151, 156,
    165, 167–168, 176, 179, 207
  risks of defunding, 91, 104
  September 11th, 35, 44, 50–51,
    110, 187
  state, 151–152, 156, 158, 160, 165,
    167–168, 172–173
  unsanctioned activities (*see*
    prohibited activities)
  volunteer mobilization, 84, 113,
    130–131
alienation, 130, 167, 212, 216
Allman, Paula, 10, 14, 16, 26, 145,
  161, 202, 204

Bachmann, Michelle, 150
Bannerji, Himani, 21–22, 70, 218
bifurcation, 94–95, 104, 167–168
Bush, George H.W., 46, 49, 154
Bush, George, W., 50–51, 77, 96,
  110–111

Campus Compact, 39

capitalism
  accumulation of, 46, 58, 173
  citizenship, 6, 28, 43, 176, 190,
    192–197
  constitutive social relations of, 8, 22,
    31, 67, 203, 209
  critical education, 204–205
  crisis within, 1, 174, 181
  democracy and, 2, 34, 144, 169,
    174, 176, 182–184, 186–190,
    203
  dialectical analysis of, 7, 18–22,
    210, 214
  labor, 52, 57, 171–172
  local/trans-local, 159–161
  reproduction, 86, 198–199, 211–213
  state, 33, 186–190, 202
civic engagement
  abstraction, 52
  civilian national service, 45, 53, 55
  community service, 44, 53, 56,
    62–67
  conceptual ambiguity, 40–43, 95,
    112, 121–123
  dialectical analysis, 23
  discourse of, 4–5, 7, 51
  ideology, 6, 34, 145–148, 172–173,
    180–181, 184, 190, 202–208
  movement, 31, 36–37, 40, 50, 173,
    177
  place, 157–158
  practice, 24, 30, 32
  service-learning, 31, 63–67
  time, 157–158
  theory of change, 4, 7, 97
  See also AmeriCorps
citizenship
  active vs. passive, 41, 55, 149
  capitalism, 6, 28, 43, 176, 190,
    192–197
  'good,' 2, 6, 8, 28, 31, 36–37,
    39–40, 43, 55, 60, 62, 149, 151,
    156, 161–165, 172, 198

managing inequality, 179–180, 184, 190, 193, 197–198
neoliberalism, 160, 175–176, 184
citizenship education, 7–8, 36, 39, 42, 56, 112, 198
civil society, 4–6, 39, 41, 43
  and AmeriCorps regulations, 32, 84, 97, 104, 146, 149, 206–207
  historical materialist critique, 21–23, 67, 191, 194–198
  neoliberalism, 66, 174–175, 177–178, 180
  usages, 20–21
civilian national service, 32, 37, 39, 44–53, 55–56, 154, 171. *See also* AmeriCorps; Corporation for National and Community Service; national service
common good, 57, 65–66, 113, 161
communitarianism, 38, 49, 149, 178–179
community service, 2, 4, 6, 23, 32–33, 44–45, 50–53, 55–56, 58–63, 65–66, 75, 97, 108, 110, 117, 131, 135, 142, 148–151, 158, 164–165, 171–172, 179, 206–207. *See also* AmeriCorps
Civilian Conservation Corps, 46
civic consciousness, 49, 60
class formation, 191
Clinton, William J., 44, 49–50, 108, 171
Commission for National and Community Service, 49
consciousness:
  civic, 49, 60
  critical, 42, 197, 203–204, 209, 212
  dialectical analysis, 11–12, 14, 16, 18, 21–23, 24–25, 208
  'false,' 144, 204
  idealism vs materialism, 12–13
  ideology, 25, 185

objectified social, 26–27, 29, 33, 145–148, 166–167, 193
See also AmeriCorps; praxis
Corporation for National and Community Service
  civic engagement, 108–115, 117, 131, 146, 171
  dual character, 154
  emergence, 39, 45, 49–50
  expansion, 50–51
  organization, 44
  purpose, 2, 36, 97, 148, 151
  regulation, 71–73, 77–80, 83, 87, 91, 99, 131, 150–151, 167
  service, 151, 154–155, 164, 171
See also AmeriCorps
critical education, 4, 7, 30–31, 34, 144–145, 166, 204–206, 209, 212, 216

depoliticization, 55, 124, 144–145, 165, 178, 202
deficit theory, 102–103, 190, 198
democracy
  abstraction, 19, 23, 67, 107, 141, 202, 207
  capitalism, 58, 144, 169, 181–185, 189–190, 195
  contradictions, 2–8, 20, 139, 185, 187–189
  dialectical theorization, 19–20, 23
  deficit, 2, 7, 31, 38–40, 171
  educational research, 43
  historical emergence, 185–187
  fetishism, 161, 202
  ideology, 144–145, 147–148, 165–169, 191
  learning, 10–12, 14, 19, 23–30, 37, 39, 52, 55–56, 59–60, 62–67, 70–72, 104, 107, 116–117, 141–142, 145, 147, 149, 169, 199, 202, 203–205
  liberal, 57, 142

democracy *(continued)*
  neoliberal, 105, 173–174, 177–181
  philosophies of, 40–42, 59, 62
  public/private, 161–162, 179
  reification, 203, 206–208
  revitalization, 37, 49, 171
  scale, 159–161, 179
  schools for, 35–36
  See also AmeriCorps
Dewey, John, 14, 31, 55, 59, 62–66, 129
dialectics
  civil society, 21–23
  consciousness, 12, 14, 16, 24–27, 146, 167, 172, 205
  historical materialist, 9–12, 19, 26, 30, 32, 172, 190
  mode of analysis, 9–12, 20, 184–185, 206, 209–210
discourse
  civic engagement, 3–4, 50–55, 207
  community service, 45, 52
  limits, 24, 27–28, 67, 145, 147, 212
  institutional discourses (IE), 25–30, 33, 166
  neoliberalism, 172, 175, 198
  regime, 53–57
  division of labor, 21, 191–196

Edward Kennedy Serve America Act, 2, 41, 55
emancipation, 187, 190, 195–197
entrepreneurial(ism), 50–51, 84, 113, 160, 180
epistemology, 6, 12, 15–16, 18, 66, 144, 205
Etzioni, Amitai, 178–179
experience *(see* praxis)
experiential learning, 16, 61, 65, 67, 70, 104, 129

fetishism, 160–161, 172, 179, 202, 205, 207. *See also* AmeriCorps
feudalism, 20–21, 185–187, 189, 191
freedom, 174, 181–183, 185, 187–190, 192, 196

governmentality, 53, 55, 160, 176

Hegel, G.W.F., 9–10, 20–21, 196
higher education, 2, 4, 31, 35, 37, 39–40, 56, 60–61
historical materialism, 7, 9–12, 14–15, 19, 21, 24, 26, 28, 30, 32, 181, 184, 205

idealism, 11, 14–15, 19, 26, 43, 60, 195, 205, 208
ideological frame, 33, 142, 145, 147, 172
ideological practice, 103, 145, 166
ideology
  abstraction, 18, 213–214
  civic engagement, 6, 34, 145–148, 172–173, 180–181, 184, 190, 202–208
  critical education, 7, 30, 144–145, 166, 204–206, 209, 212
  democracy, 144–145, 147–148, 165–169, 191
  institutional ethnography, 27–30, 33, 142, 145, 147, 172
  logic models, 72, 99–101, 161
imperialism, 2, 34, 46, 52, 205, 215
institutional ethnography: 7, 9, 12, 23, 25
  differentiation from discourse analysis, 24–28
  ideological frame, 33, 142, 145, 147, 172
  institutional discourse, 27–30, 145

INDEX

ruling relations/relations of ruling, 25–29, 165
objectified social relations, 26, 167
standpoint, 27–28
trans-local relations, 26, 146, 159–160, 172

labor
AmeriCorps, 77, 81, 86, 105
citizen, 41
civil society, 20–21
gendered, 22, 57, 164, 191–192
institutional ethnography, 29
materialism, 12, 15–16, 21, 211
racialized, 22, 46, 192, 197–198
service-labor, 171–172
volunteer, 7, 32, 45, 47, 52, 57–58, 76, 171
waged/unfree, 57, 186–190
See also capitalism, constitutive social relations; division of labor; praxis
local
domain of action, 66, 70–72, 77, 84, 88–89, 108, 121, 155–159, 175, 177
fetish, 146, 160–161, 179
relation to trans-local, 24, 26–29, 101, 107, 144, 146, 158–159, 172
scale, 159–160
state-citizen relation, 121, 148, 160, 172
logic models, 72, 87–88, 96–99, 101, 114, 128, 161

management of inequality, 179–180, 184, 190, 193, 197–198
Marx, Karl, 7, 10–12, 14–15, 18–19, 21–22, 24–26, 29, 86, 144, 160, 167, 172, 184–185, 187, 189–197, 202, 208, 210, 212–213

materialism, 11–19, 21, 24–30, 41–43, 50, 52, 64, 67, 104, 116, 145, 147, 159, 161, 166, 169, 172, 181, 184–189, 193–197, 208–213, 218

nation, 4, 8, 37, 42, 45, 49–50, 60, 110–113, 143, 146, 148–149, 155–156, 160, 163, 168, 189, 198, 201
nationalism, 51, 201
National Community Service Act of 1990, 108
National Community Service Act of 1993, 108
National Service Fellows Program, 109
National Commission on Civic Renewal, 39, 109, 198
National Civilian Community Corps (NCCC), 44
national service, 5, 37, 46–54, 77, 83–84, 104, 108–109, 114, 117, 143, 148, 152–154, 171. *See also* civilian national service
National Service Secretariat, 47
neoliberalism: 34, 160, 172–181, 202
citizenship, 33, 54, 105, 173, 184
civil society, 66, 105
education, 113
not-for-profit organization: 32, 44, 48–51, 55, 175, 178, 180, 202. *See also* AmeriCorps

Obama, Barak, 1–3, 51, 143, 150, 154–155, 168, 171, 213
objectification, 10, 27, 209

performance measures, 33, 78, 96, 99–101, 105, 108, 112–116, 118, 120–121, 124, 130–131

politicization, 42, 55, 124, 141, 144, 198
political socialization, 37, 42, 52, 55–56, 59, 141
praxis, 7, 12, 14–16, 18–19, 24, 26–27, 30, 109, 139, 145, 166, 185, 204, 208–209
  critical/revolutionary, 203–205, 208, 212
  ideological praxis, 145, 148, 166–167, 169, 214
  uncritical/reproductive, 145, 172, 214
privatization, 21, 46, 84, 148, 171, 177–178, 186, 191, 204
President's Council on Service and Civic Participation, 50–51

reflection
  critical, 28, 141
  service-learning, 61, 64–65
  See also AmeriCorps
reification, 10, 16–17, 24–25, 33, 139, 161, 202–203, 206–210, 212, 214
relations of ruling/ruling relations, 25–29, 165

settlement house movement, 35, 58, 66
service-learning, 4, 31, 52, 56, 61–65, 67, 103, 116, 129, 131, 142
Smith, Dorothy, 7, 12, 23–30, 86, 146–147, 166, 208
social capital, 37–38, 102–103, 164
social inequality, 32–33, 62, 103, 105, 107, 148, 162, 165–166, 172
Social Innovation Fund, 44, 51

state, 6, 32, 37, 43, 45, 67, 71–72, 104–105, 144, 151, 183
  and capital, 33, 67
  citizen relation, 33, 37–38, 41, 45, 50, 52, 58, 148–149, 160, 168, 172–173, 180, 202
  civil society, 20–22, 206, 66, 180, 206
  conservative communitarian, 178–179
  imperialism, 221
  Foucauldian analysis of, 53–55
  Marx's analysis of, 19, 21, 184, 187–197
  nation-state, 149
  neoliberalism, 174–178
    violence, 1, 176, 201, 214
  welfare state, 3, 41, 52, 178, 181, 184, 198
  See also AmeriCorps
subjectivity, 92, 171, 175–176

theory of change, 4, 97, 99
Trilateral Commission, 38

unfreedom, 181–183, 187–190, 192
USA Freedom Corps, 50, 110

vacuity, 107, 116, 142, 145
Volunteers in Service to America (VISTA), 44, 47–48, 51, 82, 93
volunteerism, 2, 46, 49, 51, 56–60, 110, 117, 122, 158

War on Poverty, 47–48, 53, 171
Wood, Ellen Meiksins, 2, 185–186, 191

www.ingramcontent.com/pod-product-compliance
Ingram Content Group UK Ltd.
Pitfield, Milton Keynes, MK11 3LW, UK
UKHW041917140426
5217IPUK00013B/190